REVIEWING POLITICAL CRITICISM

Public Intellectuals and the Sociology of Knowledge

Series Editors
Dr Andreas Hess, University College Dublin, Ireland
Dr Neil McLaughlin, McMaster University, Canada

The sociology of knowledge has a long and distinctive history. Its function has always been that of attempting to bridge the aspirations of the discursive and institutional founding fathers of sociology with that of modern attempts to define the discipline through the study of the emergence, role and social function of ideas. However, since Mannheim first outlined his program in the 1920s, the sociology of knowledge has undergone many changes. The field has become extremely differentiated and some of its best practitioners now sail under different flags and discuss their work under different headings. This new series charts the progress that has been made in recent times—despite the different labels. Be it intellectual history Cambridge-style, the new sociology of ideas which is now gaining strength in North America, or the more European cultural analysis which is associated with the name of Bourdieu, this series aims at being inclusive while simultaneously striving for sociological insight and excellence. All too often modern attempts in the sociology of knowledge, broadly conceived, have only looked at form while they downplayed or disregarded content, substance of argument or meaning. This series will help to rectify this.

Reviewing Political Criticism
Journals, Intellectuals, and the State

ELISABETH K. CHAVES
Virginia Tech, USA

ASHGATE

© Elisabeth K. Chaves 2015

All rights reserved. No part of this publication may be reproduced, stored in a retrieval system or transmitted in any form or by any means, electronic, mechanical, photocopying, recording or otherwise without the prior permission of the publisher.

Elisabeth K. Chaves has asserted her right under the Copyright, Designs and Patents Act, 1988, to be identified as the author of this work.

Published by
Ashgate Publishing Limited
Wey Court East
Union Road
Farnham
Surrey, GU9 7PT
England

Ashgate Publishing Company
110 Cherry Street
Suite 3-1
Burlington, VT 05401-3818
USA

www.ashgate.com

British Library Cataloguing in Publication Data
A catalogue record for this book is available from the British Library

The Library of Congress has cataloged the printed edition as follows:
Chaves, Elisabeth K.
　　Reviewing political criticism : journals, intellectuals, and the state / by Elisabeth K. Chaves.
　　　pages cm
　　Includes bibliographical references and index.
　　ISBN 978-1-4724-3004-5 (hardback) – ISBN 978-1-4724-3005-2 (ebook) – ISBN 978-1-4724-3006-9 (epub) 1. Political science--History. 2. Political science--Philosophy. 3. Intellectuals--Political activity--History. 4. Criticism--Political aspects. 5. Journalism--Political aspects. 6. State, The. I. Title.
　　JA81.C5264 2015
　　320--dc23

2014028898

ISBN 9781472430045 (hbk)
ISBN 9781472430052 (ebk – PDF)
ISBN 9781472430069 (ebk – ePUB)

Printed in the United Kingdom by Henry Ling Limited, at the Dorset Press, Dorchester, DT1 1HD

Contents

List of Tables		*vii*
Preface		*ix*
Acknowledgments		*xiii*
	Introduction: The View and the Re-view	1
1	The Beginnings of the Re-view	11
2	The "Great Re-views": The Institutionalization of Critical Practice	31
3	The Re-view of War, Intellectuals, and the State	55
4	*The Public Interest*, *Telos*, and the Re-view of Welfare State Politics	75
5	The Professionalization of Re-view? The New "Critical" Journals	105
6	The Present Disconnect Between View and Re-view	131
	Conclusions: The Future of Re-view?	155
Bibliography		*157*
Index		*171*

List of Tables

5.1	Sample of "Critical" and "Radical" Journals and their "Impact"	117
5.2	*NPS* Themed Issues	123
5.3	Comparison of Submission Numbers	126

Preface

Barbara Epstein, co-founder and co-editor of *The New York Review of Books*, passed away as I was starting this project. A number of obituaries and retrospectives appeared, and they left me with a sense that there was, or is, a real intellectual community out there somewhere. To the eyes of a studious suburbanite raised in a mass-media entertainment soaked environment, this community existed in a some-place where ideas and writing are paramount, perhaps influential and even a little alluring. When my first academic article appeared in a respected scholarly journal, I flipped through the pages of the issue in which my article appeared and felt no allure or influence. While ideas were discussed, they were not paramount and mostly lay heavy on the page. There was a divide, a disconnect, between the community of scholars and the intellectual community. The scholarly journal is the home of the academic, and the journal of opinion that of the intellectual.

An article on Epstein and *The New York Review of Books* by James Atlas (2006) in particular attracted my attention. It portrayed the environment, accurately or not, of an intellectual community, writers rubbing elbows with other writers, erudite editors dictating letters to eager interns, and the production of a periodical described as the "premier journal of the American intellectual elite." Moreover, a journal like *The New York Review of Books* was a place where questions of politics and culture could be investigated side by side. Any issue could contain politics, economics, philosophy, history, art, sociology, psychology, astronomy, and literary criticism, as well as original poetry. One was not confined to disciplinary boundaries. In the journal's first issue in 1963, the lengthy table of contents included, among others, a piece by Dwight MacDonald titled "To the Whitehouse," a review essay by Oscar Glass on Russian economic development, a review essay by Susan Sontag on Simone Weil, a review essay by Nathan Glazer on Herbert Gans's *The Urban Villagers*, and poetry by Robert Lowell, John Berryman, and Robert Penn Warren.

Critics have rightly described *The New York Review of Books* as political, its politics progressive or to the left. However, Philip Nobile (1974) argued that by the early 1970s the *Review*'s politics lacked any bite. While this may have been true, the *Review*'s politics reemerged strongly after 9/11 and the Iraq War (Sherman 2004; Atlas 2006). However, the *Review* itself has never put forth an explicit political program. It has only published one statement of editorial intent and that appeared in its first issue as a letter "To the Reader." In it, there was no mention of politics whatsoever. Instead, the editors expressed their hopes that the review would serve as the type of literary journal that is "needed in America." They would not spend time on books that "are trivial in their intentions or venal in their effects." The only explicit description they gave of the new endeavor was that it would be a "responsible literary journal" (Epstein and Silvers 1963). They left open the questions of responsible to whom and to what.

I had a fairly parochial upbringing and education, and growing up, I did not really know of the existence of reviews and journals such as *The New York Review of Books*. I had seen *The New Yorker* and read a few issues. I had read *The Economist* and browsed other 'current affairs' magazines at bookstores. But prior to my doctoral degree, no professor had ever urged me to pick up the latest issue of *Dissent*. They had never assigned essays from *Salmagundi* as part of my course reading. Course readers, packets of articles that supplemented textbooks, might contain articles from scholarly journals or even from some of the leading news magazines, but I do not remember them containing anything from journals of opinion, like *The New York Review of Books*, *The Nation*, or *The New Republic*, or from other less widely read, non-academic journals, like *Telos* or *Monthly Review*.

I have re-read Atlas's article on *The New York Review of Books* several times since 2006. As I read it yet again in order to write this preface, I noticed something new almost immediately, something that I had previously ignored or glossed over. His depiction of Epstein's work and the *Review* itself is suffused with glamour. First, there are the parties. Atlas writes of "literary cocktail parties," "Truman Capote's Black and White Ball at the Plaza"; he even describes how "their [the Epsteins'] parties were famous." The settings are enviable and exotic: "a leafy street lined with elegant old apartment buildings known for their wood-paneled walls and double-height living rooms," "marble pillars and chandeliers," the "remote farmhouse in Provence," France! A "Thames River barge … moored … on the right bank of the Seine," Paris! The lifestyle is luxurious: "pot-au-feu, coq au vin, boeuf bourguignon," "bottles of champagne," "high-toned benefactors," "trust fund," "hunting dogs," a man "coiffed and tanned, in a beautiful suit like someone out of a movie."

Then there is the *Review*'s headquarters: "The office was chaos." It is filled with loose papers, smoked cigarettes, shabby secondhand furniture, walls of galleys, and mountains of books. They may party hard but they work harder, is the moral. They may be privileged, but they aren't slackers. They are not just intellectuals, but intellectuals with distinction. I now wonder what attracted me first, the intellectual community or the status and prestige. I believe it is the former, although the latter does not detract. Still, the intellectual's work is always affected by the concern for status position in relation to other intellectuals and to society, the need for intellectual differentiation and social esteem, what Richard Hofstadter refers to as "status anxiety" and what Pierre Bourdieu calls "distinction." By 1969, one critic of *The New York Review of Books* described its political voice as "cocktail-party revolutionary" (Goodman 1969, p. 71).

Still, another tribute to Epstein and *The New York Review of Books* appeared in *The Chronicle of Higher Education*. In that piece, Mark Oppenheimer argued that Epstein's intellectual status may have rated high within "literary circles, but in the wider world, she was hardly known" (2008, p. B14). Within the intellectual and cultural fields, she occupied a position of distinction in comparison to editors of more mainstream or middlebrow journals. However, she and the *Review* take on entirely new weights depending upon who is doing the weighing. This is perhaps the trap of most writing about intellectuals. The intellectuals loom large among their peers, who are often the ones writing about them, but may be wholly insignificant to almost everyone else.

How then does one judge the influence of an Epstein on society at large, when most Americans have never heard of her? Oppenheimer argues that not even graduate students at Yale are reading opinion journals like *The New York Review of Books* or *Dissent* or *Commentary* or, even, *The American Scholar*. He doubts that most professors read them. Perhaps the argument could be made that such journals no longer enjoy the same influence in American society that they did in the pre-radio, pre-television and pre-internet eras. Still, even if almost no one has heard of *The New York Review of Books* or of any of the other periodicals that I discuss in this book, journals still constitute one of the most frequently used mediums of communication for the transmission of ideas. They also allow intellectuals to connect with an audience, even if it is comprised largely of only their immediate peers.

Many authors who write about these journals, journals "at the intersection of academe and the culture at large," as Oppenheimer describes them, value them as contributors to intellectual culture. Oppenheimer details the number of ways that reading such journals can foster the life of the mind among graduate students and also possibly encourage them to act as "public intellectuals." Disciplinary and professional pressures in the academy steer many students and professors away from non-specialist periodicals. However, sometimes those pressures may steer intellectuals into beginning a journal when other avenues available to them have been cut off. Two hundred years ago, the founding members of the *Edinburgh Review* were trained as lawyers yet their intellectual and political views prevented them from pursuing careers at the bar or in politics, because they ran counter to the dominant reactionary politics in Scotland following the French Revolution. In the 1970s, Paul Piccone, founding editor of *Telos*, devoted himself full-time to that journal when denied tenure at Washington University, St. Louis.

By writing this book, I have been able to inhabit the world of journals, for a time. I think I would quickly trade the life of a professor for a career at *The New York Review of Books* in the 1960s or at *Partisan Review* in the 1930s or somewhere similar today. There is definitely a strong attraction exerted by the idea of the literary intellectual and the opportunity to live in a world of ideas that knows no disciplinary boundaries where leisure, freedom, and maybe even enjoyment is possible. This desire, however, likely suffers from the same malady of most other "grass is always greener" illusions. As Stefan Collini puts it, the concept of the "intellectual" is "an object of desire, and it is in the nature of desire simultaneously to pursue and to resist total satisfaction" (2006, p. 500). Perhaps part of the role that journals play in society is to keep this desire alive. Arguably, this is also the role of political imagination, to keep in view the desire that "another world is possible." While this book primarily traces the political interventions made by journals in relation to a number of historically important critical moments, the book also explores journals as mediums of desire. After all, what is critique, even when unglamorous, but a desire for change?

Acknowledgments

This project began almost eight years ago when I told my dissertation adviser, Tim Luke, University Distinguished Professor of Political Science at Virginia Tech, that I wanted to study the "literary communities" of political theorists. Eventually that interest narrowed to journals that make, or attempt to make, some political intervention upon the world. Tim has been an invaluable mentor over this period, even after he was no longer my official adviser. He read numerous drafts and provided wonderfully helpful feedback. He also pushed me to publish, and I thank him for his encouragement and support. This book benefited enormously from his involvement.

I also thank other colleagues for their guidance and thoughtful input, especially Patricia Mooney Nickel, Wolfgang Natter, Scott Nelson, Janell Watson, and the community of scholars in the College of Liberal Arts and Human Sciences and the School of Public and International Affairs that make Virginia Tech an exciting and stimulating place to work. Many thanks to Peter Beilharz and Trevor Hogan for their inspiring conversation about *Thesis Eleven* that motivated this project. Thanks also to Nicholas Kiersey for productive discussions about the sometimes strange political inclinations of certain journals. Nancy Love and Mark Mattern provided me with very useful information about *New Political Science*. And Emily Hauptmann shared her work on *democracy* and her interest in my project. Thanks also go to Jesse Richardson, Max Stephenson, and Paul Knox for their professional support. Anne Khademian and the School of Public and International Affairs at Virginia Tech gave me the needed time to complete this project, for which I am very grateful.

Series Editors Andreas Hess and Neil McLaughlin also provided beneficial reviews of the project at several stages. I would like to thank them and the editorial staff at Ashgate, especially Claire Jarvis, Carolyn Court, and Elaine Couper, for their assistance and for including the book in this unique series.

There have been many friends who sustained my spirits throughout. I would like to especially thank Katie Butler, Jessica Gottstein, Natalie Hart, Stani Licul, Nicole Sanderlin, Angela Shafer, and Heather Switzer. My love and deep thanks to my family who have always been there for me.

Finally, a huge and heartfelt thanks to Andy Scerri. His critical insights and thoughtful conversations about the project gave me the necessary motivation to pull this book into shape, and make it sharp! I am so happy to know him. And I look forward to returning the favor.

Introduction
The View and the Re-view

This book develops a social history of the "review" form of journal publication. It also proposes something of a theoretical framework for interpreting the role that the "review" journal form plays within the broader field of political criticism. Through a series of historical examples, I explain the "review" as a means of political practice, one that essentially serves as a re-view of the state's view of how society, in particular the economy and cultural norms and values, should be ordered.

The earliest eighteenth-century reviews, like Daniel Defoe's *Review of the State of the British Nation* or the early American journal *A Monthly View of the Political State of the British Colonies*, as their titles suggest, trained their re-viewing practice upon the state. That is, they published reports and opinion on affairs of state. These early publications evolved in the nineteenth century into the so-called "great reviews," such as the *Edinburgh Review, The Quarterly Review*, and the *Westminster Review*. These later journals institutionalized the review form, and also published reviews of other texts, whether books or political pamphlets. Still, these "book" reviews, the ancestors of *The New York Review of Books* or sister publication the *London Review of Books*, embraced political criticism, both deepening the sophistication of and making more explicit, particular political opinions or viewpoints.

While periodicals in Europe and then the United States may not have called themselves "reviews" until the eighteenth century, the review belongs to a long line, or genre, of written political criticism that dates back to at least the thirteenth century in Western Europe. This body of work first advised, then revised, and with the increased confidence afforded to civil society by the rise of market capitalism, subsequently challenged and even transformed the state's view on what and how it governed. This book then traces the development of the review from the eighteenth century onwards. I use the review form of the journal to develop an ideal type, which I model on the "great reviews." This conceptual schema allows me to describe in detail a dialectic of view and re-view, one in which contributors and editors see themselves as sometimes conservers and, sometimes, critics of the state. Toward the end of the book, I examine how contributors and editors continue to undertake the tasks of viewing and re-viewing the state, even amidst the very different circumstances in which they find themselves in the early twenty-first century.

I recognize that "the state" is a freighted term, conceived differently by lay-people and across disciplines, and as an empirical fact, operating in many different ways depending on social historical and, indeed, geographical contexts.

Some of the re-viewing practices that I examine specifically take aim at "the state," while others refer more to the apparatus and personnel of government, and others more nebulously focus upon the ordering of society that may involve a role for the state or government but, as in the case of the late twentieth-century anti-state journal *Telos*, not necessarily. That is, while some may be critical of "the state" in sum total, as an institution, others are not critical of "the state" *per se* but are critical of *how* the state orders a particular society or societies at or up to a particular moment. So, those critics, unlike anti-statists, may embrace "the state" as the desirable form of government, even demanding a strong state along Continental *dirigiste* lines, while still criticizing how the liberal-democratic Anglo-American state functions.[1] Still, I use "the state" as something of a shorthand to narrow attention to the ways in which intellectuals and journals challenge the *political* orderings of societies. This use of the concept "the state" is more inclusive than that of "government," as it represents not only the governing practices that order a society on a daily basis, but also how a political society envisions how and to what degree it should be governed. It points to that institution that legitimately or, at least, without resistance sufficient to topple it, organizes the rules for life held in common in a given territory. The trajectory of re-viewing practices that I trace in subsequent chapters brings to the fore the increasing importance granted by intellectuals to the concept of "the state," even in the Anglophone tradition. This is noticeable especially in the US over the twentieth and twenty-first centuries, where growing elitism, militarism, imperialism, bureaucratization, and routinization were contributing to an increasing statalization of politics. "The state" thereby gains greater quiddity over this period as critics of "the state" publish their criticisms of it.

Also, while I pay almost exclusive attention to how Anglophone critics[2] re-view the state, I note that journals additionally offer re-views of civil society, the family, the economy, technology, art, culture, and so forth. Indeed, the early modern intellectuals assigned various objectives to their critical practice: dictating taste and morals for an emerging civil society; setting that civil society off from the state; offering targeted partisan critique of those holding power within it; satirizing colonial power and imperial pretensions; vindicating or defending rare, controversial or simply unique political views; supporting or stabilizing the

---

1   Is criticism different in those countries with a strong state tradition versus those without? Perhaps it is, but since this book largely focuses on the latter, further research may be required to determine fully the answer.

2   I realize this may be viewed as a shortcoming in my analysis. However, I argue that the Anglophone journals I concentrate upon are worthy of study due to the strong influence their home states exerted over large portions of the globe throughout the time period I address. Further, they existed in societies where public discourses and intellectual culture were comparatively free to develop. This then is perhaps a starting point for a more extensive analysis that other scholars may complete in order to provide a fuller picture of political criticism in journals across states, societies, and cultures.

dominant cultural ideological view or seeking reform of a prevailing morality or ethics. However, I only include here those practices which are germane to my discussion of the political ordering of society: that is, to the view and re-view of the state. In examining these multiple practices of criticism, therefore, I examine how the early reviews laid the groundwork for and institutionalized a particular radical or oppositional relationship between intellectuals and the state. The review form offers a space where critics present new alternative views on the state and politics, or recover "discarded possibles," many removed from view by the state. This book then centers upon a critique of the state, government, and politics undertaken by intellectuals, and their multiple actions of power seeking in their writing. Throughout the book, I elaborate on this double practice—the "view" of the state being "re-viewed" by its critics and sometimes taken on or censured.

Before moving too far, it goes without saying that criticism of the state occurred in forms other than, or outside of, the journals that flourished, and gained some degree of influence, in early modern Europe. Further, the liberal public sphere of civil society brought into being in part through these periodicals is well documented. This book continues the focus on the liberal public sphere, because even later "radical" periodicals appear to trace their ancestry and tradition of criticism to it. My account of the function of early journals is situated within complementary discussions of state formation (Anderson 1983; Foucault 2009; Mitchell 1988; Scott 1998), the liberal public sphere (Habermas 1991 [1962]; Koselleck 1988 [1959]; Sennett 1976), investigations into the historical effects of print technology (de Certeau 1984; Eisenstein 1979; Kafka 2012), and the sociologies or histories of knowledge and thought that focus on the emergence of intellectual communities and the central role played by institutionalized forms of writing in their founding (Bourdieu 1969, 1991; Burke 2000, 2012; Collins 1998; Grafton 2009; Siskin 1998). Journals are often mentioned in these accounts, although sometimes only in passing. I therefore link these various research agendas to the journal, offering a more concentrated account of it as a home for the critical practice of re-viewing the state. This study, then, contributes to the political sociology of criticism or critique, a subfield of the sociology of knowledge (Chiapello 2013).

Today, reviews are a familiar form of periodical. Publications from the political *New Left Review* to the literary *Sewanee Review* to the cultural *Hedgehog Review* include the word "review" in their titles. Yet not all publications that call themselves "reviews" may engage in the practice of political re-view that I outline here. Further, journals and magazines that do not refer to themselves as reviews or make the review of other literature the central concern of their publication, but may instead act as policy journals, such as *The Public Interest*, or theory journals, such as *Telos*, should still be included within the category of "review" I describe. This is because they direct the bulk of their attention to the state's view. Still, there are many more periodicals that may fit my argument of "re-view" than I can give sustained attention to here. So, I have limited my focus to select publications that re-viewed during important critical moments in history.

Often journal projects are brought into being due to a perceived crisis, a moment of decision. Such projects hope to answer, or more so, to bring about clarity of the crisis through their criticism. Crisis, as understood in the medical sense, as a climax or turning point, will end in recovery or death. Crisis, as a moment of decision-making, requires the exercise of political judgment, but also as Raymond Geuss (2010b) suggests, political imagination. Walter Benjamin's and Bertolt Brecht's *Krise und Kritik* in the 1930s and Maurice Blanchot's *Revue internationale* in the 1960s were both planned to respond to a moment of crisis. However, neither journal moved beyond its planning stage; their founders were unable to materialize their utopian aims (Schmidt 2010). Benjamin and Brecht referred to their journal project, *Krise und Kritik*, as "interventionist thinking." Further, the journal's aims were not just to intervene but also to bring on a particular crisis. They identified the crisis as one of ideology or false consciousness. Similarly, Blanchot envisioned his new journal as responding to a crisis in early 1960s France that would "only make our critical situation more manifest" (2010 [1960], p. 38). Moreover, Blanchot argued that it was this very crisis that necessitated the journal project and which demanded its success. "[No]t only do I not doubt that it [the journal] will be realized, as it meets a demand one might call historic, but I am tempted to believe that the intellectual future may depend on the way in which it will be realized" (p. 39). The critical moments that I focus on throughout this book are therefore historical times requiring the exercise of political judgment to which the reviews believe they can contribute.

As Reinhart Koselleck (1988 [1959]) argues, "critique" and "crisis" are historical categories. In the era of enlightenment in eighteenth-century Western Europe, critique became a central category and disposition as the powers of the absolutist state were increasingly challenged. The encyclopedist Denis Diderot wrote that *critique* was sovereign over everything (Goodman 1989). However, as Koselleck contends, many critics were also ambivalent about the political nature of critique. Early critics of the modern state operated within the private sphere, of the so-called "republic of letters," rather than the public sphere of the state. Critique was also often the preserve of a secret sphere, that of Masonic lodges and guildhalls. These private spheres belonging to "society" were kept separate from the absolutist state to the advantage of actors in each. Thomas Hobbes' Leviathan could ideally govern free of moral or religious concerns, and the occupants of the private spheres could ideally practice religion freely and privately.

The early critics of absolutism grounded their critique in moral law and only indirectly challenged the authority of the state. In England, where the absolutist state was shorter lived, criticism perhaps more quickly became directly political, and the critics' "re-views" solidified into a regular practice in periodicals. This took place as private opinion gradually congealed into what Jürgen Habermas (1991 [1962]) labeled the "bourgeois public opinion" of the seventeenth-century mercantile and later, industrial capitalist classes. With the displacement of the pilgrimage and tithe economy by market capitalism, the state was forced by circumstance to respond to the public's publicized interests and demands.

Interestingly, the criticism of the state that this new public of private property owning middle-class individuals generated was considered non-political, even while it increasingly had political effects. That is, as Habermas shows, opposed to the arbitrary non-order presided over by the aristocratic and ecclesiastic classes, bourgeois public opinion was self-understood as giving expression to the "natural order of things."

As Jason Edwards (2007) argues, the bourgeois public's radical criticism of the state—radical in its opposition to what were dominant or prevalent ways of thinking, talking about and acting in politics in its context—also had an ambivalent relationship to the object of political critique, the state. "Public sphere" critics viewed the modern state as a "vital agent" of transformation. Meanwhile, as an emergent political faction, they remained wary of the dangers that the state posed to those private domains in which the newly understood concept of human freedom could be expressed. In other words, the emergent bourgeois public sphere those theorists such as Koselleck, Habermas and Richard Sennett so keenly describe saw the state not as something to be overthrown but as an institution subject to political contestation and control. The state's capture promised the victors the power to impose upon it their view of how society should be governed. However, this political power, while often out of reach of the state's most radical critics, was also considered by them to be dangerous and requiring subordination to social, moral and religious domains. I contend then that the radical critics used the review form to police this political power, continually re-viewing its exercise and offering new theories on how it could best govern.

Fashioning a View

One of the key thinkers of this institutional transformation, from a state form premised upon the arbitrary will of a hereditary monarch advised by faith-based counsel to one premised upon a constitution or constitutional monarch advised by counsel who drew legitimacy from techno-scientific knowledge of the natural order, is of course Michel Foucault (1979; 2009 [1978]). Foucault's example of Louis XIV inspecting his troops in 1666 demonstrates the need to recognize the fact that the grandest view belongs to those holding power within the state. I suggest that Louis XIV's claim "L'état, c'est moi" implies that the state is at once view and viewer, defining both what is, and what is important to, the healthy functioning of society. The holder or holders of power in the state are therefore, especially where rivals exist, compelled to publicize and disseminate their view, which is the view of how things are and should be. The state's view and all critical counterviews can in this sense be thought of as competing, coexisting or perhaps codependent visions, maps, or inventories. These views and re-views of order represent differing narratives of power, and are the product of what Foucault saw as differently constituted technological assemblages. The overarching authority and legitimacy of the state allows it to command the resources necessary to impose and distribute one particular view, one particular ordering discourse upon society.

The state's view remains partisan. This is perhaps most readily seen in the workings of colonial states, if only because such states imposed order from afar, without, and over, many less than willing people. One of Foucault's more recent interpreters, Timothy Mitchell, offers a compelling illustration of this point. For Mitchell, the French colonial mission to Egypt of 1798 arrived to conquer that country with a printing press. Upon landing at Alexandria, Napoleon's first act was to issue a printed proclamation to the Egyptian people (1988, p. 134). Mitchell, as well as Benedict Anderson and James Scott, shows how, as the modern state developed, it increasingly relied upon the medium of print, which improved the efficiency of various functions, such as census taking, resource inventorying, and mapping, allowing the state to more precisely and predictably govern its citizens and impose its authority. One method by which the colonial state in Egypt governed its subjects was the daily record, or *jurnal*, an administrative practice undertaken by government inspectors to report upon the production of cotton and other commodities by rural laborers whose performance was carefully monitored. The state's view was then recorded in its journals. Fifty years later, the first satirical political journal, *Abu al-nazzara al-zarqa*, would appear in Egypt, which was quickly shut down by the colonial powers. Indeed, the colonial government in Egypt attempted to suppress any publications it did not control (Mitchell 1988). The state's viewing practice, as embodied in its journals, was appropriated by the state's critics and used against it. It is this tension between official and unofficial uses of the printing press and mass circulation networks that Michel de Certeau (1984) calls the "scriptural economy" of modern societies.

I suggest that since the state is able to institute its view through such an economy, the work of the critic may be conceived of as one of bringing "back into view the conflicts and confrontations of the early beginnings and therefore all the discarded possibles, [retrieving] the possibility that things could have been (and still could be) otherwise" (Bourdieu 1998, p. 40). It may also involve making the state's view visible, especially when the state's exercises of power are purposefully secret. The re-view mounted by the critic challenges the state's view by questioning that "'possible' which, among all others was actualized" by the holders of power in the state at a particular historical moment (p. 40). The re-view then often operates as a "practical utopia" because it rescues what could have been, rather than attempting to bring into being what may be in the future. Additionally, it accepts the presence and permanence of political power, unlike a more radical utopianism, and instead of seeking its abolition, attempts to organize or reorder an actually existing order to meet specific goals (Edwards 2007).

Organization of the Book

Of course, the re-viewing functions of the intellectual or critic are made difficult by the censoring powers of the state functionary, and also previously the church (Febvre and Martin 2010 [1958]). Because the state by definition seeks to monopolize real and symbolic violence, those inhabiting it have often felt the need to set in place mechanisms for censoring re-views—publication "in the sense of a procedure aimed at rendering a state or act public, at bringing it to everybody's knowledge" (Bourdieu 1998, p. 63 note 31). Indeed, in both England and the United States across the seventeenth and eighteenth centuries, state censorship prevented the publication of parliamentary or assembly proceedings. Due to state control, the first periodical did not appear in England until 1622, while in 1690 the first American newspaper was published. Early colonial journals faced even greater censorship. Indeed, the narrative developed in Chapter One takes off from this period, when an increasingly restive class of private individuals, seeking to make public their opinion of how the state should manage the political economy, cultural values and legal norms of their societies, began to oppose through journals the state's use of censorship to stifle dissent and monopolize information about the natural order of things.

By the nineteenth century, the view that the state should govern absolutely had been largely discredited in theory and in practice. In Chapter Two, I examine the age of the so-called "great reviews" in Britain and the institutionalization of the review form. The re-views of the emerging liberal-democracies reached their zenith as their criticism more directly intervened in the state's practices. In a sense, the radical spirits of the American and French Revolutions became embodied in this method of critique.

War, however, may be the most critical moment at which a journal can intervene and also the moment at which a journal's intervention may be most ineffective. Chapter Three then discusses such efforts during World War I, the Vietnam War, and the Iraq War. While intellectual efforts in journals did not stop these wars, they reminded the public about the importance of critical dialogue even when it is most unwelcome. Further, these interventions chastised those intellectuals who uncritically supported the state, thus undermining the role of re-view.

Intellectuals may have achieved a new prominence during the middle of the twentieth century in the United States. Although their influence in government throughout this period may be overstated, they helped institute "an academic technocratic discourse" that translated into power for those who best wielded it (Townsley 2000). In Chapter Four, I review some of the best adopters of that discourse, *The Public Interest* crowd, who ushered in the neoconservative movement in the US. I compare their journal to that of a different crowd, the developers of North American critical theory at *Telos*. Interestingly, I find parallels in their critical re-views of the transitioning liberal welfare state. Both sought a smaller role for the state, although for different reasons. And both journals were challenged by the transforming nature of state authority as it morphed into neoliberal forms.

The late 1960s and 1970s are the opening setting for Chapter Five. In part, this chapter continues the focus upon the professionalization of criticism, albeit now in academic journals, especially those that claim to be "radical" or "critical." Specifically, it considers the challenge to the American Political Science Association by the Caucus for a New Political Science and their eponymous journal, *New Political Science*. It asks whether the institutionalization of re-view impairs the effectiveness of its critique and what can be learned about the power of criticism in light of the proliferation of "critical" journals at this time.

In the late twentieth century, re-viewing may have lost a lot of its political influence. Moreover, its practices of re-view no longer resembled the clear political focus that sought to check the state's exercises of political power. Power was increasingly diffuse and dispersed, and an increasing anti-statism looked to alternative means of ordering society and the economy. Chapter Six then argues that postmodern themes of anti-statism, deradicalization, and aestheticization of political critique have transformed and perhaps undercut the re-view.

The return of crisis however has spurred the growth of a new crop of critical journals and perhaps refocused the practice of criticism. I conclude the book by considering the recent digital environments of journals and states. I ask whether the review form of journal has outlived its original purpose, or whether digital forms of governing and electronic means of organizing and disseminating political criticism have breathed new life into an old form.

Providing a "Re-view"

Liberal-democracies depend upon visible government. Ideally, democratic government implies a system in which state actions are made visible to a public. Democratic government can take form as representative democratic government, which further implies that representatives are tasked with making the public, the *demos*, visible to the state. Similarly, liberal government implies some form of rule of law that constrains the actions of those holding power within the state, the people's representatives to the state and the people themselves, as citizens. One important role that political critics play in liberal-democracies then is that of revealing the state's shortfalls in relation to either.

Visibility does not only mean that the workings of power are in view. Power is often visible, or at least, the operation of power is readily felt (which often translates into various conspiracy theories). Visibility also entails having the means to address and control the workings of power. Government is visible to the public to the extent that the public not only knows how the government is operating but also has a say in the operation of government. Visibility is then not just about a form of sight but of oversight that, in liberal-democratic contexts, offers a bulwark against arbitrary or inegalitarian application of ordering principles, of the so-called "rule of law." For example, "sunshine" laws, such as open meeting laws, do not only cast light on the workings of government but also ideally make them open to the public so that they are knowable, accessible, and ultimately controllable (Bobbio 1982). Still, liberal-democratic states will not always operate in the open. Unlike autocratic states, however, they permit "free criticism and the expression of diverse viewpoints" which can act as correctives to abuses of authority and bring some of the secret workings of government into view (Bobbio 1982, p. 53). This criticism then can act as a re-view of the state, challenging or correcting its operations, as well as making its perhaps unjust orderings of society and the economy visible to the public.

Max Horkheimer argued that the social function of philosophy is the "criticism of what is prevalent" (1972, p. 264). The prevailing thought or opinion, belonging to the ruling class, is known as *doxa*. Thinkers from Plato to Pierre Bourdieu (1998, p. 7) referred to its proponents as *doxosophers* or "technicians of opinion who think themselves wise." The role of the philosopher or theorist is to challenge the *doxosophers*. Such criticism assumes a negative function. It challenges the dominant vision.

If *doxa* is the prevailing opinion, an orthodoxy, which represents the point of view of the dominant thinkers as well as the powers of domination, then any criticism that undermines this view by offering an alternative becomes a re-view of those theories and authorities. Sheldon Wolin argues, "political philosophy constitutes a form of 'seeing' political phenomena" (2004, p. 17). However, his definition of "seeing" more closely adheres to the definition of vision of "something seen in the imagination or in the supernatural" rather than the descriptive "act of seeing, sight, things seen."

If the review form of journals acts as a writing practice where criticism is articulated, then we can also say that journals act as re-viewing practices. The word "review" dates back to the mid-fifteenth century and derives from the Middle French *revue*. It was first used to describe an inspection of military or naval forces, especially a ceremonial display and formal inspection undertaken by a monarch or high-ranking dignitary. However, "review" can also be defined as the act of looking a second time, of seeing again. The word also refers to the action of looking over something with the aim to correct or improve it.

The etymology of the noun, "review," would be enough if we considered a review (or journal) to be an object, a passive assemblage of essays or articles. However, if we consider the more active construction of a review—who writes for a review, where and how did the review originate, what role does it play in society, how is it institutionalized—any and all of these questions speak to a practice of "re-viewing." Therefore, more appropriately, the etymology of the verb "review" should be investigated. How then are the writers and their reviews "re-viewing"? What do they "see again"?

This points to another understanding of the re-view, or re-vision. "Seeing again" can be both future and past oriented. A re-view can be a theoretical imagining of something that does not yet exist—the holding out of a Platonic ideal and measuring it against the state, as it actually exists. A re-visioning, however, can also be an act of revisionism—re-reading the past and revising the perception of what occurred. The critics often undertake both of these roles. They may attempt to change our understanding of history, and they may offer a vision for the future.

To understand critical activity, one must reflect on where this activity takes place—on the institutions of criticism that give rise to it. Journals then are a merger of intellectual and material activity. They are both ideas and the active containers of those ideas, which give shape to critical thinking (Williams 2009). As W. J. T. Mitchell argues in respect to the journal he edits, *Critical Inquiry*, critical activity is not autonomous or independent; it is always bound up in institutional form. "And yet the idea that criticism has, or should aspire to, this sort of autonomy is a persistent illusion that has prevented criticism from taking a clear look at itself" (1982, p. 610). This book then pays attention to the institutionalization of political criticism in the review form in order to explore how critics re-view the state and how this practice of re-view has transformed from the early eighteenth century to the early twenty-first century.

Chapter 1
The Beginnings of the Re-view

This chapter first identifies what I call the critical practice of journals. It does this by exploring the relationship between the early modern state and its critics, perhaps the first generation of so-called "public intellectuals," including Daniel Defoe, Joseph Addison, and Richard Steele. These critics of the state developed their journals, *A Review of the State of the British Nation*, *The Tatler*, and *The Spectator*, into the early reviews. The chapter describes a narrative of change over time, wherein hitherto diffuse critical voices contesting absolutist government in seventeenth- and eighteenth-century Europe were concentrated in the journal form. Even though criticism of the state predates criticism of absolutism in the eighteenth century, such political discourse did take on a more adversarial position *vis-à-vis* the modern state at this time. This coalescence of critique around challenges to absolutism is of course often described as a product of "the Enlightenment." In this chapter, I look in particular at how English, Scottish and North American critique, carried on a rising tide of bourgeois public opinion, forced the state to deal with "reasoned" criticism by deflecting, absorbing, ignoring, or censoring it. Either way, with the emergence of the journal as a form of critical practice, those holding power within the state found that they could no longer simply suppress criticism. By examining how the holders of power within the formative modern state dealt with criticism of how they governed, this chapter argues that criticism of "the state" is perhaps better understood as criticism of a particular ordering of society, of politics, the economy, and culture. On the one hand, those holding relatively more authority or say in how society is ordered were through the prevailing technologies of governance, able to represent the state's view, that is, to normalize, or following Foucault, naturalize a distinct order of things. On the other hand, critics, possessing less authority, yet disseminating before and shaping an increasingly restive public opinion, offered alternative ideas about what the good, right or just order consists of: in essence, a re-view of the state. As such, the critical moment that provides the focus for the discussion in this chapter is that of the rise of Habermas's bourgeois public sphere, and the slow crisis that unfolded as this new class challenged the authority of the traditional holders of power within the state, the landed aristocracy and their allies, the high church.

From State View to the Critical Re-view

What Habermas (1991 [1962]) identifies as the bourgeois public sphere and the reviews that helped shape it are historically located within a line of developing written criticism aimed at public authority. This line of critical practice began with advice books directed at royals, aristocrats and courtiers, which appeared as early as the thirteenth century in Italy, and the "mirror for princes" literature of the Renaissance, the most famous example being Niccolo Machiavelli's *The Prince* (Skinner 1989). For my purposes, such early texts instituted the genre of political literature, which has since taken many forms and that, with the rise of the Habermasian self-conscious public sphere, morphed into the journal or "review." They were "a product of new and distinctive forms of political organization that arose within late medieval Italy," and through their pages, they helped form the concept of "the state" (p. 96). Their most important piece of advice, or reformist criticism, centered on how to maintain one's state as a prince by keeping power over existing structures and institutions of government. They thereby transformed the meaning of *stato* from a personal term that referred to the state or condition of princes to an impersonal one that referred to institutions of government and means of coercive control that organized and preserved order within political communities (Skinner 1989). The distinction between the institutions of a state versus those that have control of the state was also encouraged by the tradition of Renaissance republicanism, which advocated self-governing institutions as the optimal form of the state. Authority would not belong to particular rulers or magistrates but to the rule of law and public institutions whose administration was entrusted to rulers and magistrates, who in turn governed for a "common" good. The latter's priority then was a duty to maintain these institutions for the republic, rather than as earlier advice-books argued, a duty to preserve power for oneself.

Arguably, this impersonality of the state culminated in the writings of Thomas Hobbes (1991 [1642]). Hobbes's "artificial man" or Leviathan was a double abstraction, the state as separate from ruler and ruled. Taken in historical context, this concept of the state was essentially conservative. It challenged the ideologies of popular sovereignty emerging in the French religious wars and English Revolution of the seventeenth century and argued that political power was not delegated by the people to the state but absolutely transferred. The coercive authority of the state was then justified by its capacity to protect the public and ensure the common good. Sovereign authority then needed to be distinct from both ruler and ruled to serve this role. Hobbes searched for a term to describe this authority and settled on "the state." The concept of the state was the outcome of one particular theory of politics grounded in a counter-revolutionary movement (Skinner 1989).

As such, political criticism experienced a major transformation with this release from its function as the "mirror for princes" and transference to "the public." Dena Goodman (1989) chronicles this change, albeit across the Channel in France, by focusing on the work of Charles-Louis de Secondat, baron de Montesquieu. His work broke with the "mirror for princes" tradition and was directed at those who could effect reform. For Goodman, Montesquieu's *Lettres persanes*, written in 1721, educated the reader in how to analyze and criticize the political system "on a radically fundamental level," even if it did not provide instruction on how to change it (p. 28). This form of political criticism, more radical than the reformist criticism of the advice-books and "mirror for princes" literature, was further advanced with the publication of Denis Diderot's *Supplément* in 1772. The Supplement helped to transform the radical critical attitude into action, by explaining, to the critical reader addressed by Montesquieu, what was required to become an agent of political change (p. 225). Critical practice therefore emerged as the epistemological adversary of absolutist thinking, which had depended upon dogmatic reiteration. I now turn to demonstrate how such critical practice came to be housed in the early reviews, journal publications that contained a multiplicity of views, some more impactful than others. What united these views is that they all served in some way to re-view the state, whether seeking an audience amongst those holding power within it or amongst those subjected to the state's order.

The Critics' Re-views, or the Di-visions within the Ordered Vision

Publication of periodicals really did not begin until the early seventeenth century in England due to a combination of licensing restrictions, Star Chamber regulations, and the royal prerogative in news circulation, along with religious conflict. The first English periodical appeared in 1622. It was a periodical pamphlet dealing with foreign wars and authorized by the King (then James I). Early periodicals did not contain running titles. The pamphlet form of the periodical followed the broadside ballad. The first isolated pamphlets were known as *Relations* of news. When early periodicals began to appear with titles, or "catchwords," they were known as *Coranto*, or "current" of news. Essentially, the *Coranto* was a *Relation* of news that made repeat appearances, rather than being confined to one pamphlet. According to *The Cambridge History of English and American Literature*, all *Corantos* dealt exclusively with foreign news until 1641 (Ward and Waller 2000). After that time, the *Diurnall*, or "newsbook," of domestic news began publication. These newsbooks contained no editorial comment. Official journalists, sanctioned by the crown or Parliament, were also established in the 1640s.

Under Oliver Cromwell's rule, much journalism was suppressed or strictly controlled. In 1660, under the Restoration, parliament prohibited printed reports of its proceedings and did not remove that embargo until the end of the century.[1] In the late 1600s, new journal forms that avoided concerns typically regarded as

---

1 In 1681, parliament began to allow the publication of its "votes." However, they were published through licensed journals that were partial to the government. Rules of confidentiality continued to operate in parliament through the eighteenth century. As a Member of Parliament from 1713 to 1714, Richard Steele used his position to breach these rules and publicize parliamentary proceedings in his journals (Knight 2009). In 1738, parliament increased the prohibition on the publication of its proceedings so that publication of its debates *between* sessions was also disallowed. As Habermas reports, only in 1771 did Wilkes, then alderman of London, nullify the law "in fact if not in law" (1991 [1962], p. 61).

belonging to the state began to appear. One of the earliest academic journals in England is thought to be the *Philosophical Transactions of the Royal Society*, which began publication in March 1665 (McCutcheon 1923, p. 626). It was a scholarly or scientific journal and consisted of the papers read before the Society and was not principally a review of books. Its first editor Henry Oldenburgh kept his personality and opinions hidden from the reader, as the re-viewer as "author," or one who had "authority," had yet to develop. It appeared around the same time as the French *Journal des Sçavans*, considered the earliest academic journal published in Europe and containing reviews of works pertaining both to science and the arts. This journal was published by *privilege*, or royal permission, and publications governed in this way could not judge or reflect upon matters that affected the state. It is possible though that the journal had not received permission from the crown, which may have contributed to its brief lifespan consisting of only 13 issues (Brown 1972). Whichever the case, the journal tried to maintain as much independence of thought as it could. Its main purpose was to help working scholars establish networks of learning, but it also sought an audience among amateurs who wished to be informed of the latest developments in knowledge. Still, its main contribution was to the sciences, and it helped establish authority for them as well as a means for conveying information and organizing debate among a collective that did not depend upon face-to-face interaction. Following its publication, more than 1,000 journals would be founded in France over the next century (Burke 2000, p. 48).

Habermas's *The Structural Transformation of the Public Sphere* tells the story of the consolidation of state power through the domination of representation, aided by the medium of print, which was then re-appropriated by the public and used to critique the state. Habermas's analysis highlights the interconnectivity of state and public. The early "newspapers" were often trade letters that transmitted important information to merchants. The state then co-opted this medium to use for its own administrative purposes, as the state was being captured by the mercantile classes, before it was re-appropriated by "the public" to oppose perversions of or the granting of privilege to certain mercantile factions by the state. In his account, Habermas stresses the historically constituted double binary of private/public that led to the creation of "the public sphere" (Siskin 1998, p. 163).[2] The first binary refers to the divide between public and private, where the former is the state and the latter society. The second binary is the division within the private sphere of society, which contains a public realm, figuratively represented by the coffee house, table society and salon, but constituted by private persons, and the private realm, best represented by the family. As Habermas contends, the public sphere became "public" in a double sense when its critique of the state challenged the state's authority, represented through the confrontation between state and

---

2 As Clifford Siskin states, "Print … overwrites the category of public-as-state, by instituting, within the private realm of society, a new kind of publicness—one that is accessed and thus produced in private terms" (1998, p. 164).

press (1991 [1962], p. 60). However, Habermas may not make clear enough the interdependence of the two "publics." As Mara Loveman argues, "the state's power is not derived from autonomy from society, but rather from the webs of interconnections to actors and institutions outside the state" (2005, p. 1,678).

Habermas stresses the role of the press, and journals in particular, in helping to constitute this public authority of the state. Similarly, the development of "public opinion" depended upon the existence of a literary public sphere that "institutionalized a form of rational-critical discourse about objects of common concern that could be carried over directly into political discussion" (Calhoun 1992, pp. 13–14). Social advice and moral instruction, much of it critical of prevailing mores, was extended to political criticism by the journal-ists of the eighteenth century and early nineteenth centuries. However, Craig Calhoun questions whether Habermas may have overstated "the prominence of a strictly literary public sphere in grounding the eventual political one" (1992, p. 48 note 54). In part, this could be a twentieth-century epistemology unnecessarily dividing literary from political concerns in an eighteenth-century world that saw no such strict division. Or it could be a lack of attention to the historical record of political concerns who organized outside literary journals but whose record may not be as preserved as those of print periodicals.

Again, early journalism was almost exclusively taken over and controlled by the monarchical state.[3] Early political journals served the state's purposes by recording its visual displays and disciplinary practices, whether by reporting on a ball or reproducing a sovereign ordinance (Habermas 1991 [1962], pp. 21–2). The press was intimately tied to political power; it was of and for reigning power cartels. Although, the "public" at this time was a limited one, comprised of a relatively wealthy and well-educated mercantile elite, they began to view themselves as a counterpart and counter agency to the state's authority (Calhoun 1992, p. 9). This was the self-understanding Habermas and others such as Sennett (1976) famously saw coalescing in the Coffee Houses of London, Amsterdam, Hamburg, Danzig, Vienna, and Paris. As markets became increasingly important to the state, this elite public was then able to re-appropriate the authority of the press from the state. Creating new di-visions of power, the "public" was then able to contest the state's vision of power as it repurposed the press to function as criticism, a coexistent and codependent force. The journal or review form, as a text that contained critical readings of the state, became a means for those out of power to influence politics. The journal form in effect challenged the state's monopoly of symbolic violence, and the scriptural economy it theretofore largely controlled.

At this time, importantly, the political re-view becomes a diverse critical practice. Some states bring some re-views into their internal political debates and divisions while others are policed as examples of external political resistance. Further, a range of political viewpoints can be represented among the critics and,

---

3   English journalism became freer of the Crown and Parliament's influence with the end of the licensing act in 1695.

depending upon who the state functionaries are, the re-view can contain both conserving (conservative) and transforming (radical) voices.

Defoe's Review of the State

In the late 1600s, the periodical press that reported daily news and economic activities was supplemented by journals that went beyond the supply of information to give pedagogical instructions, as well as criticism and reviews. In part, these new journals may have favored opinion over news, because slow print production could not keep up with the speed at which news traveled by word of mouth. Creating a market for opinion was then somewhat fueled by a response to the available media technology.[4] In the early eighteenth century, criticism, or critical reasoning, began to dominate the press and created this new genre of periodical (Calhoun 1992, p. 9). It was criticism, or judgment represented as so-called "public opinion," and the emergence of public opinion itself that became regarded by many in the seventeenth and eighteenth centuries as a countervailing force against the state. The criticisms of Habermas's "public sphere" are already known. While the "public" may have come into existence at this time, it was by no means a wholly representative public. Rather, it mainly consisted of middle- and upper class white males. So, "public" opinion was similarly restricted.

Within the "public's" opinion were likely many opinions, or di-visions, that challenged the state's vision of order, especially when that vision intruded upon what was then considered "private" life. Habermas's public sphere "defined as the public of *private* individuals who join in debate of issues bearing on state authority" has become the ideal (and idealized) expression of modern democracy, although it first appeared as a temper on the more absolutist powers of the state (whether monarch or parliament) than as rule by the people, per se (Calhoun 1992, p. 7). This ideal forum then is grounded in an Enlightenment understanding of the public use of reason as necessary to improving public life. Criticism meant that the public was no longer un-self-conscious and immature, but could think for itself.

One of the first known reviews to bear the name was Daniel Defoe's *Review of the State of the British Nation*, begun in 1704, about 80 years after the first English periodical was published. Observing closely Defoe's chosen title, I contend that the early critics of the modern state challenged the state's view through a practice of re-view. Early political criticism was a viewing and re-viewing practice. For example, *The American Magazine*, one of the first magazines to appear in the New World, was published in 1741. Edited and printed by Andrew Bradford, the magazine bore the subtitle, *A Monthly View of the Political State of the British Colonies*. Despite a print run of 400 copies, Defoe's *Review* marked a turning

---

4 Arguably, with the development of the steam engine and then steam-powered press in the late eighteenth and early nineteenth centuries the ability of print technology to keep pace with the news greatly increased (Briggs and Burke 2009).

point in British journalism. The circulation figures are somewhat misleading as researchers have pointed to the fact that rather than purchase journals, most Londoners read them in coffee houses. People who were illiterate gathered in the streets to hear them read aloud. As Secord argues, "[i]t is obvious that the *Review* had an influence all out of proportion to its sales" (1965, p. xxii).

No longer concerned only with facts, Defoe, a religious nonconformist, printed his opinions, marking the beginning of the periodical essay form and the journal of opinion.[5] Lasting until 1712, Defoe's *Review* initiated a new era, as the better known papers of Richard Steele and Joseph Addison, *The Tatler* and *The Spectator*, appeared in 1709 and 1711, respectively. With their arrival, the press no longer existed only to report the news but to shape it, and thereby, to shape public opinion. These journals quickly emerged as the front-runners of the bourgeois public sphere (Mackie 1998). They also capitalized on a burgeoning reading public and emerging literary market that could provide solid returns to the providers of print material.

Defoe began the journal while in prison for libeling the High Church party. The party then ruled in Britain and laws like the Act of Uniformity, the Test Act, the Five Mile Act and the Conventicle Act made life very difficult for dissenters. Defoe used the *Review* to weigh in on religious controversies, such as the granting by James II of an indulgence to dissenters and on the subject of "occasional conformity." As a reviewer of his literary and political career later noted: "There appears to be no reason for doubting the statement that his polemical power, coupled with the keenness of his logic, did more to thwart the schemes of the High Church party than the efforts of all the other opponents of the measures combined" (Harrison 1891, p. 516).

Daniel Defoe's *Review* presents an interesting case in that he claimed an authority to speak of political, religious and economic affairs in his journal as a political activist rather than a man of letters. In fact, his novels, *Robinson Crusoe* and *Moll Flanders*, were published well after the *Review* ceased publication. Although a Member of Parliament supported the journal, Defoe's case still raises the question of how the critic's view gains authority and legitimacy to speak on politics from the pages of a periodical. In other words, what power accrues to a journal that re-views the state? This is a key question to ask of critics and their reviews. Obviously, the answer will change depending upon when and of whom it is asked. A critic's view, and its authority, depends not only on its content but also on how it is transmitted, what position it occupies within the intellectual field, and the make-up of the media environment of which it is a part.

From the first, Defoe's *Review* was a partisan paper, in that Robert Harley, then Secretary of State, sponsored it. Defoe's journal largely focused on political and trade issues of the day, unlike Steele's and Addison's papers that largely focused

---

5 Defoe's *Review* was not the first publication to provide opinion in addition to the news. However, his publication, along with the arrival of Steele's and Addison's journals, are the periodicals remembered and heralded as the initiators of the form.

on issues of morals and manners.⁶ Habermas devotes the majority of his attention to the papers of Steele and Addison, mentioning Defoe's *Review* almost in passing. He emphasizes Defoe's connection to Harley and writes of the *Review* as if it were wholly a piece of propaganda. This could be in part because Defoe's partisanship and attention to politics put him more closely in the primary public sphere of state authority, rather than the secondary public sphere belonging to society, which is "the" bourgeois public sphere of Habermas's account. However, the nineteenth-century reviews, which are discussed in the next chapter, have more in common with Defoe's *Review* than the papers of Steele and Addison. They were also more concerned with matters of state policy than morals and manners. Additionally, they also were shaped by partisanship, although they were not strictly partisan journals. While Steele and Addison may have set the bar in matters of writing style, Defoe's *Review* made matters of state a legitimate subject for writers to take up.

Further, Defoe's *Review* sincerely sought an audience among those members of the public interested in state affairs. As William Payne argues, Defoe's very subject matter, as well as style, sought an audience neither among the aristocracy nor the masses, but among those so positioned as to be concerned with matters of state and educated enough to follow his essays (1951, p. xvii). Defoe believed that his role as writer for and editor of a review was to cry "fire!" against other narratives of power that might usurp the state's disciplinary practices and impose their own view. As different factions wrestled for control of the state, the review's job, in the service of or aid to whichever faction, was "to open the eyes of the deluded people, and set them to rights in the things in which they are imposed upon" (quoting Defoe, Payne 1951, p. xvi).

Telling the Public What to Think (and How to Act)—*The Tatler* and *The Spectator*

On April 12, 1709, the first issue of *The Tatler* appeared on London street corners. It sought a readership among the "politic persons, who are so public spirited as to neglect their own affairs to look into transactions of state" and were enjoying a steady diet of the "other Papers," publications which *The Tatler*'s editors would subject to much critique (Addison and Steele 1803, pp. 1–2). They worried that those papers failed to educate the public in right thinking, or in "the public use of

---

6 Defoe's *Review* did include a section titled "Advice from the Scandalous Club," which censored morals and manners and provided some entertainment. Addison and Steele largely borrowed from the idea of the club in their own papers. Defoe did not enjoy writing the section and separated it into its own paper, titled *The Little Review*, and then abandoned it altogether. He realized though that his audience required some entertainment, and he hoped that the inclusion of the Club would "hand on the more weighty and more serious part of the design into the heads and thoughts of those to whom it might be useful" (quoting Defoe's *Review*, Vol. 1, "Preface," February 1704, Payne 1951, pp. 6–7).

their reason," which they found to be more important than any particular politics (Habermas 1991 [1962], p. 27). Those "politic persons" then more likely to give priority to political news than managing their own affairs would be the persons that *The Tatler* and then *The Spectator* would attempt to reform through a course of moral instruction. Their greater interest in reforming morals and manners and teaching the bourgeoisie how to act also cemented or naturalized class distinctions and socioeconomic difference as matters of taste (Eagleton 1984; Siskin 1998; Mackie 1998).

Editor and founder of *The Tatler* and later *The Spectator*, Richard Steele (1672–1729) was a journalist and playwright who led a somewhat bohemian life but would also serve in parliament for the Whig party. Co-founder and contributor Joseph Addison (1672–1719) was a diplomat and Whig politician who occupied the position of under-secretary of state. Periodicals flourished in the eighteenth century, and Steele's and Addison's, published on newssheet, set the standard for the era. "Addison and Steele were perhaps the first to be star newspaper essayists. They did so in part by shrewdly focusing on manners and mores for their middle-class readers who wanted to imitate the aristocracy" (Lopate 1995, p. xlviii).[7] Both periodicals became so popular that they were reprinted in their entirety for centuries afterward.

The Tatler appeared three times a week, making it perhaps more closely resemble what we consider to be a newspaper today, rather than a journal. However, the dividing line between newspapers and magazines in the eighteenth century was very blurred. The paper quickly reached a circulation of 4,000, with a readership that well exceeded this figure, but ceased publication only two years later (Habermas 1991 [1962], p. 260 note 37). Its first four issues were offered for free, presumably to build an audience, and the following issues would cost one penny each, a price that Steele forbade street hawkers from raising (Mackie 1998, p. 50). Addison and Steele ended *The Tatler* in January 1711 when they began publication of *The Spectator*, a daily, in March of that year, which would have an even shorter lifespan, its first series closing in December 1712, and a second series appearing briefly from June to December 1714. The second paper was discontinued due to the stamp tax that made printing the paper a loss. While *The Tatler* and *The Spectator* may have filled most of their pages with admonitions about how to dress and act, vices to avoid, and charities to sponsor, it was in these pages that the bourgeois public came into being (Habermas 1991 [1962]).

An issue of *The Tatler*, published May 17, 1709, reemphasized the periodical's chosen audience as those "worthy citizens who live more in a coffeehouse than in their shops" and needed to be cured of this malady (Habermas 1991 [1962], p. 260 note 36). Still, Addison and Steele wrote the papers as reports on the activities of the coffeehouses and depended on these places for the consumption and

---

7   Still, neither paper was particularly new or unique, as Mackie argues. However, she notes, they stood apart in their use of "continuous and well-developed fictional personae" and their "refinement of the single-essay format" (1998, p. 25).

distribution of their papers (Mackie 1998, p. 16). Steele promised to distinguish the paper from "the other papers, which are published for the use of the good people of England, have certainly very wholesome effects, and are laudable in their particular kinds" but do not steer their patrons correctly in understanding and seizing upon the essential matters of the day (Addison and Steele 1803, p. 1). Contrary to these weak efforts, *The Tatler* foresaw its main purpose as

> both a charitable and necessary work [that would] offer something, whereby such worthy and well-affected members of the Commonwealth may be instructed after their reading, *what to think*; which shall be the end and purpose of this my paper, wherein I shall, from time to time, report and consider all matters of what kind soever that shall occur to me, and publish such my advices and reflections ... (Addison and Steele 1803, p. 2).

As papers with editors who believed their duty was to tell the public "what to think," *The Tatler* and its successor, *The Spectator*, served an important editorial function that discerned between what was worthy of publication and what was not, what was worthy of conversation and what was not.

The Tatler and *The Spectator* sought an audience among a group of individuals already unreasonably concerned with the affairs of state, but at the same time, it could be argued that the new publications not only found such an audience but also created it. This recalls Michael Warner's (2002) argument of the circularity of publics, or as Kathy Ferguson names it, the "chicken and egg" problem—"the public has to exist in order for us to address it, but it can't exist until we address it" (2010, p. 212). Did this public in fact already exist or did periodicals and editors such as Steele and Addison bring it into being? Determining causality is probably a futile endeavor, as a variety of factors likely contributed to the formation of "public opinion" and to emphasize any one may skew the picture. Or perhaps there is another way to conceptualize the public, which takes into account the criticisms of Habermas's theory of the public sphere. It may be that the viewers/re-viewers, whether representing those in power or out, are the public *in nuce* made public or publicized via these new publications. As John Smolenski argues: "... the long-term story is not whether ritual or print is constitutive of provincial public culture. Both are implicated. Rather, it is the history of particular forms of public expression claiming to voice, embody, or articulate a common public good" (2005, p. 50).

While addressing this public, both Addison and Steele liked to write in the periodicals under assumed names or characters, such as Isaac Bickerstaff of *The Tatler*, and could bring a "diversity" of viewpoints to an otherwise homogenous perspective. Additionally, the personalities they assumed and the essay form may have helped them gain a critical distance from the personal subject matter about which they wrote. The development of the personal essay as a form in eighteenth-century Great Britain corresponded with the rise of periodicals during the same period. The periodicals provided an institutional base from which the essay writers could gain an audience and earn a living. However, the very style and even titles of some of these periodicals suggests a certain distance between the essayists and their newfound institutionalization. As Phillip Lopate remarks,

> As part of their ironic modesty, personal essayists frequently represent themselves as loafers or retirees, inactive and tangential to the marketplace. The shiftless marginality of the essayist's persona is underscored by the titles of some of the most famous essay series: *The Idler, The Rambler* (Samuel Johnson), *The Spectator, The Tatler* (Addison and Steele). Perhaps by affecting the role of lazy scribblers, essayists make themselves out to be harmless, thereby able to poke fun at will (1995, p. xxxiii).

The Tatler and *The Spectator* had an ambivalent relationship to the public sphere and the coffeehouses that largely housed it. They depended upon them for their circulation, but they also warned of their negative effects. Satires of life in the coffeehouses could also be found in other periodicals, painting a different picture of the supposedly "rational" public sphere. These satires in part ridiculed the notion that every person could comment on matters of state and be a politician or critic. One satire described the coffeehouse as "a *High Court of Justice*, where every little Fellow in a *Chamlet-Cloak* takes upon him to transpose Affairs both in Church and State, to shew reasons against *Acts* of Parliament, and condemn the Decrees of *General Councels* ..." (quoted in Mackie 1998, p. 138). While the papers then may have contributed to the formation of a public sphere, their editors and writers likely did not hold the belief that anyone, or perhaps even most, who entered it should be listened to in equal measure. Instead, the public to be found in the coffeehouses, as described by some of the writers who sat among them, was a collection of Dickensian odd types and characters.

> As you have a hodge-podge of Drinks, such too is your Company, for each man seems a Leveller, and ranks and files himself as he lifts, without regard to degrees or order; so that oft you may see a silly *Fop*, and a worshipful *Justice*, a griping *Rook* [con artist], and a grave *Citizen*, a worthy *Lawyer*, and an errant *Pickpocket*, a Reverend *Nonconformist*, and a Canting *Mountebank*; all blended together; to compose an *Oglio* [mishmash] of Impertinence (quoted in Mackie 1998, p. 139).

Steele and Addison in the pages of *The Tatler* and *Spectator* warned of the overconsumption of news and posited their papers as antidotes to the malady of the brain likely to develop from such overconsumption. To Steele and Addison, the newspapers produced negative effects, inflaming men and filling their heads with contradictory opinions that were of little substance. They peddled the latest facts and rumors of the day, rather than teaching men how to think or encouraging wisdom. In No. 155 of *The Tatler*, Addison commented upon an upholsterer he knew who had become so obsessed with the news and affairs of state, that he neglected his own affairs and was descending into poverty. "For tho' his Wife and Children were starving, I found his chief Concern at present was for this great Monarch" (quoted in Mackie 1998, p. 59). Addison followed the upholsterer to a bench in a park where they encountered four other "Politicians," men similarly inclined to spend too much of their time discoursing on matters of state, informed by nuggets of knowledge gleaned from the paper. Before leaving, the Upholsterer asked Addison for some money.

> In Compassion to so needy a Statesman, and to dissipate the Confusion I found he was in, I told him, if he pleased, I would give him Five Shillings, to receive Five Pounds of him when the Great Turk was driven out of *Constantinople*; which he very readily accepted, but not before he had laid down to me the Impossibility of such an Event, as the Affairs of *Europe* now stand (p. 61).

While Addison appears to ridicule the upholsterer, there is also sympathy for his plight, and the charity to be provided by his paper, which Addison refers to in the opening number of *The Tatler*, appears to be aimed at such figures. Addison, charitably, will disengage them from such obsessions more likely to land them in Bedlam than Parliament, and foster more interest in one's self than the affairs of state. As Addison concludes in his account of the encounter with the upholsterer:

> This Paper I design for the particular Benefit of those worthy Citizens who live more in a Coffee-house than in their Shops, and whose Thoughts are so take up with the Affairs of the Allies, that they forget their Customers (p. 61).

It may appear that Addison is criticizing involvement, or over-involvement, in the public sphere, those that spend too much time in the coffee houses while neglecting their own business—that market interests and care of one's self should take precedence over re-viewing the state. Perhaps that was in part Addison's opinion. But he seems even more interested, not in encouraging "civil privatism," as Habermas refers to it, but in training men's and women's minds to be more discerning, to be able to exercise judgment, and to cultivate in them an ability to think that transcends the immediate and current—what the newspapers offer—and looks to what is lasting and "good."

Indeed, in No. 178 of *The Tatler*, Steele in turn took up the problem of "news-addiction." He also reported on the mad upholsterer: that "unfortunate Tradesman has for Years past been the chief Orator in ragged Assemblies, and the Reader in Alley-Coffee-houses" and who Steele claims to have helpfully dispatched to Bedlam (St. Mary of Bethlehem, a hospital for the insane), after their meeting in a coffee-house (quoted in Mackie 1998, p. 67). To warn others off a similar fate, Steele emphasized the negative effects of the newspapers:

> The Tautology, the Contradictions, the Doubts, and Wants of Confirmations, are what keep up imaginary Entertainments in empty Heads, and produce Neglect

of their own Affairs, Poverty, and Bankruptcy, in many of the Shop-Statesmen; but turn the Imaginations of those of a little higher Orb into Deliriums of Dissatisfaction, which is seen in a continual Fret upon all that touches their Brains, but more particularly upon any Advantage obtained by their Country, where they are considered as Lunaticks, and therefore tolerated in their Ravings (p. 69).

Steele promises to do his utmost to prevent these "evils" in the pages of *The Tatler*.

In the last issue of *The Tatler*, Steele apologized to his reading public for the need to end the paper. He remarks that because his paper was in the habit of correcting the public's vices, and that while not naming names in print, he still found that his friends were "in pain to act before me," worried that their faults would be highlighted in the next issue. He cites that reason and "a thousand other nameless things" as cause to cease publication. Steele also makes the claim that "the least excusable part of all this work" was that he at times had to write about matters of church and state. He defends such writing by saying that when those matters affected every Christian and freeholder in England, he "could not be cold enough to conceal" his opinion on them (quoted in Mackie 1998, p. 77). Again, in that sense of charitable guardianship, Steele would *even* engage in political criticism if it meant that his readers would be improved by it. Contemporary critics thought that *The Tatler*'s end was likely due more to some political intrigue than Steele's worry that he could no longer live comfortably among his friends. John Gay, an English poet and dramatist, in an evaluation of the periodical market at the time, commented that the paper likely had been laid down "as a sort of Submission to, and Composition with the Government for some past Offences" (quoted in Mackie 1998, p. 151). Erin Mackie argues that Steele may have given up the paper as part of a political deal that would allow him to keep his lucrative post as commissioner for stamp duties. This would then underscore Steele's regret over having published his political opinions.

Gay, Steele's contemporary, praised him and the writing found in his papers. Gay remarked that while other papers flattered the public's opinions, encouraging their "fashionable Vices, and false notions of things," Steele went against the grain and through his fictional persona Isaac Bickerstaff "ventur'd to tell the Town, that they were a parcel of Fops, Fools, and vain Cocquets" (quoted in Mackie 1998, p. 152). Steele corrected opinions rather than served them, and also convinced his readers of the value of learning, rescuing it from "the hands of Pedants and Fools" (p. 152). What Gay most admired in Steele's writings was that they offered "a new way of Thinking" that would be copied, if imperfectly, by other writers: "I think we may venture to affirm, that every one of them Writes and Thinks much more justly than they did some time since" (pp. 152–3). Still, this "new way of thinking" had to be balanced against the demands of the periodical readership. As Addison commented, contrasting periodicals with books, essays must be lively and grab the reader's attention.

> We must immediately fall into our Subject and treat every Part of it in a lively manner, or our Papers are thrown by as dull and insipid: Our Matter must lie close together, and either be wholly new in itself, or in the Turn it receives from our Expressions (quoted in Mackie 1998, p. 95).

Essay writers did not have the "benefit" of book authors, who had the space and readers expectations, to include "flat Expressions, trivial Observations, beaten Topicks, and common Thoughts, which go off very well in the Lump" (p. 95). Periodical essays then introduced a new style of writing, for which Addison's and Steele's became the touchstone. They had to negotiate a balance between earning the time and attention of "forty or fifty thousand Readers" while instructing them in "Wisdom and Virtue" (p. 95). They could not treat their audience as captive and had to get their point across quickly and clearly. One wonders if this shift was not somewhat instrumental—the performativity demands of the new form reflecting a broader interest to extract what is useful from knowledge and learning with the least amount of effort or strain, or at least, as efficiently as possible, so that the emerging bourgeois society could prosper and grow as quickly.

And while there may have been a seriousness of intention behind both *The Tatler* and *The Spectator*, Addison could also make light of their purpose, noting the "material" benefits of the paper, which he contrasted with its "formal" benefits, namely improving and delighting the reader's mind. The "material" benefits included not only the consumption of paper manufacture, the employment of printers, and business for many indigent persons who distributed the paper, as Addison remarks, "while I am writing a *Spectator*, I fancy myself providing Bread for a Multitude," but also the many uses to which the paper was put after being read, such as lighting pipes, wrapping spices in, and serving as a "good Foundation for a Mutton-pye," making the paper highly desirable the last Christmas (1998, p. 101).

Despite this joking, Addison believed that those wanting to make the world wise should utilize the advantages provided by the technology of print. The news-writers and party zealots made poor use of print, and Addison's apolitical focus was made clear again as he called for "instruction in Wisdom and Virtue" rather than politics and the making of "good Fathers, Husbands, and Sons" than counselors and statesmen (p. 95). After *The Spectator* ended, Steele and Addison followed with yet another paper, *The Guardian*, but it did not enjoy the same success. Steele also found himself under pressure to publish a more political paper, so he began the Whig *Englishman* in October 1713. Addison meanwhile briefly resumed *The Spectator* with the help of Eustace Budgell and Thomas Tickell (Mackie 1998, p. 2). The papers though that Steele and Addison are remembered for are *The Tatler* and *The Spectator*. Their adherence to standards of critical judgment and priority of intellect over politics would be emulated in the "great reviews" that began publication 100 years later.

The Spectator had continued *The Tatler*'s admonishment of overconsumption of the news and over involvement in party politics. The figure of the apolitical

Spectator would serve as a model for the necessary distance required to develop a critical judgment. Introducing himself in the first issue, "he" wrote:

> Thus I live in the World, rather as a Spectator of Mankind, than as one of the Species; by which means I have made my self as Speculative Statesman, Solider, Merchant and Artizan, without ever meddling with any Practical Part in Life. I am very well versed in the Theory of an Husband, or a Father, and can discern the Errors in the Oeconomy, Business, and Diversion of others, better than those who are engaged in them; as Standers-by discover Blots, which are apt to escape those who are in the Game. I never espoused any Party with Violence, and am resolved to observe an exact Neutrality between the Whigs and Tories, unless I shall be forc'd to declare my self by the Hostilities of either side. In short, I have acted in all the parts of my Life as a Looker-on, which is the Character I intend to preserve in this Paper (p. 81).

Addison, writing as the figure of the Spectator, recommended this critical distance and likened the distraction from politics that its cool reasoning provided to that offered by the Royal Society, who had diverted "many of the greatest Genius's of that Age" to scientific discovery, producing the air-pump, barometer, and quadrant. If not for this diversion, they may have engaged in politics "with the same Parts and Application," and may "have set their Country in a Flame" (quoted in Mackie 1998, p. 99). Addison hoped to enlarge his readership by recommending the paper to his fellow Spectators, those

> who live in the World without having any thing to do in it; and either by the Afluences of their Fortunes, or Laziness of their Dispositions, have no other Business with the rest of Mankind but to look upon them. Under this Class of Men are comprehended all contemplative Tradesmen, titular Physicians, Fellows of the Royal Society, Templers that are not given to be contentious, and Statesmen that are out of Business. In short, every one that considers the World as a Theatre, and desires to form a right Judgment of those who are the Actors on it (pp. 89–90).

What they were to do with those judgments, Addison leaves unclear. But he also recommends his paper to the "Blanks of Society," those who have no ideas of their own and fill themselves with the news of the day, and to the "female World."

It is easy to draw an analogy here between the media culture of early eighteenth-century England and the media culture in the United States, and other Western liberal democracies, today. The criticisms commonly made are that the media appear ever more partisan, that the line between news and analysis or news and opinion is increasingly blurred, and that shallow thinking prevails. Arguably, these criticisms could be applied, to some degree, to the news media since its inception, as Steele's and Addison's thoughts on the newspapers of their day make clear.

[T]his Way of Writing [in newspapers] falls in with the Imagination of the cooler and duller Part of Her Majesty's Subjects. The being kept up with one Line contradicting another, and the whole, after many Sentences of Conjecture, vanishing in a Doubt whether there is any Thing at all in what the Person has been reading, puts an ordinary Head into a Vertigo, which his natural Dulness would have secured him from (Steele quoted in Mackie 1998, pp. 67–8).

The review's role then, or the role of the long-form essay format that *The Tatler* and *The Spectator* provided, was to deepen thinking, improve critical judgment, and move past partisanship where it leads to one-sided thought. As Addison declared in No. 262 of *The Spectator*, "my Paper has not in it a single Word of News, a Reflection in Politicks, nor a Stroke of Party … I have rejected everything that savours of Party" (quoted in Mackie 1998, p. 97). What may be the difference though between the time of Steele and Addison and today is the degree of influence that the reviews have upon the public. Addison surmised in No. 10 of *The Spectator* that it was read by at least 60,000 readers in London *and* Westminster, as 3,000 issues were printed and each issue he estimated to be read by 20 persons. He referred to his readers as "disciples" (quoted in Mackie 1998, p. 88). Six thousand readers may not seem like many, but its influence appears to have been large. The figure relative to the total number of literate readers able and willing to engage with these texts may be higher than today. Additionally, the ability of those readers to intervene in politics may also have been different. As Addison claims, his readership included not just people in London, the inhabitants of coffeehouses, but also people in Westminster, the inhabitants of Parliament. The extent to which the news and punditry influence politics today may unfortunately be much greater than the influence of the *London Review of Books* or *The New York Review of Books*.[8]

Censors of Opinion—From Morals to Politics

The formation of "public opinion" then was not just a spontaneous amalgamation of the general middle-class population's ideas and thoughts. Rather, writers and editors who told the public *what to think* privately sought to direct "public opinion." As Charles A. Knight writes, rather than consider them the reflectors of consensus, "they might equally be thought of as efforts to define, elicit, or impose such a consensus in a period of dynastic rivalry, war, religious contention and political uncertainty" (2009, p. 3). Defoe gave himself the role as censor[9] of opinion when

---

8 Jacobs and Townsley (2011) detail the changing nature of the space of political opinion, arguing that new media, such as television, have increased the influence of political opinion while also decreasing its autonomy from politics and its critical rationality.

9 The word "censor" comes from the Latin word *censere* meaning "to appraise, value, judge." It first appeared in English in the 1530s to refer to the Roman magistrates who took

he wrote in the preface to the first volume of his review that "my firm resolution in all I write to exalt virtue, expose vice, promote truth, and help men to serious reflection, is my first moving cause and last directed end" (Payne 1951, p. 7). The censor's remit as re-viewer was to shape public opinion by informing them on how to view the state.

Steele referred to himself, or his fictional persona Bickerstaff, as the "Censor of Great Britain," stating that "In a Nation of Liberty, there is hardly a Person in the whole Mass of the People more absolutely necessary than a Censor" (quoted in Mackie 1998, p. 55). In his first expression of censorship, Bickerstaff criticizes the general expense and affectation in equipage, the means by which London citizens got around the city other than by foot, often a horse drawn carriage with attendants, but he also critiques the use of sedan chairs used to carry people through the streets. If Bickerstaff were to propose a tax, he says it would be on coaches and chairs, because they take up space on the road and impede the movement of everyone else. In support of such a tax, Bickerstaff argues,

> We hang a poor fellow for taking any Trifle from us on the Road, and bear with the Rich for robbing us of the Road it self. Such a Tax as this would be of great Satisfaction to us who walk on Foot; and since the Distinction of riding in a Coach is not to be appointed according to a Man's Merit, or Service to their Country, nor that Liberty given as a Reward for some eminent Virtue, we should be highly contented to see them pay something for the Insult they do us in the State they take upon them while they are drawn by us (quoted in Mackie 1998, p. 56).

Bickerstaff's "policy recommendation" for a tax on equipage begins as something like a political critique, condemning a use of the road that seems to privilege the wealthy but also the pretenders. The critique though resolves to a more moral one by its end, as he condemns the pretensions and evil vanity that are the source of the problem. This example fits Koselleck's (1988 [1959]) argument that the public sphere's dominion was over morals and that the moral order put forth there became a critique of the state, whose job it was to regulate things like traffic upon the roads and to impose taxes. The moral and seemingly apolitical re-views presented an alternative means of evaluation and eroded, perhaps marginally, the state's power to enforce its view, because they offered and drew from the public a different set of criteria from which to judge how society should be ordered. They translated the political views of their party, the Whigs, into socio-cultural instruction.[10]

---

censuses and oversaw public morals. *The Tatler* and *The Spectator* similarly oversaw public morals and advocated for social reform.

10 Both papers were also wartime publications and according to Mackie, translated the "ongoing military and political battles against the French onto the domestic and social theater of cultural war" (1998, p. 24).

According to Knight, Steele leveraged his authority as a moral writer into that of a political writer. "A key issue was the authority of writers, as writers, to speak of political matters" (2009, p. 2). In essence, the question was whether writers could participate in politics and also whether writing was a form of political participation. Could the state, specifically the Crown and Parliament, who officially occupied the realm of politics, be challenged in their field by an authority derived from the realm of letters? Many writers previous to and during Steele's and Addison's time published unacknowledged pieces, such as Jonathan Swift, or maintained distinct personas as writer and politician, such as Matthew Prior (Knight 2009). However, Steele especially, who served as a Member of Parliament from 1713 to 1714, sought to combine these roles. The "critic" and its counterpart could be embodied in the same person, operating side by side.

By the early 1700s, periodicals had developed into a variety of forms, which recognizably persist today—newspapers, tabloids, scholarly journals, journals of criticism, journals of opinion, and special interest journals, such as journals of trade. Even the latter, while concentrating on subjects such as agriculture, could use reviews to provide criticism on affairs of state.[11] Moreover, within the fairly broad category of journals of opinion, a split could already be seen between publications like *The Tatler* and *The Spectator* that paid more attention to culture and society and publications like Defoe's *Review* that gave more attention to politics and economics.

In 1713, Parliament levied a tax of a halfpenny on half-sheet news magazines, a penny tax on whole sheets, along with a tax of 12 pence on advertisements (Payne 1951). Defoe wrote about the proposed tax in Volume VIII, No. 172 of his *Review*, arguing that the tax was not meant to raise revenue for the state but to stop the press.[12] While Defoe was not opposed to putting certain publications out of business or even forbidding all papers from discussing public affairs, he effectively argued that the economic, educational and religious benefits of periodicals and other pamphlets outweighed their harms.[13] While the tax drove many publications out of business, the boom of periodicals rebounded by century's end. By 1800, at least 264 periodical publications existed in England (Coser 1997, p. 72). In addition to fighting the state's censorship, early political journalists often also

---

11 John Houghton, a seventeenth-century editor, published several journals including the *Collection of Letters for the Improvement of Husbandry and Trade*. That journal while concentrating on economic and agricultural articles also contained reviews of titles such as Thomas Firmin's *Some Proposals for the Employment of the Poor* and Cook's *A Discourse of Trade*, which was the subject of a review titled "An Essay to prove that 'tis better for *England* to have *Ireland Rich* and *Populous*, than *Poor* and *Thin*" (McCutcheon 1923, p. 257).

12 Habermas (1991 [1962]) also writes that the stamp tax put some journals out of business while others printed fewer copies and with less volume.

13 Here he took a paternalistic view, arguing that the stop in trade would harm the poor, that the unavailability of religious tracts would keep them in spiritual darkness, and a lack of publications would deprive them of the advantage of reading.

risked their personal well-being. Defoe was imprisoned multiple times for his writings, and Steele was ousted from Parliament for writing a piece of propaganda, which he later won recognition for in the award of a knighthood. Despite their efforts, however, the institutionalization of the review form did not occur until the beginning of the nineteenth century.

Chapter 2
The "Great Re-views":
The Institutionalization of Critical Practice

This chapter examines the institutionalization of the review form, specifically focusing on the *Edinburgh Review, The Quarterly*, and *The Westminster Review*. These so-called "great reviews" began publication during times of rapid political change. They followed the American and French Revolutions, wielding their greatest influence in the years leading up to the Reform Act of 1832 in Great Britain, which extended voting rights to a large number of male citizens who held substantial property (remaining males would gain the right to vote in 1918, while women gained the right in 1928). This, the period of the "great reviews," saw a solidification of the domination of liberalism as a political doctrine and of capitalism as the means of organizing a state's economy. It is this rise to predominance of the liberal-democratic state form that provides the critical moment around which discussion in this chapter is organized. Although the three selected journals represented different views on the state's current policies and had different hopes for its future, they shared a commitment to the critical practice that had come to define the review form. As with the early reviews, the "great reviews" were held up as a forum for critical debate that sometimes erupted into partisan rancor. Importantly, the "great reviews" provided "men of letters" with a position from which to critique those holding power within the state. In exploring the genesis of the great reviews, I contend that, while providing a home for the intellectual or theorist intent upon making a critique of the state, from its beginnings, the reviews' very users critiqued the form itself. The reviews' editors, contributors and readers were engaged in a self-reflective process of questioning the value of their critical practice: asking whether or to what degree the review could be expected to effectively challenge the prevailing order of things.

A New Institutional Home for the Practice of Politics?

In the opening decade of the nineteenth century, the tradition of the so-called "great reviews" began. The first was the *Edinburgh Review, or Critical Journal*, launched in 1802. Its subtitle is significant, because it defines the new review form as a practice of criticism. After *Edinburgh*, two more noteworthy reviews began publication—*The Quarterly Review* in 1809 and *The Westminster Review* in 1824. Beginning in the 1820s, a second generation of reviews proliferated in Great Britain, including but not limited to, *The Foreign Quarterly* (1827), *The British*

Critic (1827), *The British and Foreign Review* (1835), the *London Review* (1835), *The Dublin Review* (1836), *The Church of England Quarterly* (1837), *The Foreign and Colonial Quarterly* (1837), the *English Review* (1844), *The North British Review* (1844), the *British Quarterly* (1845), the *Prospective Review* (1845) and its successor the *National* (1855), *The Irish Quarterly* (1851), the *Scottish Review* (1853), the *London Quarterly* (1853), and *The Home and Foreign Review* (1862) (Shattock 1980, p. 96).

What separated the reviews from other institutions of thought? In an essay titled, "The Great Reviews," R. G. Cox (1937a) writing for *Scrutiny*, a twentieth-century English literary quarterly, laid out the three historical functions of serious reviews. First, they fostered an exchange of ideas, much like the coffeehouses, by "providing a focus for current movements of thought and opinion" (p. 2). In this sense, they operated as a print public sphere—this sphere was neither unified nor universal but rather represented many di-visions. However, even if room existed for a variety of reviews and other periodicals, they, taken together, created a critical milieu that contributed to the critique of the state's view, whether or not the critique was ever complete or uniform. Second, the reviews professionalized writing and reviewing by providing a decent living from it, thereby creating an institutional home for writers. This not only materially provided for the writers, but it also gave them a platform from which they could express themselves and find an audience. In other words, the reviews gave writers "a means of livelihood *and* a field of action." Third, the reviews built and maintained a critical tradition, through "an authoritative expression of critical standards" (p. 2). They told people what to think, like *The Tatler* and *The Spectator* and Defoe's *Review* before them. Denys Thompson likened this role of nineteenth-century journalism to one of the functions of the church, citing Stead on Morley, who wrote, "To him a newspaper was simply a pulpit from which he could preach" (Thompson 1935, p. 30).

Cox also argued that the function of the critical reviews served as a replacement for the "conversation and personal contacts of a small and compact society" by focusing critical discussion (1947, p. 267). Lewis Coser writes about the reviews as the British equivalent of the French salon (1997). They comprised an institutional setting for intellectual activities. They became necessary as the public who visited the coffeehouses became larger and more separate. As Coser writes, "authors ... grouped themselves around the [*Edinburgh*] *Review*, sharing in a common universe of ideas. For many, the *Review* provided not only intellectual contact but also the setting for personal meetings. The editorial office became a kind of informal forum where writers would meet with one another, the editor, or, upon occasion, a reader" (1997, p. 77). Early eighteenth-century papers like *The Tatler* had already begun the substitution of a print public sphere or public culture for the face-to-face culture of the coffeehouses. The reviews continued this trend, linking together writers and readers. However, as the quotation above makes clear, they also brought writers and sometimes writers and readers back together to that face-to-face immediacy that print lacks.

Cox also articulated the "ideal function of the literary review," something he noted to which "founders of serious periodicals during the last thirty years have devoted much thought" (1947, p. 264). He began with T. S. Eliot who advocated the ideal review as a *tendency* rather than a program, which is "residual from the play of the individual opinions of the editor and contributors" (p. 265). Rather than being the expression of a haphazard group, a review unified a diverse group of thinkers by providing a common space for publication. This "corporate personality" of a review allowed room for disagreement but still demonstrated a tendency in its thought. By serving as institutional "group" homes, the "great reviews" became places where men of like (a)vocation could interact. Moreover, this practice allowed a common "ideological" voice to develop. Often, the reviews did not publish signed articles, preferring a collective "we" or corporate personality (Coser 1997).[1] Rather than a collection of opinions, the reviews were editorial collectives and advanced a particular mode of thought.

The practice of anonymous reviews not only encouraged the reviewers to be more forthright in their opinions but also assigned the authority of the opinion to the review itself. This represented a change from the papers of Defoe and Addison and Steele where the authority of opinion resided within the man itself.[2] By transferring the authority to the institution, the "great reviews" could outlast any one editor or contributor. Moreover, they gave authority to criticism as an institution rather than to a particular critic. Institutionalizing this authority within an impersonal publication increased the perception of its infallibility. As George L. Nesbitt writes, "[t]his assumption of infallibility added much to the vigor and incisiveness of the articles. Apparently it awed the reading public ... For both [the *Edinburgh* and the *Quarterly*] prospered exceedingly" (1966, p. 5).

The American journal, the *New Englander*, a largely theological organ, sought a similar authority from a more corporate voice. It made a distinction between journals that publish a variety of opinions and reviews that speak their own mind and actively censor opinions.

> Its functions therefore in its proper department are analogous to those of the American Journal of Science, rather than to those of a popular Review, which aspires to be a censor of opinions and of parties, and to speak its own mind on whatever topic it undertakes to handle (Kingsley 1843, p. 5).

---

1 However, Sir William Molesworth, the proprietor of the *London Review* begun in 1834 and later merged with the *Westminster Review* in 1836, required that "some signature" be attached to each article to make the review only responsible for the "general principles advocated, not for the particular development of them, and to attach a certain degree of responsibility to each writer" (quoted in Grote, 1970 [1866], p. 10).

2 Even though in the case of the persona Isaac Bickerstaff or The Spectator, the "man" was fictional.

As it had stated in its prospectus, the *New Englander* sought to align itself with the latter type of periodical. Like the "popular Review," and unlike the scholarly *American Journal of Science*, it would present its opinions in a common voice. In other words, as Steele stated in the first issue of *The Tatler*, it would tell people what to think and not present all opinions "objectively" side by side. Further, the journal made it clear that while a variety of topics would be discussed, there would be a consistency to rather than a diversity of opinions.

> It will claim the privileges of a corporation in the republic of letters, a person in law, with an individuality and character of its own, and with its own opinions to profound and defend (Kingsley 1843, p. 2).

The journal chose to buck the trends of relying upon the names of its contributors for its success and presenting a variety of opinions to appeal to a wider audience. Instead, it chose to have a particular point of view. This perspective would be ensured by a collective method of management. A committee of six men, including the quarterly's owner, would make the editorial decisions.

The "corporate personality" of the reviews can be thought of in terms of the distinction between the universal and specific intellectual along with Bourdieu's attempted reconciliation of these types. This dichotomy in the theorizing of intellectuals arose in France. Jean Paul Sartre perhaps both created and embodied his self-defined role of the universal intellectual. Embracing the position of the ultimate *engagé*, Sartre, and others like him, returned to the Platonic ideal of the intellectual as critical adviser on all matters important to state and society. Similarly, Edward Said (2002) saw the intellectual as the one who "speaks truth to power." Opposing the seeming self-importance and the necessarily transcendent position of a universal intellectual, Foucault proposed the role of the specific intellectual, who would only speak to the body of knowledge that constituted that intellectual's domain. Since Foucault's archaeologies and genealogies were only supposed to be read for themselves as such and not transported into other discourses, it made sense that an intellectual should also not intervene in a discourse that he/she had not studied. Bourdieu attempted to combine the universal and specific intellectual by outlining a program for a universal intellectual that is a composite or *corporative* association of specific intellectuals (Bourdieu 1989). Achieving the best of both worlds, intellectuals could speak more truth to power *and* know what they were talking about. In many ways, the "great reviews" anticipated Bourdieu's corporation of intellectuals and created an authoritative "we," which while still allowing for differences, embraced a common tendency of thought.

The reviews and other forms of "higher journalism" also "provided many intelligent people with a livelihood and an opportunity of using their talent without feeling that it was wasted" (Thompson 1935, p. 30). The fact that the reviews paid their authors further institutionalized the form and the vocation of the critic. The *Edinburgh* paid rates that had not been seen before and forced its authors to accept payment, so there would be no division between "dilettantes" and "professionals"

(Coser 1997). Being able to earn a living through criticism allowed reviewing to become a profession that attracted the best.

It also offered an opportunity to educated and intelligent men who lacked other vocational avenues due to their politics. Young men started the *Edinburgh* and the *Westminster*. The *Edinburgh*'s founder was 31, its founding editor, 29, and its two most active contributors, 24 (Coser 1997). Three were lawyers and all were highly educated but poor. Tories dominated the Edinburgh bar at that time, making it difficult for Whigs to gain a foothold. The *Westminster* was founded at Jeremy Bentham's initiative and with his support. However, the group most active in the journal was the Utilitarian Society, and its leader was the 17-year-old John Stuart Mill.

Defoe, Addison, and Steele may have helped legitimize the profession of author and editor. However, being a journalist continued to be considered a rather degrading occupation. An exception was made for those associated with the "great reviews." A friend supporting John Gibson Lockhart's decision to become editor of the *Quarterly* wrote,

> Your accepting the editorship of a newspaper would be infra dig and a losing of caste; but not so I think accepting of the editorship of the Quarterly Review ... An editor of a Review like the Quarterly is the office of a scholar and a gentleman; but that of a newspaper is *not*, for a newspaper is merely stock-in-trade to be used as it can be turned to most profit (William Wright, quoted in Innis 1942, p. 6).

Still, Francis Jeffrey, a founding editor of the *Edinburgh* and Henry Cockburn, a regular contributor, were ashamed of their connection to the review. When Jeffrey and his friends first planned the review, they wanted to establish a policy of no compensation. Sydney Smith had to convince them otherwise (Weir 1852). To be paid to write opinions was apparently *déclassé* at the time.

Although begun by young men, the reviews quickly generated significant audiences. The *Edinburgh* in time reached a circulation of almost 15,000, about six times more than the *Westminster*. Further, the former estimated that at least three people read each copy, ensuring that most members of the intellectual and elite circles comprised its audience. As a direct comparison, the "great reviews" attracted a larger audience than the many twentieth-century reviews, and that is not taking into account the differences in population (Cox 1937a, p. 2). Their audience also constituted a more coherent reading public. Cox stresses that the reading public in 1820 was not very stratified: "It was still possible to write for the reading public as a whole, just as it was still possible for the reviewers to examine the whole output of publishers" (1937a, p. 3). A more coherent and educated reading public allowed these quarterlies to practice a style of criticism that was lengthy and intellectual.

Unlike the early journals of Steele and Addison, as well as Defoe, which appeared bi- and even tri-weekly, most nineteenth-century reviews appeared as quarterlies, and according to Walter Bagehot, a co-founder of the *National Review*, they were successful because they met a timely need (Shattock 1980). After the stamp tax was passed in 1713, early journals shrunk even more, publishing fewer pages albeit also using smaller type. Sometimes reaching 40 pages in length, the essays found in the nineteenth-century reviews allowed writers more room to expand and expound upon the issues of the day.

> The *Spectator* and the *Tatler* had 'opened a similar vein' but they were too small: 'They could only deal with small fragments, or the extreme essence of a subject. They could not give a view of what was complicated, or analyse what was involved. The modern man must be told what to think—shortly, no doubt—but he must be told it. The essay-like criticism of modern times is about the length which he likes. The *Edinburgh Review*, which began the system, may be said to be, in this country, the commencement on large topics of suitable views for sensible persons' (quoting Walter Bagehot, Shattock 1980, pp. 98–99).

Other critical reviews, like the *Monthly Review* and the *Critical Review*, had begun in the mid- to late eighteenth century and achieved success but reviews during this period often were "puff" pieces that booksellers and publishers produced to sell their wares (Coser 1997; J. Gross 1969).

In the United States, the *American Review* (1845–52), a Whig journal, contrasted its role with that of the mainstay of the partisan press, the newspaper. Although it acknowledged the valuable role of the newspapers, especially those of the Whig party, it also pointed out their shortcomings—mainly brevity and impermanence. On the other hand, "[t]he Review will be a means of presenting more grave and extended discussions of measures and events, and of better preserving them to after times" ("Introductory," 1845, p. 2). Like its opponent, the *Democratic Review*, however, the *American Review* argued that a focus solely on politics could not be and would not be the entirety of the new periodical. While it recognized the importance of national politics, especially to a party journal, the review found that literature, philosophy, and morals were of equal or even greater importance. "It is not to be doubted, indeed, that these, from the nature of things, are so closely blended with all other elements that go to compose a state, as to make whatever influences affect these vitally, affect also, for evil or for good, the entire political fabric" ("Introductory," 1845, p. 3). The "great reviews" similarly took a wide lens to the important matters of the day, reviewing works on art, literature, travel, and other subjects not explicitly political.

The type of criticism practiced in the reviews may not have appealed to all audiences. That could be said to limit the distribution or transmission of the reviews' views. To an extent, it may be true. However, the reviews' political perspectives also traveled through the other types of periodicals, as their opinions influenced the monthlies, and the weeklies, and so on. Remarking on this refraction, Cox argued that the quarterly reviews, along with the periodicals that appeared weekly or monthly, all contributed to the foundation of criticism or the "irrigation of the surface of society" (1937a, p. 3). H. A. Mason similarly argued that while the quarterly review may provide the best form for the type of criticism *Scrutiny* admired—criticism that could dig deep into a subject and adhere to principles rather than passing fashions, it also gave support to publications with a greater frequency. Weeklies and monthlies could still be valuable in disseminating opinion, as long as the quarterlies existed to provide the backbone of a critical milieu. Mason reflected on the ideal hierarchy of M. Duhamel who proposed a pyramidal authority of book, quarterly, weekly, and newspaper. Even if ideal, all, in practice, Mason argued, contributed to the creation of a critical milieu, each "completing a certain stage in the dissemination of opinion" (1938, p. 259). However, he made the caveat that "[s]ome kind of consensus of opinion, and a coherent view of society as a whole (however sketchy be the coherence) is, of course, a necessary preliminary to this process" (Mason 1938, p. 259). While the nineteenth-century British reviews may have provided the necessary support to the other periodicals, Mason found the critical milieu of the twentieth century to be lacking.

The Politics of Re-viewing: Visions and Di-visions

The *Edinburgh Review* adopted a more selective approach to reviewing that rejected the inclusive manner of casting an eye over all the latest publications and instead chose to focus on those whose review could advance the political opinions held by the journal's authors and editors (Siskin 1998). John Gross gives two reasons for why reviews became more salient in the nineteenth century: 1) "their irrepressible passion for discussion which succeeded the fall of old systems on the French Revolution," and 2) "the stirring-up of fundamental social questions by the steady advance of industrialism" (1969, p. 2). Nesbitt presents a similar argument, writing that "[p]olitics was the subject of greatest interest and importance to the reading public" (1966, p. 6). The most interesting and important question of the day was reform, including the expansion of the electorate.[3] The politics of the reviews closely aligned with the parties holding different positions on the reform question, the *Edinburgh* giving voice to Whig views, the *Quarterly* to the Tories, and the *Westminster* to the as yet non-institutionalized philosophical radicals. Conservative forces, embodied in the Tory party, feared the expansion of the electorate and sought to oppose it. The Whigs, similarly fearful, sought a careful program of reform, and also office. Both parties opposed the radicals. Each criticized radical politics, but the Tories also accused them of bad morals (Nesbitt 1966, p. 7).

When the *Edinburgh* began, there was virtually no liberal party in Scotland, the country's politics then dominated by Tories, who made up the majority of the population. Expression of liberal opinions ran the risk of trials for sedition. Still, the politics of the minority Scotch Whigs were fairly moderate:

---

3   In 1818 and 1819, both the *Edinburgh* and the *Quarterly* reached their maximum circulations of around 14,000 copies each.

that there were a great many abuses in the Scotch political and administrative system which might be remedied, that the people had too little power and the lairds too much, that the Revolution in France had not been unmitigated madness, [and] that at any rate the fear of its influence in this country had been monstrously exaggerated (Masson 1856, p. 435).

There was a need though for an institution to give voice to these opinions, hence the arrival of the *Edinburgh Review*, which began during a brief and perhaps necessary interlude of Whig power.

The reviews were all partisan, although the *Edinburgh* and the *Westminster* were not intended as party publications. Nesbitt also argues that the question of reform was seen as too important or perhaps too large to leave to the journalists. Therefore, it required the critical analysis of the reviews. Reminiscent of Steele's and Addison's distinction between the newspapers and their own journals, a dividing line was created between providing the news and providing people with the means to judge it.

Indeed, while calling themselves "reviews" and writing their essays allegedly as reviews of other work, the journals focused more on politics than literature. As Terry Eagleton notes, "the journals tended to select for review only those works on which they could loosely peg lengthy ideological pieces, and their literary judgments, buttressed by the authority of anonymity, were rigorously subordinated to their politics" (1984, p. 38). In 1810, about half of any issue of the *Edinburgh* or *Quarterly* contained articles on current affairs; only one or two reviews would be literary (Nesbitt 1966, p. 5). Further, unlike Defoe, who aimed to make his review an organ of moderation,[4] the tone of the early nineteenth-century reviews was the antithesis of moderation, even and perhaps more so, when criticizing literature.

The journals' reviewing function, while aimed at books, had a higher purpose—to critique politics and advance the positions of their respective political parties (Fender 1986, p. 198). Further, while originating as reviews, the quarterlies did not only review books. Sometimes, they "reviewed" pamphlets or whatever other publication served their goals. For example, in an 1834 issue of the *Edinburgh*, a review begins:

---

4 Defoe lamented the partisan rancor of his day, writing in the last issue of the *Review*, "I acknowledge I cannot find that either recent as in memory or remote as in history, I ever saw, heard, or read the story of any nation, or of this nation, when such heats, such feuds, such rage of men among themselves ever went off without blood" (Vol. IX, No. 104, June 6, 1713; Payne 1951, p. 67). Defoe later referred to the feuds as "party madness." While reviews like Defoe's, Samuel Johnson's and Steele's and Addison's may have avoided the rancorous tone that the early nineteenth century "great reviews" are said to have adopted, the rancor itself was nothing new to the nineteenth century. Rather, the new eminent periodicals partook in it, whereas the earlier generation of model reviews mainly avoided it.

> We place the titles of these pamphlets at the head of this article without any design of entering upon the discussion of their contents, or going into the subjects to which they are directed; but in order to make some observations upon the present condition of the Party which still holds out against all reform—all change of any kind—all liberal opinions—all the principles suited to the age we live in, abroad and at home;—we mean those who used to be called Tories, and have lately taken the name of Conservatives (pp. 457–8).[5]

Reviews were lengthy, often at least 15 pages, and while they referenced the object of the review, their authors usually used them as opportunities to put forth their own, often political, opinions that took them further afield then what they were ostensibly reviewing (Nesbitt 1966, p. 4). What took priority often was the political writing; the so-called review was a means to an end.

While all three reviews at times exhibited fierce partisanship, however, Joanne Shattock contends that their party allegiances should not be so strictly defined (1980). She argues that neither the reviews nor their audiences always adhered to party divisions. Their audience was in great measure homogenous, comprised of similarly educated, intelligent, and politically interested individuals with some common cultural ties (Shattock 1980, p. 96). For the reviewers, who were a comparable group, sometimes a paycheck was more important than party affiliation, as reviewers published where they could (Fontana 1985). Both James and John Stuart Mill published in both the *Edinburgh* and the *Westminster*, and many other reviewers of lesser stature could be found in multiple publications with competing politics.

In the case of the *Edinburgh* the murkiness of its party allegiance may have been due to the vagueness of its political opinions. Moreover, its leading editor Jeffrey was no lover of politics. William Weir (1852, p. 108) argues that while the politics of the *Review* consisted of "vague, amiable sentiments, rather than of definite opinions or measures," this very indistinctness may have made the journal the effective propaganda organ that it became. It united a diverse group of "straggling and partial liberalism" into a powerful force in Britain. Weir also argues that it served as a medium of communication between the great thinkers of the day and a busy public. "It acted as a fly-wheel to quicken and increase the power of the action of the intellectual machine" (Weir 1852, p. 109).

The reason for the creation of the *Quarterly* in 1809 was as an explicit response to the popular *Edinburgh* and its politics. Its founders feared the criticisms being put forth by the Whigs and reformers, which could undermine church and state (Innis 2006 [1943], p. 316 n. 10). Tory leaders in London sponsored the new review, giving it political rather than literary aims (Nesbitt 1966, p. 4). Although

---

5 The titles of the two pamphlets being "reviewed" were "A Protest against 'The Reform Ministry and the Reformed Parliament.' By an Opposition Member" and "A Refutation of the Calumnies against the Lord Chancellor in the last Number of the 'Quarterly Review;' in an Article on 'The Reform Ministry and the Reformed Parliament.'"

it was formulated with a definite political purpose, to combat Whiggism, the Tory *Quarterly* still maintained a learned tone. One of its founders was Sir Walter Scott, who previously published in the *Edinburgh*, leaving the latter when it began to assert its Whiggishness too assertively. Moreover, the *Quarterly* saw itself as a review rather than a party paper. Emulating the review form of the *Edinburgh* was a political and tactical strategy. The *Quarterly*'s editor recognized that the authority of the review's opinions derived, in large part, from its form. The only way to combat philosophical Whiggism in a review was with another review of opposing political opinion.[6]

Understanding the partisanship of the reviews therefore also requires understanding their views on political parties themselves. Biancamaria Fontana (1985) emphasizes the complexity of the *Edinburgh*'s relationship to the Whig Party. She notes that the reviewers themselves were never a unified group, and that they had recurrent disagreements about how explicit the political commitment of the review should be. When Henry Brougham, one of the founders of the review, joined the Whig Party in 1807, the *Edinburgh* took a more partisan turn. However, some of the reviewers felt the journal had gone too far. Fontana argues that the identity of the review was more intellectual than political, and writes that "their sharing of a common theoretical project exemplified more of the reviewers' attitude than did the determination to sustain a common party allegiance" (Fontana 1985, p. 7). The review became the site where the new ideology of nineteenth-century Whiggism had its early formation. Perhaps its editors felt that a review too tightly bound to its party affiliation would not have had the freedom to participate in such a theoretical project.

The *Edinburgh* also helped to redefine the nature of parties, taking its cue from Edmund Burke's contemporaneous arguments on the role of political parties. Burke envisioned a party system whose partisanship was explicit and aggressive (Fontana 1985). Parties were not to be merely parliamentary factions. Rather, as the *Edinburgh* expressed, parties should operate throughout the country reflecting di-visions within society and public opinion. The *Edinburgh* found its audience and its "party members" among the people and public opinion, rather than within Parliament (Fontana 1985, p. 45). In other words, it sought the alternative resources of power present in the public sphere and further blurred the division between state and society.

While the *Quarterly* was closely tied to the Tories, the *Westminster* did not like political parties, which could have been in part because it lacked one. Over time, however, there would be philosophic radical Members of Parliament.[7] Still,

---

6 Sir Walter Scott, the *Quarterly*'s first editor, wrote, "he did not wish the projected review to be principally or exclusively political. That might even tend to defeat its purpose" (Ward and Waller 2000, Sec. 4, VI, Vol. XII).

7 Sir William Molesworth, the proprietor of the *London and Westminster Review*, which J. S. Mill edited, was a MP and philosophical radical, who during his ownership of the review wished to quit his political role in order to focus exclusively on the review,

John Stuart Mill writing in the first volume of the *Westminster* considered political parties to be institutions that made public interest subservient to private interests (Collini, Winch, and Burrow 1983). Attacking a Jeffrey essay on the subject of parties, Mill argued that the party speaking for the general interest would be the party to end all parties. The review's prospectus stated:

> The other critical works of the same kind are the saw powerful and efficient advocates of their respective parties, but it is the firm and decided determination of the Editors of the Westminster Review to take part with no faction, to support no body of men, and to perform the duties of the office they have undertaken, and in which they are not untried, as uninfluenced by personal enmity as by personal friendship (quoted in Nesbitt 1966, p. 35).

Watching from the United States, the *North American Review* noted the new journal's arrival and took aim at the assertion of non-partisanship from the *Westminster*.

> As to being of no party, a position in which the reviewers take pains to make it appear they stand, this is a very good string to strike in the beginning; it will vibrate with notes of melody to the people's ears;[8] but the thing itself is plainly impossible, in the present state of politics in England. Whoever are not for the ministry are against them; ministerialism is party, and opposition is party; there may be different shades of opposition, and consequently different gradations of party; but still, it is party, and nothing else ("Miscellaneous Notices," 1824, p. 423).

The *North American* commended the *Westminster* on identifying the shared aims of the *Edinburgh* and *Quarterly*, describing them as Scylla and Charybdis, each in different ways supporting tyrannical aristocracy. However, even though the *Westminster* had set a course between these two parties with a common purpose, and while

> their [the *Westminster*'s] work may be emphatically styled the *People's Review*; they are of the party of the people; but, after all, this is a *party*; and

---

where he thought he would be more useful and influential. He also argued that his political views on the Corn-laws, especially as expressed in the review, negatively affected his seat in Parliament. As he wrote to his friend Harriet Grote: "You would not have wished me to compromise those questions, nor could I have done it with my *Review*; indeed, I knew it (the *Review*) would lose me my seat, and it was the first pretext against me" (quoted in Grote, 1970 [1866], p. 20).

8 It could be that the *North American* was speaking from experience. The review had over its life span cultivated an appearance of non-partisanship and largely steered clear of political questions.

by the reviewers' own showing, it is a party marked by much stronger lines of distinction from the other two, than they are from each other ("Miscellaneous Notices," 1824, p. 424).

The *Westminster*'s first essay, "Men and Things in 1823," ostensibly a review by W. J. Fox of James Shergold Boone's poem, pays little attention to the poem under "review." The seventeen-page essay only discusses the poem and its author within the last page or two. The remaining 15 pages are given to an exposition of the politics of the day and the *Westminster*'s leading argument that government is best entrusted to the people. Arguing for the increasing importance of "the people," the radical philosophers of the *Westminster* spoke of a "new power," tapping into the critical moment when political decisions would be made about extending the vote in the liberal-democratic state (Fox 1824, p. 3). However, this new power belonged "of course" to the middle class, not the common masses: it "was championing certain 'outs' who wished to get in" (Nesbitt 1966, p. 42).

> The people have made themselves of more importance, and they are felt and acknowledged to be so, by every man that speaks, or writes, upon whatever subject. The manners and spirit of the higher classes would no longer be the sole, or the leading, topics of a dissertation on the state and prospects of the country. They are reduced to their proper dimensions. They have their chapter in the volume along with others, and stand in the index instead of being in the title. The people no longer sit quietly by as spectators, while Whig and Tory, that is, a few great families with their connexions and dependants, and a few pensioned or expectant creatures, play out the political game, in their own way, and for their own benefit (Fox 1824, p. 2).

With demands for alternative views making their way into the public sphere, the practices of re-viewing reflected this fragmentation and division. In the discussion of politics, the views of "the people" must also be taken into account. The review speaks of members of the House of Commons who now direct their speeches to the gallery, not only to the benches.

The public opinion and its "growing intelligence" is being recognized, the *Westminster* argues, but this recognition also contributes to its increasing wisdom and importance, being both "cause and effect" (Fox 1824, p. 6). The recognition comes from both politicians and men of letters along with the institutions that support them. The people represent both votes and new markets for literary products.

> The most abstruse controversies, on which the learned used to write in Latin, and discuss as in a secret sitting with closed doors, are now canvassed in cheap tracts, and debated in every village. The book-manufacturers show that respect for the people which all manufacturers show for a new and extensive market. All the standard works of our language make their appearance in cheap editions, or weekly numbers (Fox 1824, p. 2).

It is because they can purchase literary products that book-manufacturers and sellers are making titles available to them. In other words, the democratization of knowledge in large part depended upon its profitability.[9] Boone, the author of the poem under review, deems this democratization of knowledge a "revolution."

> It is justly remarked, however, that 'beneath the surface of the present conflict a far wider revolution is going on; and its mainspring, its vivifying principle, is the diffusion of knowledge. The pen is become a far more powerful and effectual weapon than the sword; and they who would oppose the arm of power to the influence of the press, must soon have occasion to rue the hopelessness of the contest' (Fox 1824, p. 17).

However, Boone fears this revolution, as political power may fall into the hands of "political enthusiasts, hair-brained speculators, soldiers of fortune, ambitious rebels, [and] hungry, desperate, unprincipled adventurers" (p. 17). To the editors and contributors of the *Westminster*, this fear might be justified, but the solution is not to take the power away from the people and place it in the hands of government, but to trust the people with that power.

Still, J. S. Mill famously later wrote of his fear of the tyranny of the majority and thought that political questions should be decided by a small number of persons specially educated for the task (Habermas 1991 [1962], p. 136). So, public opinion and public decision-making were distinct; the former could inform or revise the state's view, but its authority could not replace the state's, as guided by wise critics equipped for the task. The *Westminster* may have been willing to trust the people with power when it began publication, but over time, the opinion of at least one of its major contributors changed.

While other quarterlies like the *Edinburgh* and the *Quarterly* may have sought to re-view the state by proposing moderate reforms, improving upon it to meet the needs of their respective parties, the *Westminster* saw beyond the current state and sought to de-legitimize power sharing arrangements between Whig and Tory factions. The *Westminster Review,* as belonging to no party at its inception, expressed a critique of the political status quo. Its editors, contributors, and readership imagined a democratic state ruled not by the aristocratic classes, but by "the people." Prior to the publication of the *Westminster Review*, utilitarianism

---

9   The reviews themselves would not have existed if there was no market for them. The *Westminster* originally attained the services of the publisher Longmans of London. As Nesbitt argues, "Longmans would never have launched into any such expenses without good ground for assurance that Radicalism would either promote, or not prevent the accession of a proportionate number of customers" (1966, p. 35). After reading the attack on the *Edinburgh* within the *Westminster*'s first issue, Longmans decided to terminate their relationship, as they were also the publisher of the *Edinburgh*, which was one of its most profitable publications. James Mill then persuaded his own publisher, Baldwin, Cradock, and Joy, to undertake publication of the *Westminster*.

had little influence among Whigs (and of course, none among Tories) (Ward and Waller 2000, Sec. 3, III, Vol. XI). It acquired institutionalization and a publication to represent it only with the creation of the *Westminster Review*. Representing the position of those who were at the time radicals, the Westminster was the launching place for the utilitarian's political assault upon the holders of power within the state at the time.

The Institutionalization of the Reviews: A Home for Symbolic Action

In short, I am arguing that political writing that shapes politics requires institutionalization in some form and that such writing, in order to be politically effective, also requires the distance afforded by institutionalization. In the early nineteenth century, the reviews acted as their own "schools" for the production of effective political writing. They were "self-instituting institutions of criticism" (Fekete 1981/82) because they created a new form of political writing that was shaped not only by its "organized matter" (the apparatus) but also by its "materialized organization" (the institution) (Debray 2000). In other words, it was the institution itself that produced the authority of the reviews and largely shaped their contents. Additionally, and perhaps most importantly, while the reviews were primarily concerned with issues of politics, their first loyalty was to a standard of thought or criticism, not to a party. This meant that, first, they were institutions of criticism, or intellectual institutions, and only second, that they provided a home for programmatic political strategy or action, what today would be called "policy." The reviews assumed a position within a broader intellectual field, not the political field, and used this positioning capacity to influence politics. And, they met with a great deal of success. Harold Innis attributes a number of political successes to the various reviews and their editors and authors:

> Godwin, Shelley, the Hunts and Hazlitt sponsored an interest in revolution. The energies of Cobbett, and Place and the radicalism of James and John Stuart Mill, Bentham, and writers for the Westminster Review stiffened the influence of the Whigs for reform. Sydney Smith and writers in the Edinburgh Review and Albany Fonblanque[10] in the Examiner were effective in securing Catholic emancipation, the Reform Acts, the reduction of taxes on knowledge and eventually the destruction of the mercantilist system. Robert Burns gave a fatal blow to ecclesiasticism in Scotland (1946, p. 116).

While a Whig journal, the *Edinburgh* did not toe as strong a political line as the more radical and dogmatic *Westminster Review*. In fact, Coser's study of nineteenth-century British reviews in his book *Men of Ideas* specifically focuses on the two journals, because in his opinion they represent the two major varieties

---

10 Fonblanque was also a regular contributor to the *Westminster*.

of modern reviews: "the first, the broad review of opinion and the second, the more narrow mouthpiece for a particular set of doctrines" (1997, p. 73). James Mill in the first issue of the *Westminster* criticized the *Edinburgh* for circumventing major political questions in order to have a broad appeal (Mill 1824). The success of the *Edinburgh* and the review form—its popularization—had the effect of fragmenting philosophic Whiggism, dissipating the very identity of this political ideology (Fontana 1985). Over time, as more people read the reviews and as the reviews catered more to the tastes of their enlarged readerships, the pure elitism of the reviews and the "philosophical" side of their political thought was lost. The *Westminster* and its attention to "the greatest happiness of the greatest number" helped bring this about. However, when the reviews began, they measured themselves against high standards of criticism and thought that anchored their political opinions and philosophy. The motto found on the cover of the *Edinburgh* read "*judex damnatur cum nocens absolvitur, Publius [Publilius] Syrus*," translated as "the judge is condemned when the guilty is acquitted."

Similarly, the *London and Westminster Review*, the outcome of the joining of the two reviews in 1834, contained a quotation of John Locke from his *Essay on Human Understanding* on its title page:

> Those who have not thoroughly examined to the bottom all their own tenets, must confess they are unfit to prescribe to others; and are unreasonable in imposing that as truth on other men's belief which they themselves have not searched into, nor weighed the arguments of probability on which they should receive or reject it.

Interestingly, and again drawing on the Koselleckian framework, Locke's treatise blurred the boundary between state and moral law, giving the citizen as critic the right to pass moral judgments on the state, which eventually made the state's law dependent on the public's consent or rejection. But the reviews tried to elevate moral criticism and maintain the intellectual integrity modeled by Locke. The intellectual standard then of the re-view allowed it to challenge the public authority of the state's view from the private authority of the literary sphere.

The reviews may not have always met the standard they set. Some critics looking back find the reviews lacking critical depth (J. Gross 1969). Later literary criticism in certain small circulation periodicals like T. S. Eliot's *The Criterion* or the Leavis's *Scrutiny* may have improved upon their "great review" predecessors. Still, for that time, the seriousness and insightfulness of the reviews' criticism, particularly in matters of politics, is evident. Cox writing in *Scrutiny* had the following to say about the quality of the "great reviews": "The critical vigilance of the Reviews when faced with the unequal, the mediocre, or the utterly worthless, could be illustrated from almost any number" (1937b, p. 169), and "[t]hey consistently refused to pretend that excellence was 'common and abundant,' and with their extraordinary influence and authority, they played the major part in creating for the writers of their age that informed, intelligent and critical public without which no literature can survive for very long, and which is so conspicuously lacking to-day" (p. 175). These were not just shouting matches between partisans transcribed, although there was some shouting. The reviews' essays practiced a relatively high level of discourse and a willingness to train their critique upon their own assumptions and parties.

What distinguished the partisanship of the reviews from the party press was this level of discourse and the willingness to turn their criticism inwards. Reviews like the *Edinburgh* and *Westminster* supported Whiggism and radicalism, but their partisanship was of a philosophical kind. As I point out above, the ideology of the *Westminster* was labeled "*philosophic* Radicalism." This emphasis on thought and ideas was not only a matter of content but also a matter of style: "The exact mind which of all others dislikes the stupid adherence to the *status quo*, is the keen, quiet, improving Whig mind; the exact kind of writing most adapted to express that dislike is the cool, pungent, didactic essay" (quoting Walter Bagehot, Shattock 1980, p. 101). Shattock writes about the fine line the *Edinburgh Review* tread between being viewed as a ministerial journal and criticizing the Whig establishment in the government. As a re-view, it was careful to maintain a distance from the "view," perhaps wary of losing its credibility as a source of independent critique. She quotes correspondence from Thomas Macaulay, a contributor to the *Edinburgh*, and Lord John Russell, a Whig politician.

> Both Macaulay and Lord John Russell among others were insistent that although the *Edinburgh* was a Whig review it should on no account feel obliged to support all government measures and consequently never to offer criticism. 'I do not think that the Edinburgh Review ought to be under the same restraints under which a Whig Cabinet is necessarily placed,' Macaulay wrote. 'It should expound and defend the Whig theory of government; a theory from which we are forced sometimes to depart in practice.' Russell echoed the sentiment: 'I must repeat that, although a general concurrence of views between the Edinburgh Review and the bulk of the Whig party is very desirable, it would injure both the party and the Review, if the writers in the Review were checked in their general observations, or the party bound to enforce practically all that is speculatively beneficial' (1980, p. 101).

Perhaps more of the dispute between the *Edinburgh* and the *Westminster* was a disagreement over method and style rather than the political proposals for reform (Collini, et al. 1983). Jeffrey, the first editor of the *Edinburgh*, charged James Mill, a contributor to the *Edinburgh* in addition to helping found the *Westminster*, with Jacobinism. Macaulay, a contributor to the *Edinburgh*, believed that the philosophical Radicals' or Utilitarian's deduction of the "Science of Government from the principles of human nature" was "utterly impossible" (quoted in Collini, et al. 1983, p. 101). The group around the *Westminster* was charged with following the tradition of the French *philosophes*, which they did not deny, since the thought of the *philosophes* had produced results. In 1837, J. S. Mill explained the meaning of "philosophic radicals," writing in the *Westminster*,

> Those whom ... we call philosophic radicals, are those who in politics observe the practice of philosophers—that is, who, when they are discussing means, begin by considering the end, and when they desire to produce effects, think of causes ("England Under Seven Administrators," quoted in Collini, et al. 1983, p. 91).

Further, reviews like the *Edinburgh*, the *Quarterly*, and the *Westminster* maintained an independence that earlier reviews may not have achieved. This allowed them to practice a criticism more autonomous from social and market forces (Coser 1997, p. 76). The *Edinburgh* "broke upon a stagnant political and literary world" (Innis 1942, p. 7). Innis also writes that "[t]he deterioration of English journalism and restrictions on newspapers" and lower printing costs in Edinburgh were in part responsible for the appearance of the *Edinburgh Review* (1942, p. 7). At the time of the *Edinburgh*'s birth, "there was no critical journal worth reading" (Nesbitt 1966, p. 4). The inheritors of the Scottish Enlightenment used the review as a forum to continue discussions primarily of political economy, following the example of its short-lived namesake to which Adam Smith contributed.[11] As the first publication to successfully establish the new review form, the *Edinburgh* became and remained the standard against which other reviews were measured. "Almost from its inception the *Edinburgh* became the review for which most reviewers wished to write and in which authors wished to be reviewed" (Shattock 1980, p. 99).[12] Fontana similarly notes that it was the "first major vehicle for the popularization of the doctrines of political economy in nineteenth-century Britain" (1985, p. 2). Further, it also was "a most fertile and influential workshop for their application to the political and social problems of the time" (1985, p. 3).

The print run of the *Edinburgh*'s first issue in 1802 was 750 copies. By 1814, its circulation had reached 13,000. Fontana writes that the promotion of political economy, a branch of moral philosophy, remained the "star achievement" of the review (1985, p. 111). She also argues that political economy organized the thought of the *Edinburgh* because the driving question after the French Revolution was "on what basis could one hope to design political institutions suitable for modern commercial society?" (p. 10). Again, the focus of criticism was how best to order society to achieve certain aims. As the review aged, its politics pushed more to the foreground, and its political opponents took notice. As noted above, this is one of the main reasons why the *Quarterly*, the Tory publication, began.

---

11   The first *Edinburgh Review* began in 1755 but lasted only two issues.

12   The *Edinburgh* also exercised its influence in the United States where pirated copies were sold. Ralph Waldo Emerson wrote to Margaret Fuller, "Why should we read many books when the best books do not now avail us to yield that excitement and solid joy which fifteen years ago an article in the Edinburgh ... would give?" (quoted in Shattock 1980, p. 99).

For the *Edinburgh*'s editors and authors, the opportunity to answer the questions presented by political economy was not only "an effort to discuss productivity, but to *be productive*" (Siskin 1998, p. 45). As Friedrich Engels argued, political economy, as a line of inquiry and new form of knowledge, was brought into being by changing economic conditions, namely the expansion of trade. At the same time, the intellectuals who studied political economy and wrote about it in the pages of the *Review* sought not only to theorize those changes but also direct them (Siskin 1998, p. 45). Re-viewing was not a passive activity, but a purposeful intervention into the governance of society.

Whatever partisanship the reviews displayed, it was tame to what occurred in other publications, mainly newspapers. Arguably, this increasingly venomous discourse was a product of the impingement of outside forces on the "public sphere": "What distinguishes these polemics from the bellicose exchanges of earlier Whigs and Tories is their class-function: they are at root reactions to a threat to the public sphere itself from organized social interests beyond it" (Eagleton 1984, p. 38). Such organized interests arose in what Eagleton identifies as the "counter-public sphere," made up of the working-class and radical organizations of London's "Corresponding Societies, the radical press, Owenism, [William] Cobbett's *Political Register* and [Thomas] Paine's *Rights of Man*, feminism and the dissenting churches" (1984, p. 36). The *Westminster*'s general denunciation of the periodical form, discussed below, was aimed not only at the *Edinburgh* and the *Quarterly* but also at this radical press. For the *Westminster Review*, such interventions all equally substituted immediacy, what grabbed attention, for measured thought. Of all the radical publications then in existence, only the *Westminster* would attain the legitimacy and authority of the review form, soon constituting a triumvirate with the *Edinburgh* and *Quarterly* as the "publications that mattered," despite their different politics.

Evaluating the Review Form: A Re-view of Reviews

Fashioning a point of view is a necessary step in exercising authority, or at least of representing one's view, one's ordering, of the world. Although over time the *Westminster Review* achieved some success in legitimizing a form of radical criticism and institutionalizing the philosophy of its founders, at its outset, the *Review* questioned whether the review form could achieve these gains and bring about the political reforms it espoused in its pages. First published in January 1824, the *Westminster* was created to directly challenge the preeminence of the *Edinburgh* and the *Quarterly*. While the issue's first essay gave some indication of the *Westminster*'s political opinions, it would be an essay titled "Periodical Literature" found toward the back of the issue that would attract the most attention.[13]

---

13 The conservative American *New Englander* later reported: "The assault made a sensation at the time, but the object of it [the *Edinburgh*] survived and continues still to

Following the practice of other publications at the time, the *Westminster* included a "review of reviews," aiming most of its arrows at the *Edinburgh* and the *Quarterly*. While this essay written by James Mill is often read for what it says about the other reviews' politics as well as those of the *Westminster*, it also calls into question the review form itself. Specifically, the *Westminster* appears reluctant to utilize a medium whose characteristics appear inimical to the philosophical radicals' aims. The *Westminster* called then for a practice of reflexivity: "It is indeed a subject of wonder, that periodical publications should have existed so long, and have come at last to occupy so great a portion of the time and attention of the largest class of readers, without having become subject to a regular and systematic course of criticism" (Mill 1824, p. 206). In other words, the reviews should review *other* reviews, and, in the case of the *Westminster*, re-view the very role of reviews.

The "review of reviews" first turned its attention to the qualities of periodical literature in general, observing that due to their nature, periodicals must sell immediately. Because of this imperative, periodicals must give immediate effect and grasp at the applause of the moment. To do so, periodicals flatter opinions rather than guide them.

> To please the great body of men, which is the object of the periodical writer, he must flatter their prejudices. Instead of calling in question the opinions to which they are wedded, he must applaud them; and the more he can furnish such men with reasons for being in love with their opinions than before, the more he is sure of commanding their approbation, and of increasing their zeal to promote the reputation of his work (Mill 1824, pp. 207–8).

Those opinions most flattered are the fashionable opinions belonging to the ruling classes. It is the propagation of those opinions, the *Westminster* argues, on which periodical literature's success depends. For the *Westminster*, such a practice is unacceptable.

> The favourite opinions of people in power are the opinions which favour their own power; those opinions which we have already characterized as being the grand instruments of evil in this world, the ultimate and real cause of the degradation and misery of the great mass of mankind (p. 208).

Although the opinions belonging to the ruling class might be the fashionable opinions of the day, the review argued that over time wiser *critical* opinions would be commonly held. While wise opinions may begin with only a few people, through a slow process of transmission, they become the opinions of many. However, the review argues, periodical literature runs counter to this slow process of transmission because as noted above, it depends on immediate success. The

---

hold its leading position as an exponent of the sound conservative thinking of the times, as they move on" (1874, p. 610).

two dominant journals, the *Edinburgh* and *Quarterly*, were in no way immune to this characteristic.

The new review recognized that a large audience was not being served by either the Tory or the Whig journals. Their audiences, despite the seeming differences between the two reviews, were still comprised of the "aristocratical" class. The *Westminster* clarified what it meant by "aristocratical," defining it like an oligarchy, or rule by the few, and not confining it to the nobility. The *Edinburgh* and *Quarterly* catered to this ruling class and its fashionable opinions. In fact, the *Westminster* argued, the only real difference between the Tories (the ministerial party) and the Whigs (the opposition party) was that at any given time one party might have more power than the other, and that whichever had less was also trying to get more. The reviews' objective was either to maintain power for their party or overthrow the party in power. "The plan, therefore, is, to excite disapprobation of the principles and conduct of those who retain the distribution, and to excite approbation of the principles and conduct of those whom they wish to hold it in their stead" (p. 217). Whichever party was in power, politics would be exercised by the few and not the many. The review noted that just 200 leading families returned a majority of the members of the House of Commons each election.

The supposedly different audiences which the *Edinburgh* and *Quarterly* addressed themselves to, according to the *Westminster*, was really just the ruling class divided by the share each side had in the powers of government. As the representative of the opposition party in 1824, the *Edinburgh* had to play at "seesaw" between the positions of "the people," who it claimed to address, and the "aristocratical" class, to which it in actuality catered.

> If a portion of the discourse has been employed in recommending the interests of the people, another must be employed in recommending the interests of the aristocracy. Having spoken a while on the one side, they must speak a while on the other. Having written a few pages on the one side, they must write as many on the other ... In this game, o aristocratical and popular, it is sufficiently evident on which side, at last, the winnings remain (p. 218).

The *Quarterly* had an easier job, as it only claimed to represent the aristocracy and spoke for them. It offered its opinions as the opinions of the country and denigrated any opinion that might be construed as belonging to "the people." The *Edinburgh*'s seesaw act, on the other hand, required that it disparage both sets of opinions referring to those of the ruling class as "despotical" and those of the people as "anarchic" and affirming its own as belonging to the "middle," by which "they always desire to be understood *wise*" (p. 220). Its seesaw act also required, according to the *Westminster*, the use of vague language.

> Words which appear to mean much, and may by those to whom they are addressed be interpreted to mean much, but which may also, when it suits the convenience of those who have used them, be shown to mean little or nothing, are of singular

importance to those whose business it is to play the game of compromise, to trim between irreconcilable interests, to seesaw between contradictory opinions. Language of this description is peculiarly needed in making declarations which are meant to gain favour with the people (p. 220).

The *Westminster* stressed that its critique of the reviews applied to their politics and not their writings on literature and other subjects. The *Review* then turned to specific essays published in the *Edinburgh* and *Quarterly*, spending more time with the former. Through a practice of deconstruction, the *Westminster* supported its argument that the *Edinburgh* did in fact seesaw between the opinions of the aristocracy and the people, although its earliest volumes seesawed between the opinions of the aristocracy and established philosophy.

The *Westminster* noted that the review seemed disposed "to avoid grappling with any important and tender subject" (Mill 1824, p. 234). In fact, the *Westminster* makes clear that the subjects the *Edinburgh* chose to review, such as political economy, abolition of slavery, and Catholic emancipation, are those least likely to disrupt the opinions of the ruling classes.

The hold possessed by the aristocracy upon the powers of government, was not likely to be weakened, by any opinions propagated on the subjects of political economy, and the slave trade ... These were subjects, therefore, on which a reputation with the liberal, the enlightened, and the disinterested part of the public, might be courted, without risking much with the aristocratical and prejudiced (p. 234).

The prospectus of the *Westminster* sought to differentiate the new review from the *Edinburgh* and *Quarterly*, writing

'The Editors have great satisfaction in stating that they are the organs of an able and active society of individuals, who have seen with regret and somewhat of indignation that the name of criticism has been usurped with sinister views, and that the interests of literature and of a wise policy, and through them those of the Public have been sacrificed to selfish and unworthy purposes, are resolved to establish a tribunal where a fairer and more unbiased hearing may be obtained ... It is their ambition to make this review the representative of the true interests of the majority, and the firm and invariable advocate of those principles which tend to increase the sum of human happiness, and to ameliorate the condition of mankind' (quoted in Nesbitt 1966, p. 35).

However, no matter what its intentions, the new quarterly was still a review. In other words, despite the *Westminster*'s criticisms of the form, the philosophic radicals still went forward with the publication.

How did it reconcile its criticism with its undertaking? It argued that it would try to do things differently, in the hopes that there also was coming into being a different sort of audience that would appreciate its efforts.

> Are we, it may be asked, superior to seducements to which all other men succumb? If periodical writing is by its nature so imbued with evil, why is that we propose to add to the supply of a noxious commodity? ... We have no claim to be trusted, any more than any one among our contemporaries: but we have a claim to be tried. Men have diversities of taste; and it is not impossible that a man should exist who really has a taste for the establishment of the securities for good government, and would derive more pleasure from the success of this pursuit, than of any other pursuit in which he could engage, wealth or power not excepted ... We may be sanguine enough, or silly enough, or clear-sighted enough, to believe, that intellectual and moral qualities have made a great progress among the people of this country; and that the class who will really approve endeavours, in favour of good government, and of the happiness and intelligence of men, are a class sufficiently numerous to reward our endeavours (Mill 1824, p. 222).

The answer from the *Westminster* effectively stated that the men who operated the journal could overcome any shortcomings inherent in the review's form. They believed that somehow their intentions could counteract the review's evanescent nature, which flatters opinions rather than guides them. Periodicals are transitory, and whether a politics that aims to replace fashionable opinions with wise opinions can be accomplished in a review is a valid question. In what ways does the review form undermine its re-viewing practice? Conversely, does the form's mode enhance a re-view of the state, an object that itself does not remain constant and requires an evolving or developing critique? The *Westminster*'s choice to utilize the review form despite its shortcomings would be repeated by many future critics. In effect, critics or intellectuals would come to be associated with the journal or review as things that go hand in hand.

With the arrival of the *Westminster Review*, the *Edinburgh*, and the *Quarterly* in the nineteenth-century's first decades, the review form was solidified and legitimized. Most critical journals and reviews that have followed can trace their lineage to this group. Interestingly, they continue to point to them as exemplars of the genre and as early models. The twentieth-century literary review, *Scrutiny*, described them as something to be emulated and marking a time when the review form held a prestigious place in society and garnered a far larger audience than their modern counterparts. In the twenty-first century, a new print journal began publication. *n+1* claimed to be in the tradition of *Partisan Review* or as they put it "like *Partisan Review* but not dead" (Shapiro 2004, p. n/a). The claimed ancestor began publication in 1936 and ceased publication in 2003, just a year before the new journal began.

This act of ancestral claiming is not unique to *n+1*. Rather, many journals look to the past for their models. *Social Text* modelled itself after the "little magazine." However, its founding editors had different "little magazines" in mind. Stanley Aronowitz thought of *Partisan Review*, while John Brenkman had the French journal, *Tel Quel* in mind, and Frederic Jameson pointed to *Les Temps modernes* (Brenkman 2009). *Telos* claims similar models, namely *Les Temps modernes*, *Praxis*, and *New Left Review* (Staff 1970). *Universities and Left Review* (ULR) by its title claimed the unorthodox 1930s Marxist journal *Left Review* as its antecedent. *ULR* would merge with *The New Reasoner* to form *New Left Review* in 1960. Marking the journal's fiftieth anniversary, Collini wrote that the *New Left Review* "as a severely intellectual journal committed, in principle, to the radical transformation of society...had few models to draw on in British history" (2010, p. n/a). He then points to the Left journals, *Commonweal* (1885-90), *Left Review* (1934-38), the *New Statesman* (1913-), *Tribune* (1937-), or a more cultural journal, *New Age* (1907-22), before finally settling on the *Westminster Review* as the closest antecedent, a journal he describes as "another successful journal of ideas conducted at the highest intellectual level by a self-consciously radical group" (Collini 2010, p. n/a). These reviews, however, served as more than just models. In effect, they institutionalized the critical re-viewing practice and by so doing, defined the parameters for writing politically at the dawning of Western liberal-democracy.

Chapter 3
The Re-view of War, Intellectuals, and the State

War tests "the health of the state" and the limits of critical intervention. During times of war, as general consensus supports the state's decision to go to war, critics who oppose state policy often find themselves in the minority. Moreover, criticism is less tolerated during times of war. Indeed, war is effectively the quintessential critical moment, putting to the test not only those holding power within the state and, so, directing the war effort, but testing critique of that effort and its machinery of legitimation. Public intellectual re-views of the state are often persecuted and prosecuted for undermining the war effort. In times of war the dividing line between intellectuals acting in service of and those challenging the state becomes especially clear. This chapter recounts a handful of interventions made by intellectuals in journals opposing US wars fought during the twentieth and early twenty-first centuries. These authors, the journals and their editors were carrying on the earlier traditions of the "great reviews," but in a changing "public sphere." Importantly, in the twentieth century, mass-media institutions and other large political and economic interests muffled the voice of the independent journal. Many critics themselves began to wonder if critical re-view of the state any longer held sway in directing state reform. They trained their attention then on intellectuals who still had power, those who sided with the state, and they criticized those supporters of the state for lacking responsibility or certain ethical and moral standards. In so doing, they kept alive some hope that the work of intellectuals as re-viewers could serve in the critical renewal of the state and continue to inform "public opinion."

World War I and a "Little Magazine's" *Beau Geste*

In 1916 and 1917, a short-lived monthly, the *Seven Arts*, published the anti-war essays of Randolph Bourne. The journal's founders not only hoped that criticism could matter but also "were wild enough to believe that the artists and critics could dominate America" (Oppenheim 1930, p. 157). *Seven Arts* published just 12 issues from November 1916 to October 1917 and had an estimated circulation of about 5,000 with an annual subscription price of $2.50.[1] James Oppenheim served as

---

1   The average household wage income in 1916 was about $13,000 in 1998 dollars, or a little less than $650 in real wages.

editor, while Waldo Frank was associate editor. Members of the journal's advisory board included: Kahlil Gibran, Louis Untermeyer, Van Wyck Brooks, Robert Edmond Jones, Edna Kenton, David Mannes, and Robert Frost. The journal announced its purpose as a conduit for an emerging national self-consciousness, "a channel for the flow of these new tendencies: an expression of our American arts which shall be fundamentally an expression of our American life" ("Editorials," 1916, pp. 52–3.)

Why was it then that this "little magazine," dedicated to fostering US nationalism, would publish Bourne's political essays opposing US entry into World War I? In part, the journal was concerned with the effect of war on art and artists. The first issue's editorial expressed a concern with the development of modern art as being "for many artists, self-conscious and intellectual" (p. 56). The war demonstrated the precariousness of this trend, having "blown to pieces so much of modern art."

> Such art could not meet the tests of life and death, 'the corrective of reality.' It was a pose the artist lost as soon as he was in danger. For it takes a Goethe to stand above the battle and then go to his room and continue his work. Why should war make a difference to him? This new reality does not crowd out the old, because it is all of a piece with his experience. But he who creates an artificial world of intellect, and is suddenly confronted by the real world, loses the one and is utterly lost in the other. He is dazed and confused, a fool among men (p. 56).

The journal continued its preoccupation with World War I, whether because it directly affected, or interfered with, the journal's mission to develop the 'American' arts, or because the members of the journal were not so myopic in their focus that they ably extended their attention from art to what they considered the most pressing issue of their day, the war.

In fact, they published a special supplement to the April 1917 issue, titled "American Independence and the War." The anonymously authored supplement acknowledged that a monthly magazine might not be the best place to discuss pressing political matters. Further, a publication whose acknowledged domain is the arts may be seen as overstepping its bounds in discussing politics.

> But we are face to face with so grave a crisis, that we can very well afford to forget the rules and dogmas we have laid down for ourselves; and remember only that a democracy has no one to do its thinking for it. It must think for itself.[2] At a moment when a decision and a line of policy will determine a future epoch, it is necessary to press into service every organ of publicity, to mobilize, as it were, every medium of discussion. Action already outstrips our thinking: let us

---

2 A sentiment contrary to the one expressed by the editors of *The Tatler*, who viewed their role as telling people what to think.

consider well then before that action becomes, first, a policy, second, a tradition, and third, the very spirit and structure of our nation (1917a, p. 1).

In addition to the special supplement, the journal published six articles by Bourne opposing US entry into World War I during its brief lifespan.

Bourne's essays appeared around the same time that another "little magazine," *The Masses*, was denied use of the postal service by the Postmaster General for violating the spirit of the Espionage Act of 1917. Very few free speech cases existed before the passage of the Espionage Act of 1917 and the Sedition Act of 1918, which purportedly were enacted for national security reasons. Hundreds would be prosecuted for speech and writings under the former, including Eugene Debs, who was convicted in 1919 for obstructing recruitment to the armed forces, *Debs v. United States*, 249 US 211 (1919). Five defendants, all born in Russia, were also convicted under the Espionage Act for printing and circulating leaflets that opposed US involvement in World War I, *Abrams v. United States*, 250 US 616 (1919).[3] *Seven Arts* feared similar treatment. Indeed, the journal was accused of treason by the *New York Tribune* in an August 1917 article "Enemies Within: 'Seven Arts' Magazine Says 'Democracy is a Wornout Idea; Patriotism Is Just a Form of Anger.'" The *Tribune* pointed out that six of the 12 articles in the journal's August issue contained "outright attacks on American participation in the war." Further, these articles "follow the general lines of argument and assertion used by *German and other anti-American publications* to show that our motives for entering the war were sinful and that President Wilson betrayed the wishes of his people" (emphasis added) (1917b, p. 7). The *Tribune* piece also criticized at length anti-war articles by John Reed and Randolph Bourne to complete its condemnation of the journal. In these times, the practice of "re-view" was potentially treasonable.

Bourne's first article appeared in *Seven Arts* only after the US had entered the war in April 1917. His essay, "The War and the Intellectuals," (Vol. 2, No. 2) followed in June 1917. In that piece, he criticized eminent intellectuals, notably John Dewey, who supported US participation. Not only did those intellectuals support the decision to go to war, but many also took credit for it. While the main pushers of US entry into World War I were "the preparedness advocates who came from the ranks of big business," Bourne argued, they quickly co-opted one intellectual group after another to their cause. As a result, the intellectuals "have identified themselves with the least democratic forces in American life." Moreover, even those intellectuals who previously claimed to be socialists had also joined in the call for war, showing how thin their intellectual facade of socialism was.

> For they called us in terms that might have emanated *from any bourgeois journal* to defend democracy and civilization, just as if it was not exactly against those

---

[3] National security interests would again be invoked for restraining free speech during the Vietnam War.

very bourgeois democracies and capitalist civilizations that socialists had been fighting for decades (emphasis added) (Bourne 1917, p. n/a).

Bourne argued that the American intellectual class had reverted to primitive ways of thinking. Thought serves to rationalize what is already occurring. For him, in a crisis, rather than suspend judgment, intellectuality craves certainty. Bourne noted that a few intellectuals still kept up the "pose" of critique, but since their advice merely reflected what was already underway, "their criticism [was] little more than a rationalization of the common emotional drive."

Bourne denied that such an attitude and intellect toward the war could be described as "realist." The proponents of "realism" opposed the "idealism" of pacifists and others who opposed US involvement in the war. For Bourne, rather than sternly and intelligently facing reality, the so-called "realists" were merely surrendering to it.

> [I]s the realist who refuses to challenge or to criticise facts, entitled to any more credit than that which comes from following the line of least resistance? The realist thinks he at least can control events by linking himself to the forces that are moving. Perhaps he can. But if it is a question of controlling war, it is difficult to see how the child on the back of a mad elephant is to be any more effective in stopping the beast than is the child who tries to stop him from the ground (1917, p. n/a).

Bourne remarked that those who accept war and try to steer it with liberal principles "will be listened to as responsible thinkers." Those who object to war "have committed intellectual suicide and shall be cast into outer darkness." Bourne divided intellectuals into two camps, the "responsible" and the "irresponsible." Only the criticism belonging to the former had any chance of success.

Indeed, Dewey had been one of Bourne's "idols," and wrote essays in support of the war for journals such as *The Atlantic*[4] and *The New Republic*, the latter founded in November 1914 by Dorothy and Willard Straight and Herbert Croly. They felt that the new magazine would fill a gap in American intellectual life, being the liberal journal that *Harper's Weekly*, they believed, had failed to be. Another editorial board member Walter Lippmann, wrote in his autobiography, that the journal was created to explore, develop, and apply the ideas put forth by Theodore Roosevelt as leader of the Progressive Party. The first issue of the magazine sold 875 copies, but its circulation reached 15,000 in just a year and then

---

4 In an essay for *The Atlantic* titled "On Understanding the Mind of Germany" published in February 1916, Dewey obliquely voiced his support for the US's entrance into the war, writing "I am confident that all, except a few incurable aliens [some German-Americans] who merely happen to be physically among us, will respond with eagerness to any call which Americans who are longer acclimated may issue, to make our own experiment in responsible freedom more of a reality" (p. 262).

rose to 43,000 during World War I before declining in the 1920s. Ronald Jacobs and Eleanor Townsley's (2011) description of the magazine's importance during this time likens it to the influence of the "great reviews."

When *The New Republic* began, it took a neutral position on US entry into the war, mirroring public opinion at the time. An early article to appear in December 1914 was titled "Pacifism vs. Passivism." After a German U-boat torpedoed the RMS *Lusitania* in May 1915, the journal changed its position. When President Wilson asked Congress to declare war on Germany in April 1917, the journal and editor Croly gave the President and the war full support. Max Eastman, editor of *The Masses*, responded to *The New Republic*'s urge to war, with an essay in his journal in May 1915, writing

> They still live in a world in which fundamental democratic progress comes by telling, and persuading, and showing how, and propagating reasonable opinions, and better social feeling. The real world is a world in which privilege can only be uprooted by power.

Randolph Bourne was also upset with *The New Republic*'s back flip on the war. He had contributed pieces to the magazine in favor of neutrality and now found himself unable to publish there. His last piece appeared in November 1917. Ironically, an obituary for Bourne would appear in *The New Republic*. Written by Floyd Dell, the obituary praised Bourne for his extraordinary literary talent: "he was the promise of our specific contribution to American life." Dell also writes that Bourne was part of the revolt of youth against alienation from traditional modes of action. For Dell he embodied the spirit of such rebellion. As for Bourne's vocal opposition to the war, Dell deems it "an accident" that Bourne's critical attitude would have to confront the state and "the dominant political tendencies of the time."

> And yet this accident was one which could more perhaps than anything else try him and prove if his was indeed the lonely courage which our hearts had acclaimed in him. There are few avenues of expression for protest, however sane and far-seeing, against the mood of a nation in arms; and one by one, most of these were closed to him as he went on speaking out his thought. It is one of the more subtly tragic aspects of his death, a misfortune not only to a fecund mind that needed free utterance, but to a country which is nearly starved for thought, that he should in these last years have been doomed to silence. He who should have spoken for them—and who might still have spoken for them—went down to the grave voiceless (1919, p. 276).

Interestingly, Dewey had also authored a piece printed in *Seven Arts* in May 1917 titled "In a Time of National Hesitation" (Vol. 2, No. 1), that commented on the reigning mood of hesitation in relation to the war.[5] Dewey argued that such hesitation was due to a lack of a "national mind." Deciding whether or not to go to war would not end the hesitation, it being a product of an emerging national consciousness that viewed the United States as no longer a colony or child of Europe but still questioned its identity. In the piece, Dewey commented that hesitation should not serve as a passive accomplice to an unnamed foe, presumably Germany. Because of these writings, Bourne viewed Dewey as one of those intellectuals serving the state. While Dewey may have ultimately supported the US decision to join the war, such support reflected a general "para-nationalist" thematic, or what Francis Mulhern (1981) also describes as a "fetishism," of American intellectuals. Mulhern argues that as a nation lacking a prehistory of kinship or custom to forge a "national consciousness" from, the state, through its Constitution and other founding texts, created an identity for the United States. This para-nationalist constitutional fetishism would then become the dominant collective ideology of the American intellectuals and the country's education system, including its influential leader, John Dewey.

However, Dewey's "para-nationalism" would not embrace the state without criticism. Instead, he envisioned a nation of educated citizens who would engage in "free, reasoned participation and [value] critical independence as a cultural norm" (Mulhern 1981, p. 55). Dewey's influence upon and participation with journals such as *Seven Arts, The New Republic*, and later *Partisan Review*, also implicitly demonstrates his belief that journals could foster that participation and critical independence. As I suggest, however, Bourne questioned whether all "reasoned participation" was equal, or whether what masqueraded as "critical independence" in support of war was really just a veneer for complacent acceptance of what already was.[6]

In "Twilight of Idols" (Vol. 2, No. 6) published in October 1917, the final issue of *The Seven Arts*, Bourne again expressed dismay that intellectuals, specifically Dewey, supported the US entry into the war. Bourne condemned that intellectual disposition which favored the "instrumental attitude toward life," a disposition that he saw as being inculcated into new generation intellectuals.

> The war has revealed a younger intelligentsia, trained up in pragmatic dispensation, immensely ready for the executive ordering of events, pitifully

---

5 In 1916, Dewey published an essay titled "Force, Violence and the Law" in *The New Republic*, which argued that law cannot be substituted for force, commented on the futility of the peace movement, and boldly claimed that "Force is the only thing in the world which effects anything ..." (p. 296). In 1917, Dewey published a number of articles on the war for *The New Republic*, including "Conscience and Compulsion," "The Future of Pacifism," "What America Will Fight For," "Conscription of Thought," "War Activities for Civilians," and "Fiat Justitia, Ruat Coelum."

6 Dewey may have retaliated using his influence at *The Dial*, another "little magazine," to have Dewey removed from its editorial board.

unprepared for the intellectual interpretation or the idealistic focussing of
ends ... They have absorbed the secret of scientific method as applied to political
administration (2006 [1917], p. 184).

He argued that this new breed of expert-intellectuals was the product of a change in training from a broad classicist, liberal education to one concentrated upon political and economic values. They were more interested in technique than interpretation and while they would organize the war, they would leave the opinion-formation to "professional patriots, sensational editors, archaic radicals" (p. 185). The means-ends calculation of this "professionalized" intellectual cadre would not engage with larger questions of the public interest. Instead, they would offer "intelligent service" to those, presumably the established powers, who could put it to use.

By the end of 1918, Bourne was dead from pneumonia at the age of 32. *Seven Arts* had published its last issue in October of 1917. In effect, publication of Bourne's articles put the magazine out of business, its financial backer having pulled out over the fear of prosecution for treason. Despite that, editor Oppenheim later remarked that Bourne was the greatest thing to happen to the magazine. Still, Oppenheim referred to the magazine's attempt to stop the war effort as a *beau geste* "simply because of Randolph Bourne" (1930, p. 164). I suggest, however, that to describe *Seven Arts'* effort as a noble but meaningless gesture is problematic. To adopt such a view is to succumb to the common malaise besetting the critic who lives in and through the pages of journals and magazines, or perhaps with professionalization, the university hall. It immodestly mourns the inability of a publication to alter the world's immediate course, while perhaps overlooking, or perhaps denying, the possibility that critique has long-term effects.

Bourne's essays continue to be printed and read today. They anticipated a break some 50 years later within many disciplines, whereby alternative visions of scholarship would demand that intellectuals represent interests other than those belonging to the state or elites, and as I suggest in Chapter Five, gave birth to a number of alternative or radical disciplinary journals. In the outside world, they furthered the tradition begun by the early reviews in the eighteenth century, that of intellectual opposition to the dominant thinking of the time. Indeed, others, such as Dwight Macdonald, would repeat Bourne's critical opposition throughout the twentieth century. An important contribution that space in this book does not allow detailed examination of, Macdonald's essay "The Responsibility of Peoples," appearing in his journal *politics* questioned who bore responsibility for the atrocities of World War II. Macdonald placed the burden as much on private citizens, who fail to stop the actions of the state, as well as on its leaders.[7] Noam Chomsky's intervention in the Vietnam War, discussed further below, would take up where Macdonald and Bourne left off.

---

7 Macdonald concedes that "common peoples" are coming to have less and less control over their governments as they are being more closely identified with them.

The Critical Renewal of the State

For Bourne, "war is essentially the health of the State." One cannot criticize a war without also implicitly or explicitly criticizing the state. Further, one cannot oppose a war without also opposing the state. Bourne, however, did not mean opposition to war meant opposition to a particular state but to the very idea of the State. In an unfinished essay titled "The State" (1919), which was discovered after Bourne's death, Bourne distinguished three terms: the State, the Government, and the Country. The State was a concept of power and competition. It only became truly visible during times of war or perhaps national holidays, like the Fourth of July. The Government was the machinery that carried out the State's functions. It was of general concern during times of peace. The Country, or Nation, was a non-political concept; it represented peace and tolerance. The State was the Country acting as a political unit; the Government acted on behalf of the Country organized as a State. In this schema, criticizing the Government was different than criticizing the State. The former is reformist, the latter radical.

Bourne repeats his dictum "war is the health of the State" throughout the lengthy essay. To prove his point, he argues that wartime criticism is severely punished, as it jeopardizes the State itself, making such criticism especially difficult. He even argues that punishment for opinion, for example, objecting to conscription, is greater than punishment for undermining or opposing the war in any material fashion, for example, acts of sabotage. Further, public opinion, including that belonging to the intellectuals, often homogenizes during times of war in support of the State. "Public opinion ... becomes one solid block. 'Loyalty,' or rather war orthodoxy, becomes the sole test ... Particularly is this true in the sphere of the intellectual life" (1919, pp. 143–4). The fostering of public opinion in the support of the war and the crushing of all opinion in dissent suggests that, while intellectuals may sometimes doubt the force of their ideas, the State does not. As Bourne forcefully contends, criticizing war itself also calls into question the nature of the State.

> We cannot crusade against war without crusading implicitly against the State. And we cannot expect, or take measures to ensure, that this war is a war to end war, unless at the same time we take measures to end the State in its traditional form. The State is not the nation, and the State can be modified and even abolished in its present form, without harming the nation. On the contrary, with the passing of the dominance of the State, the genuine life-enhancing forces of the nation will be liberated (1919, p. 167).

What new form of the State then does Bourne envision, that will allow the nation or Country to thrive?

Bourne argues that the modern democratic state formed in the United States was not all that different from the monarchic state in England that it revolted against. He writes that the American Revolution began with the latent hopes that it might turn into a genuine break with the State ideal. Approving of the sentiment set forth in the Declaration of Independence, Bourne explains,

> If all governments derive their authority from the consent of the governed, and if a people is entitled, at any time that it becomes oppressive, to overthrow it and institute one more nearly conformable to their interests and ideals, the old idea of the sovereignty of the State is destroyed (1919, p. 201).

He argues that the sovereignty of the people is no mere phrase but a direct challenge to the historic tradition of the State. However, the sentiments of the Declaration remained mere sentiments: "No constructive political scheme was built on them" (p. 203). Instead, the Articles of Confederation, which Bourne favors, were replaced by the Constitution, and the powers of the ruling classes were solidified into a form of Government that would serve their interests. The possibility of continual renewal of the State was foreclosed.

Bourne's unfinished essay prematurely concludes with a discussion of the two-party system and the obstacles it poses to a new form of the State. That system—accompanied by the elimination of property qualifications for suffrage and other "tangible evidence" of public participation, he claims, cemented the popular demand for democracy and led to political complacency among the citizenry that lasted into the twentieth century. The start of the war, as much as Bourne opposed it, then can also be considered a possible impetus to the waking-up of the citizenry. When the State again becomes visible, during times of war, the citizens may be more prompted to reflect upon the nature of the State. The role of the intellectual, then, may be to help prompt that reflection, and as Bourne writes, to keep opinion from solidifying into any form of complacency.

> The intellectual who retains his animus against war will push out more boldly than ever to make his case solid against it. The old ideals crumble; new ideals must be forged. His mind will continue to roam widely and ceaselessly. The thing he [the intellectual who opposes war] will fear most is premature crystallization. If the American intellectual class rivets itself to a 'liberal' philosophy that perpetuates the old errors, there will then be need for 'democrats' whose task will be to divide, confuse, disturb, keep the intellectual waters constantly in motion to prevent any such ice from ever forming (Bourne 1917, p. n/a).

In these terms, the opposition of intellectuals is aimed at the critical renewal of the state. Theory and criticism published in journals "matters" to the extent that it calls for this renewal and offers visions of a renewed state.

The Responsibility of Intellectuals at *The New York Review of Books*

Almost fifty years after Bourne's death, the re-view form of criticism would be carried forward again, this time by linguist Noam Chomsky. Chomsky's "The Responsibility of Intellectuals," appeared in *The New York Review of Books* on February 23, 1967. "Responsibility" vigorously opposed the war in Vietnam and, importantly for my argument, spelled out anew what it meant to engage in critical practice. Chomsky echoed both Bourne and Macdonald in reprimanding other intellectuals, those he alleged were complicit in covering up the truth about the war. He did so in a review that would make its most targeted political interventions during times of crisis (Sherman 2004).

The New York Review of Books began publication in February 1963. It was founded, in part, to fill a gap created by the New York City printers' strike of 1962–1963, which had suspended newspaper production and distribution for a time. The other, and perhaps larger, reason for beginning the review was to remedy what its founders saw as a decline in the quality of literary criticism. In 1959, Elizabeth Hardwick had published an essay in *Harper's*, "The Decline of Book Reviewing." Hardwick critiqued mainly *The New York Times* for its "flat praise and the faint dissension, the minimal style and the light little article, the absence of involvement, passion, character, eccentricity—the lack, at last, of the literary tone itself." This attitude, she contended, had turned *The Times* into a "provincial literary journal." Three years later, during the strike, Hardwick, her husband, the poet Robert Lowell, and Jason and Barbara Epstein came up with the idea for the *Review*. Robert Silvers, then an editor at *Harper's*, was asked to join as editor of the new magazine, and he asked Barbara Epstein to serve with him as co-editor.

In the only editorial to ever appear in *The New York Review of Books*, Epstein and Silvers wrote that the *Review*, the first issue of which was put together quickly and by volunteers, would, they hoped, suggest the kind of "*responsible* literary journal" they felt was needed in America (emphasis added). When asked 50 years later if they felt at the time that they were creating some kind of ideological community, Silvers answered that it was not an ideological but an *intellectual* community they wanted to cultivate (Danner 2013). Yet, the *Review* would publish a great deal of political criticism that, although ideologically disparate, was unified by "a persistent, stubborn strain of criticizing US policy, at home and abroad, whenever it falls short of the high ideals proclaimed in this country's own Constitution and by its own leaders" (Ash 2013, p. 51).[8]

---

[8] Russell Jacoby (2014) in his review of the *Review* upon the occasion of its fiftieth anniversary made a number of criticisms. He argued that notable currents of thought were largely missing from its pages, such as Marxism, the Frankfurt School, critical theory, postmodernism, and recent French thought. Additionally, the *Review* appeared to favor English reviewers and did not successfully cultivate a younger generation of writers. Moreover, the journal published important writers once they were already important.

Stephen Fender (1986) wrote of *The New York Review of Books* that many Americans are surprised "that a review of books should have a politics at all," as reviews are perhaps expected to confine themselves to non-partisan literary criticism. Fender explicitly compares the "reviewing" practice of *The New York Review of Books* to that of the "great reviews," discussed in Chapter Two. He singles out I. F. Stone's "reviews" in the former, which in effect provided jumping off points for Stone's own political opinionating. In one essay, Stone "reviewed" a transcript of a hearing before the Senate Committee on Foreign Relations. As Fender notes, the Government Printing Office published this pamphlet for 30 cents—not the object of criticism most likely to be found in a periodical devoted to reviewing books, but very much in keeping with the practices of the "great reviews." The pamphlet allowed Stone to give his opinions on the Gulf of Tonkin episode (1986, p. 194). However, the vast majority of the pieces on Vietnam to appear in the journal were not reviews at all but instead essays, or "features." Of about 100 pieces, only a quarter were reviews that used either a book or government publication as a jumping off point to express the review author's own opinion. Like *Seven Arts*, the *Review* found itself caught up in war, which it chose not to ignore, and deviating from its original purpose to revitalize literary criticism.

Control of the *Review* was structured around two groups of shareholders: group "A" shareholders had decision-making power over editorial concerns, and group "B" shareholders would only benefit financially. The "A" shareholders were Silvers, the Lowells, the Epsteins, and Whitney Ellsworth, who joined as publisher after the second issue. According to Silvers, this structure gave the *Review* and its editors absolute control:

> [T]he *New York Review* was and is a unique opportunity, an opportunity to do what one wants on anything in the world. Now, that is given to hardly any editor, anywhere, anytime. There are no strictures, no limits. Nobody saying you can't do something. No subject, no theme, no idea that can't be addressed in-depth. There's an infinity of possibilities. Whatever work is involved is minor compared to the opportunity. That is the essence. That is the nature of the magazine (Danner 2013, p. n/a).

The magazine's finances further enabled this editorial freedom. After two rounds of fund-raising, the *Review* was able to exist on its own; unlike many other journals before or since, from 1966 forward, it has always been in the black. Silvers attributes this to a combination of low overhead—cheap newsprint, low salaries, no staff writers—, loyal subscribers, and paid advertisements by publishers, including a number of university presses. In the 1980s, the *Review* also launched *New York Review Books*, becoming a successful book publisher as well.

Finally, the *Review* was too provincial in that not only its editorial office but also most of its contributors could be found in the greater New York area.

The independence that this corporate structure allowed may have freed the *Review* to oppose the war in Southeast Asia, without needing to fear the withdrawal of its financial backer, as happened to *Seven Arts*.[9] Still, its subscribers and advertisers could have decided to withdraw their support. That the *Review* became financially profitable in 1966, as its coverage of Vietnam began to increase suggests that its political opinions resonated with more than a few. Some early pieces in 1964 touched on the war and US participation, which escalated after the Gulf of Tonkin resolution in August 1964. Stone warned in a piece at the end of 1964 that the Johnson Administration "may most easily stumble into full-scale war" in Indochina, after "pledging itself in the election campaign to peace" (1964, p. n/a).

A number of other reviews, reports, and essays would appear in 1965 and 66 on the subject of "Vietnam." The criticism contained in these pieces did not form a coherent view on the war or outline a single policy direction for the US. Some pieces tried to reveal another side to the conflict by offering new or alternative information on US actions, Vietnamese actions, in both North and South Vietnam, and on Vietnam itself and its peoples. A review appearing in August 1965 by Joseph M. Kraft titled "Understanding the Vietcong" argued:

> To those who think it [the Vietnam War] does make sense, which seems to include practically everybody in the United States, Jean Lacouture's new book on Vietnam will come as a kind of revelation (p. n/a).

Lacouture, a foreign journalist, would also publish a few reports in the *Review*, bringing an outside perspective not found in the mainstream media. An essay published a few months later in November on "The Vietnam Protest" showed that some opinion in the US was beginning to turn. The essay, co-authored by Irving Howe, a founding editor of *Dissent*, Michael Harrington, Bayard Rustin, Lewis A. Coser, and Penn Kimble, made "some proposals and comments" about the burgeoning protest movement. "We believe that the debate concerning Vietnam is far from over, in fact, that it has just begun; and we think that the protest movement has an important role to play."

An exchange between Staughton Lynd and Irving Howe a month later demonstrated that the *Review* was open to a variety of opinions. Lynd criticized the piece on the protest movement because it called for what he thought was the movement's taming and was vague as to its position on the withdrawal of American troops. Howe responded that Lynd was a radical who refused to be anti-Communist while Howe was a member of the democratic Left. Other pieces would also offer "policy" advice, whether to the protestors or the US Administration, like Kraft's 1966 piece "What Next in Vietnam?"

Then, in February 1967, Chomsky's "Responsibility" article appeared. Over the next five years, Chomsky authored and co-authored several pieces on the war for

---

9 The *Review* would later oppose the Iraq War from the start as well.

the *Review*.[10] Additionally, Chomsky actively participated in the "Letters" section of the *Review* on issues related to the war or to respond to readers' criticisms of his essays. It was the first essay, though, that received the most attention. As Silvers later remarked "Few essays we published had such an effect" (Danner 2013, p. n/a).[11] Like Bourne before him, Chomsky directed his criticism not at the government, or the decision-makers who, he argued, deceitfully led the United States into war, but at the intellectuals who facilitated the deceit. In this way, Chomsky's article solidified the shift from the journals as "great review," that is, re-views of the state, to journals as re-views of other intellectuals' stance *vis-à-vis* the state.

Chomsky actually refered to Macdonald's series of 1940s essays in *politics* and took up the question of war guilt. In those essays, Macdonald first asked to what extent the people of Germany and Japan were responsible for the actions taken by their governments. He then, more provocatively, asked to what extent are American or British people responsible for the bombings of civilians undertaken by their governments, such as the atomic bombing of Hiroshima and Nagasaki and the fire bombings of Dresden and Hamburg. Macdonald's indictment of everyday citizens' responsibility struck Chomsky, but he argued, in his essay, that intellectuals bore an even higher duty of responsibility. Due to their privilege—of education, status, access—, they were in a position to reveal, rather than help obfuscate, the true nature of the war.

> Intellectuals are in a position to expose the lies of governments, to analyze actions according to their causes and motives and often hidden intentions. In the Western world, at least, they have the power that comes from political liberty, from access to information and freedom of expression. For a privileged minority, Western democracy provides the leisure, the facilities, and the training to seek the truth lying hidden behind the veil of distortion and misrepresentation, ideology and class interest, through which the events of current history are presented to us. The responsibilities of intellectuals, then, are much deeper than what Macdonald calls the 'responsibility of people,' given the unique privileges that intellectuals enjoy (1967, p. n/a).

---

10 They included "On Resistance" (December 1967), "The Spock Trial" (August 1968), "The Menace of Liberal Scholarship" (January 1969), "After Pinkville" (January 1970), "Mayday: The Case for Civil Disobedience" (June 1971), and "Vietnam: How Government Became Wolves" (June 1972). Chomsky also travelled to Southeast Asia and wrote reports on Cambodia (April 1970), Laos (July 1970), and North Vietnam (August 1970). Mary McCarthy began the practice of such travel pieces in the *Review* with her April 1967 "Report from Vietnam I. The Home Program."

11 The article would also receive special mention in Timothy Garton Ash's review of the *New York Review* published upon the journal's fiftieth anniversary. However, Ash begins the piece by relating an incident where a friend berated him for a 1984 piece he published in the *Review*. The friend asks, "What kind of whining Chomskyesque relativist had I become?" (2013, p. 51).

Chomsky named names, pointing to intellectuals who he believed were complicit in the war effort, such as Arthur Schlesinger and Walt Rostow. Rather than enlighten the public as to the real motivations behind the war, Chomsky argued that Schlesinger's and Rostow's writings and opinions not only demonstrated a "growing lack of concern for the truth" but also "a real or feigned naiveté about American actions that reaches startling proportions."[12]

Chomsky also admonished Professor David N. Rowe, Director of Graduate Studies in International Relations at Yale University, and Reverend R. J. de Jaegher, Regent of the Institute of Far Eastern Studies at Seton Hall University. The former recommended to the House Committee on Foreign Affairs that the United States buy all surplus Canadian and Australian wheat to induce mass starvation in China; the latter testified to the same committee that people who lived under communism in North Vietnam "would be perfectly happy to be bombed to be free." For Chomsky, these statements by intellectuals were highly irresponsible, especially since they had the ear of policy-makers. Their ideas, then, were not merely ideas. He recommended reading the publications of the US Government Printing Office to learn more about the responsibility of intellectuals for the war.

Chomsky's essay was heavily documented and footnoted, placing emphasis on the facts. Point by point, he rebutted claims by others such as Schlesinger and Rostow. As Chomsky wrote, "There is no body of theory or significant body of relevant information, beyond the comprehension of the layman, which makes policy immune from criticism." Reminiscent of Bourne's takedown of the intellectuals of his generation, Chomsky complained of a breed of "scholar-experts," who replacing the "free-floating intellectuals" of the past, constructed "value-free technology" within the universities that was put to use to further the war. As Bourne had written 50 years earlier, "it is the technical side of the war that appeals to them, not the interpretive or political side" (2006 [1917], p. 185). Bourne also wrote that "Our intellectuals have failed us as value-creators, even as value-emphasizers" (p. 186).

Chomsky argued that it was the "scholar-experts" who embodied what Daniel Bell was describing at the time as "the end of ideology." That is, Bell's widely disseminated and read thesis offered a somewhat comforting image of a world in which ideology was no longer necessary because, at least in the West, the achieved pluralistic society of the welfare state offered alternative means of resolving political disputes that made radical transformation no longer necessary. As a result, intellectuals no longer needed to convert ideas into social levers to accomplish revolutionary change. Chomsky pointed out the flaws in Bell's thesis. Most importantly, such a consensus among intellectuals, to the degree it actually existed, was self-serving. Those scholar-experts who made such an argument were likely in positions of power and prosperity, possibly even in positions of influence with the state. They did not need to search for new levers to pull, because they

---

12 Schlesinger would later engage in an exchange with Daniel Ellsberg in the *Review* on the Pentagon Papers.

had access to the existing levers, which were no less ideological just because they served the status quo. Using an analogy borrowed from Karl Marx, Chomsky argued that Bell's "scholar-experts" misrepresent their particular interest for a general interest. Bell, at the time, an editor at *The Public Interest*, which began publication in 1965 and avoided all discussion of the war by not veering from its mission as a domestic policy journal, was not the only member of the journal to come under Chomsky's fire. Chomsky also took aim at Irving Kristol.[13]

Like Bourne before him, Chomsky also noted a distinction commonly drawn between "responsible criticism" and "sentimental," "emotional," or "hysterical" criticism, with the latter irrationally refusing to accept that the United States has a right to extend its control and power without limit. The "responsible critics" do not challenge that right but instead argue that in this particular time or place, the country probably "can't get away with it." Chomsky claimed that Kristol made this distinction in an essay he wrote for *Encounter*, the British literary journal funded by the CIA in an effort to win the Cold War. In his essay, Kristol distinguished the "responsible criticism" of Walter Lippmann, of *The New York Times*, and of Senator Fulbright from the "irresponsible criticism" of the "teach-in movement." For someone like Kristol, the ideal "responsible" intellectual is someone who is non-ideological, a claim he made for the intellectual expertise to be found in the second journal he would edit *The Public Interest*. Foregoing trafficking in ideas, these expert-intellectuals can solve technical problems by "sophisticated" methods borrowed from the sciences. Chomsky reversed Kristol's distinction and argued that intellectuals as social scientists cannot recognize the values of honesty or indignation, as expressed by "hysterical" critics, because those values cannot be expressed in the language of science, a language the social and behavioral sciences were trying so hard to imitate in their fields. Chomsky also argued that even the "anti-war movement" was falling prey to this cult of expertise.

Chomsky closed his essay by returning to Macdonald and addressing the question of responsibility. If intellectuals like Schlesinger or Kristol were the truly irresponsible ones, what actions should "responsible" intellectuals take to avoid complicity in the war? Macdonald had answered "Only those who are willing to resist authority themselves when it conflicts too intolerably with their personal moral code, only they have the right to condemn the death-camp paymaster [an active participant in the war who burst into tears when told the Russians would hang him]" (1974 [1945], p. 35). Chomsky left open the question of what should be done. A reader motivated by the essay wrote to the *Review* to press Chomsky on the issue. Chomsky replied that although he had spent a long time thinking about it, he was not sure what steps "responsible" intellectuals should take to oppose the war.

> I've tried various things—harassing congressmen, "lobbying" in Washington, lecturing at town forums, working with student groups in preparation of public

---

13   I return to a discussion of *The Public Interest* in Chapter Four.

> protests, demonstrations, teach-ins, etc., in all of the ways that many others have adopted as well. The only respect in which I have personally gone any further is in refusal to pay half of my income tax last year, and again, this year. My own feeling is that one should refuse to participate in any activity that implements American aggression—thus tax refusal, draft refusal, avoidance of work that can be used by the agencies of militarism and repression, all seem to me essential. I can't suggest a general formula. Detailed decisions have to be matters of personal judgment and conscience (Steiner and Chomsky 1967, p. n/a).

Interestingly, in the reply, Chomsky chose to focus on these more *material* actions in protest of the war, not naming his essays in the *Review* as an act of not remaining silent. In the essay, Chomsky wrote, "When we consider the responsibility of intellectuals, our basic concern must be their role in the creation and analysis of ideology." Chomsky chastised those intellectuals who not only refused to critique the state's ideology but also participated in the creation of an ideology that fostered war.

Chomsky would author his final piece for *The New York Review of Books* in September 1973, titled "Watergate: A Skeptical View." While he participated in a symposium on "the meaning of Vietnam" in the journal in June 1975, his only other appearances over the next few decades would be in the Letters section. Writing in praise of Chomsky's method of political criticism, George Scialabba (2009) commented that from the early 1970s to the late 1980s, Chomsky had not appeared in *The New York Times Magazine*, *The New York Times Book Review*, *The Washington Post*, *The Atlantic*, *Harper's*, the *New Republic*, *The New York Review of Books*, *Dissent*, *Commentary*, *Partisan Review*, *Foreign Affairs*, or *Foreign Policy*. Chomsky's disappearance from these publications, reminiscent of Bourne's blackballing, was all the more ironic in that sociologist Charles Kadushin had in 1970 found Chomsky to be one of the 10 most influential American intellectuals. Since the late 1980s, Chomsky has published brief opinion pieces in *The New York Times* (2004) and *The Washington Post* (2008), along with a "special report" in *Foreign Policy* (2002). Otherwise, he remains shut out from the publications that Scialabba listed more than 20 years ago. Chomsky continues to write and publish prolifically but often for marginal publications, titles such as *In These Times, The Monthly Review*, and occasionally *The Nation* and *New Political Science*, or the left-leaning foreign press. Chomsky also emerged as a regular contributor to the left-wing, activist-oriented *Z Magazine*.

Chomsky revisited his famous essay in a 2011 publication, "The Responsibility of Intellectuals, Redux," for the *Boston Review*. The occasion for the return was the 10-year anniversary of 9/11 and "the widespread approval in the United States of the assassination of the chief suspect." Chomsky began the piece by inquiring into who "the intellectuals" are.[14] Drawing parallels with the debates of the Dreyfus

---

14 He argues that answering the question helps provide a framework for determining their responsibility. "The phrase [the responsibility of intellectuals] is ambiguous: does

Affair in France in the late nineteenth century, Chomsky once again distinguished between those intellectuals who serve the dominant opinions of their time and those who oppose them. The latter he labeled "value-oriented intellectuals" while the former "technocratic and policy-oriented intellectuals." Dissident, or "value-oriented intellectuals," are only heralded when they live in another country and pose no challenge to US interests. When at home, they are derided by other intellectuals, or worse, punished by the government. For Chomsky, the responsibility of intellectuals is to have a value orientation that challenges the immoral and unethical behavior of the state. He then recounts a long list of the US's crimes, many of which are already familiar to his readers. He also uses the essay to chastise both *The New York Review of Books* and the *London Review of Books* for marginalizing US misdeeds against Native Americans. Chomsky closes the piece emphatically:

> As for the responsibility of intellectuals, there does not seem to me to be much to say beyond some simple truths. Intellectuals are typically privileged—merely an observation about usage of the term. Privilege yields opportunity, and opportunity confers responsibilities. An individual then has choices (2011, p. n/a).

While he says little that is new, his statement underscores that "intellectuals" have not learned to be responsible and that the state still pursues war.

Can Criticism Stop a War?

In April 2003, the scholarly journal *Critical Inquiry* held a symposium at the University of Chicago. The meeting's aim was to discuss the future of the journal itself and more broadly the criticism and theory that filled its pages. The journal's long-serving editor, W. J. T. Mitchell, had argued in 1982 that the young journal was designed to pursue an ideological agenda that would fundamentally "make it clear that criticism matters—that it makes a difference to someone else besides professional academic critics" (p. 616). Over the next two decades and as it aged, *Critical Inquiry* would publish a variety of critique, uniquely merging Anglo-American and European philosophical traditions, in an interdisciplinary pursuit of criticism as "a kind of public conscience, an ethical and political commentary on the full range of civilized life" (1982, pp. 617–8). The two-day event in 2003 brought together all members of the journal's editorial board, including well-known individuals Frederic Jameson, Stanley Fish, Henry Louis Gates, Jr., Bruno Latour, and Frances Ferguson, something that had not been done before in the

---

it refer to intellectuals' moral responsibility as human beings in a position to use their privilege and status to advance the causes of freedom, justice, mercy, peace, and other such sentimental concerns? Or does it refer to the role they are expected to play, serving, not derogating, leadership and established institutions?" (2011, p. n/a).

publication's 30-year history. One day would be devoted to a closed meeting of the board to discuss the journal's future trajectory, its "agenda for critical inquiry" (2004, p. 329). The other day would operate as a public "town meeting," and 550 people attended.

Interestingly, print media also covered the event, with articles appearing in *The New York Times* and *The Boston Globe*. Headlines reporting on the symposium read "Latest Theory Is That Theory Doesn't Matter" and "Crisis Theory." The headlines reflected comments by some of the symposium's participants—board members who did not think that criticism, theory, or intellectuals were effective politically. One participant even commented that intellectuals were often wrong and more importantly, wrong in "corrosive and destructive ways," perhaps suggesting either that other actors were better able to get it right or worse, that intellectualism had no role to play in the state's decision-making (2004, p. 328). It is important to keep in mind that the symposium convened one month after the United States had invaded Saddam Hussein's Iraq in search of "weapons of mass destruction." Despite worldwide attacks by public intellectuals and a strong on-the-ground antiwar movement, the war had still begun. The members of the journal and the audience drawn to the event wanted to know what criticism or theory could *do*. Could it stop a war? Or better, keep one from even beginning?

> What can criticism and theory do to counteract the forces of militarism, unilateralism, and the perpetual state of emergency that is now the explicit policy of the U.S. Government? What good is intellectual work in the face of the deeply anti-intellectual ethos of American public life, not to mention the pervasive sense that a radical faction of the Republican party that is immune to persuasion, argument, reason, or even the flow of accurate information has established a stranglehold on political power? What can the relatively weak power of critical theory do in such a crisis? (Mitchell 2004, p. 327).

Maybe criticism as embodied in the pages of a journal could carry no such force. But Mitchell argued in an unpublished letter to *The Times*, that even if theory didn't "matter" in an immediate sense, it does matter over time, that theories "take time to percolate down to practical application" (p. 328). Although ineffective in terms of building momentum sufficient to stop the war, the timing of the conference did help to generate interest in what intellectuals have to say about the power of criticism and theory. What many at the symposium perceived as an external crisis, US involvement in the war, revealed another internal crisis, the ability, or inability, of criticism to act as a "kind of public conscience," "to matter" to someone other than "professional academic critics."

Bourne's embrace of democracy and the American Revolution harks back to the critical moment of the "great reviews." *The Westminster* viewed the power of "the people" as a good and needed corrective to the state's exercise of authority. Chomsky's opposition to Vietnam both reflected and encouraged public opposition to the war, supporting Bourne's thesis of critical renewal, that the public if mobilized could withdraw its consent for war in a way that the state must respond to. Still, the degree to which Chomsky, among other critics who published their re-views of the state's malfeasance in Southeast Asia, led rather than followed a growing public anti-war sentiment is open to debate. *Critical Inquiry*'s Chicago seminar raised this question anew—to what extent does the critical re-view alter the political order, especially in times of conflict. It is difficult then to make any assertions about whether oppositional criticism found in journals helped stop a war, or whether such criticism was merely a *beau geste*.

Chapter 4
The Public Interest, *Telos*, and the Re-view of Welfare State Politics

Amidst the turbulence of the 1960s, consensus over the American welfare state unraveled. This unraveling was not entirely unrelated to what was appearing in the press, on television, and, importantly, in journals such as *The New York Review of Books*, as the unfolding military debacle in southeast Asia became more clear to the public (Gitlin 1993). At this time, two groups of former Marxists or soon-to-be former Marxists, mostly of immigrant and working-class backgrounds, launched journals in New York. Both groups would over subsequent decades publish critical re-views of the state and influence American politics and politicians, from the Governor of California to the President.[1] Both journals would blur the lines between left and right, while rejecting American consensus liberalism and replacing it with new styles of conservatism. All the while, the new journals would seek to navigate a cultural terrain that was slowly changing under the influence of post-Keynesian "neoliberal" economic technologies of government.[2]

This chapter uses the critical moment of the neoliberal turn as a focal point for examining the political, economic, and cultural interventions made by *The Public Interest* and *Telos* throughout the 1970s, 1980s, and into the 1990s. It traces the unlikely and uneven trajectory of both as they crossed and re-crossed

---

1   There is evidence that *The Public Interest* and its circle influenced Presidents Nixon and Reagan (Steinfels 1979; Hageman et al. 2009; Ehrman 1999). Nixon recommended that his cabinet read articles from the journal. Kristol's advocacy of supply-side economics got the ear of then-California Governor Ronald Reagan through the medium of Congressman Jack Kemp. Sydney Blumenthal argued that Kristol through *PI* almost single-handedly brought about the rise of supply-side economics. Kristol's neoconservatism continued to influence Regan as president. Daniel Patrick Moynihan, a Democrat and major contributor to *PI*, served in the Kennedy, Johnson, Nixon, and Ford administrations, before serving as a US Senator from New York from 1977 to 2001. *Telos* found an audience with former and current California Governor Jerry Brown, whose undated testimonial is featured prominently on the *Telos* website: "*Telos* remains provocative and independent in a time of intellectual banality" (www.telospress.com/testimonials/).

2   Especially theorists applied the term "neoliberalism" with reckless abandon from around 1975 onwards. For the purposes of my argument, I take it to indicate an ideological position in support of "market-based" solutions to social problems, including dismantling welfarism, de-regulating employment markets, and opposing collective wage bargaining, which in general implies policy embrace of supply-side (price signal) rather than demand-side (command and control) economic policy.

ideological paths in these decades. At their outset, each journal had an ostensibly clear purpose. *The Public Interest* wanted to improve the state of knowledge on issues of public policy so that more informed policy decisions could be made. *Telos* wanted to improve the state of philosophy so that issues of significance could be more critically explored. However, these express purposes were a sort of "mission statement," while the journals' titles reflected a far greater "vision statement." What ultimate aims, whether explicitly recognized or unconsciously motivating, drove them in their evolving practices of criticism? Without tracing all the contours of the changing political landscape that was home to these journals, this chapter examines the establishment of each, then describes in detail how their re-viewing practices shifted during this time. It investigates how these institutions of criticism and their political writings re-viewed the US liberal welfare state and its policies, whether they sought a new vision for the state, or merely sought to reform the existing vision. Importantly, I also discuss how *The Public Interest* and *Telos* viewed their own practices of re-view. Finally, this chapter evaluates the degree to which the political writing of these journals actually intervened in the politics of their times.

The More We Know, The More We Do Not Know: The Story of *The Public Interest*

The opening editorial of *The Public Interest,* written by its founding editors Irving Kristol and Daniel Bell, ran three pages long. It outlined a paradox, extemporized on the issue of ideology, explained the journal's title, critiqued public policy analysis, and pre-selected the journal's audience.[3] It announced the paradox in the first sentence: "The aim of *The Public Interest* is at once modest and presumptuous." What sort of purpose could be both modest and presumptuous? The editors continued, "It is to help all of us, when we discuss issues of public policy, to know a little better what we are talking about—and preferably in time to make such knowledge effective" (Bell and Kristol 1965, p. 3). The qualifying language "a little" must have been what they meant by "modest," because the rest of the purpose, to help know "what we are talking about" and "make such knowledge effective," is presumptuous and ambitious. It presumes not only the Royal "we," but that we, pre-*PI* (pre-*The Public Interest*), were unaware of what we were talking about, or to reintroduce modesty, may not have known *well enough* what we were talking about. The editors argued that ideologies interfered with knowing better, because they created "prefabricated interpretations of existing social realities" that resisted "all sensible revision." So, *The Public Interest* promised to publish only non-ideological articles, albeit with some expected exceptions. The editors recognized that their more scientific and "non-ideological" approach

---

3 The editorial that introduced the first issue in 1965 was one of only a handful of editorial interventions to appear in the journal.

would not appeal to everyone and acknowledged that the "ideological essay" is often more interesting than "a more matter-of-fact and more truthful essay" (Bell and Kristol 1965, p. 4). While the editors promised to make the new journal "lively," "readable," and "as controversial as possible," they also promised to publish "the occasional "dull" article that *merely reports the truth* about a matter under public discussion" (p. 4, emphasis added).

The new journal's aim was underscored by the editors' choice of Walter Lippmann's definition of "the public interest" for their opening editorial. After noting that "the public interest" is a much debated topic, there also being those that believe it to be nothing more than the aggregation of individual interests, and not wanting to presume to settle "a theoretical issue that has vexed political philosophers for over 2,000 years now," the editors argued that there does exist something *like* "the public interest," even if it is difficult to articulate (Bell and Kristol 1965, p. 5). They therefore borrowed Walter Lippmann's definition, which reads: "The public interest may be presumed to be what men would choose if they saw clearly, thought rationally, acted disinterestedly and benevolently" (p. 5). Lippmann was known for his belief that science was "the discipline of democracy" (2006, p. 165).

The journal focused exclusively on domestic policy, eschewing foreign policy as too contentious, due to the ongoing war in Vietnam.[4] Maurice R. Berube and Marilyn Gittell (1970) questioned how a journal so devoted to the question of improving American life could overlook questions of foreign policy. "This is precisely our objection to *The Public Interest*," they argued, its conservation of the status quo (1970, p. 7). It is a valid criticism to make, that no journal could tackle the question of "the public interest" while simultaneously ignoring an issue so important to the nation at the time.

Kristol's and Bell's introduction continued with a critique of contemporary policy analysis, arguing that analysis proceeds before the right questions are asked and before the right information is gathered. The policy machine then was put into motion and not easily diverted from its course. Further, the policy machine was said to be growing bigger and smoother, as Daniel Patrick Moynihan argued in his first article for *PI,* "The Professionalization of Reform." For Moynihan, the policy machine grew through the combined effects of growing industrial output, the professionalization of the middle class, and the exponential growth of knowledge. This "economic revolution" allowed states to learn how to manage their economies and to put increased revenues to some good social purposes. The professionalization of the middle class created a culture in which the professional is viewed as someone with "an independence of judgment, esoteric knowledge, and

---

4 Kristol wrote, "Vietnam was arousing a storm of controversy at the time, and we knew that our group had a wide spectrum of opinion on the issue. We did not want any of the space in our modest-sized quarterly to be swallowed up by Vietnam" (2005, p. 7). However, in order to accommodate interest in foreign policy, he began the sister journal *The National Interest* in 1985.

immunity to outside criticism" (Moynihan 1965, p. 13). The exponential growth of knowledge created the foundation for the government "to respond intelligently and in time to the changing needs and desires of the electorate" (p. 15). In all, the practice of reform, the quest to fulfill "the public interest," was made more possible than ever. "They are less and less political decisions, more and more administrative ones. They are decisions that can be reached by consensus rather than conflict" (p. 12). However, this trend toward professionalization risked, according to Moynihan, a "decline in the moral exhilaration of public affairs at the domestic level" and "a monocracy of power" (p. 16). The professional reformers will rule, and the public will lose interest in their "public interest." Still, it promised the possibility of eliminating stubborn problems like poverty and other "animal miseries," so that national attention could be turned to issues such as foreign affairs and quality of life. That Moynihan was more concerned with perils than promise is important, as his article neatly charted the journal's course as a beachhead for those who would challenge the notion that New Class "experts" could, through rationalizing state intervention, successfully reorder society.[5]

This emphasis on the limits of policy intervention picked up steam in the early 1970s. A similar refrain appeared in *PI* from a contributor who argued "[s]ociety can only benefit by those ties which combine the advantage of social science knowledge with a clear awareness of its limitations" (Armor 1972, p. 116). If policy could not accomplish desired change, then the question that the journal was driven to ask was whether the problem was with policy itself, or with the desire for change. A favorite trope of the journal would become "the law of unintended consequences" (Teles 2000).

In 1972, *PI* published "The Evidence of Busing," by David J. Armor, which analyzed the results of the Boston METCO study on integrative busing and argued that mandatory busing had few positive effects on improved student achievement or racial integration and instead could be causing harm. The article generated much controversy and was reported in the media even before it was published. The journal's editors accompanied the article with this statement: "While his manuscript was being copy-edited in our office, its findings were being 'reported' in the national press … and they have been denounced publicly by critics who have never seen the results of his studies themselves" (1972, p. 90). Two issues later, *PI* published a response to Armor's article in which the authors argued that the study was too limited for the conclusions he drew and took issue with some of his assumptions and interpretations of the available evidence (Pettigrew, Useem, Normand, and Smith 1973). Regarding the debate, James Q. Wilson, a regular contributor to the journal, decided he could only come to two conclusions, or "general laws," regarding social science evaluations of public policy programs

---

5 Moynihan (1995) revisited his article, "The Professionalization of Reform," upon the journal's thirtieth anniversary. There he pointed to an earlier comment he made in *The New York Times* that "there is a movement to turn Republicans into Populists, a party of the People arrayed against a Democratic Party of the State …" (p. 40).

(1973). First, policy interventions produce the intended effect if those implementing the policy or their friends carry out the research, and second, policy interventions do *not* produce the intended effect if research is carried out by independent third parties, especially if they are skeptical of said policy.

From the outset, *The Public Interest* put little hope in a liberating social science of policy analysis and development, a hope that diminished with time. Instead, it offered an alternative role for like-minded social scientists as *critics* of those social scientists and policy professionals that they saw as members of the New Class, those who believed that policy in particular and social science in general could be deployed to expand human liberty. The journal's audience would likely be middle-aged, revanchist professionals, scholars, and writers who were drawn to question the welfare state project. *PI* developed a significant, if modest, readership. Early issues made announcements of reprints for sale in order "to meet the constant stream of requests."

Warren Demian Manshel, a wealthy friend of Kristol's, who had served as Ambassador to Denmark and was also the founder of *Foreign Policy*, initially funded the journal.[6] Manshel gave Kristol and Bell a $10,000 grant to begin and established a company, National Affairs, Inc., to publish the journal.[7] Over its lifespan, the journal secured substantial foundational and institutional support, notably from the American Enterprise Institute, a conservative think tank. The new journal's masthead listed Bell and Kristol as editors and Manshel as publisher.[8] The journal's editorial office address was "in care of Basic Books," the publishing house in New York City where Kristol was employed. The journal's subscription office address was care of Freedom House, also based in New York City.

Bell and Kristol solicited articles by calling on friends and acquaintances, who they believed "to be on our 'wave length'" (Kristol 2005, p. 6). This "wave length" was skepticism toward or, more arguably, a strong critique of the welfare state and President Johnson's declared War on Poverty. The first issue contained the article from Moynihan, articles by Robert M. Solow and Robert L. Heilbroner, Nathan Glazer, who would later replace Bell as co-editor, Eveline M. Burns, Robert A. Nisbet, Daniel S. Greenberg, Jacques Barzun, Timothy Raison, and Bell. As with these authors, contributors were mainly university professors, federal government employees, and other policy analysts in the private and public sectors, often at various think tanks and foundations. A sampling of topics covered in the

---

6   It is not clear how much money Manshel gave to the journal over the 25 years of his support. The increased circulation of the journal caused the subsidy from Manshel, by definition a patron, to increase to several tens of thousands of dollars per year (Kristol 2005).

7   The corporation now publishes the quarterly opinion journal *National Affairs*, the company's eponymous inheritor of *The Public Interest*'s mantle.

8   The journal also had a "Publication Committee," whose members included Murray L. Silberstein (chairman), Leo Cherne, Daniel P. Moynihan, Arthur J. Rosenthal, Leo Rosten, Martin E. Segal, and Stanley Simon.

early years include, but are not limited to: the question of automation, technology and unemployment, welfare, the high cost of hospitals, suburbia, education, crime, housing, the draft, public television, class, and pollution.

The journal devoted entire issues to single topics of domestic importance. Special issues were often funded by outside donors such as the special issue on New York (Issue 16, Summer 1969) funded at least in part by the Carnegie Corporation and the Ford Foundation, or their series on professional education, which began with Issue 79 (Spring 1985), and was funded by a grant from the Alfred P. Sloan Foundation. Special issue topics included: 'the Universities' (Issue 13), 'Focus on New York' (Issue 16), 'Capitalism Today' (Issue 21), 'The Great Society: Lessons for the Future' (Issue 34), and the 'Crisis in Economic Theory' (Special Issue, no number, 1980), among others. Glazer argued that the journal's cessation of such issues after 1990 helped push it in an ever more conservative direction.

Mark Lilla, a later editor, described *The Public Interest*'s articles as "gentlemanly essays, not dissertation chapters" (1985, p. 68). Written for a more general audience, the early articles did not overly rely on statistics or "science." This changed in the 1970s when economics began to dominate policy analysis, and the articles grew more specialized.[9] Presumably, the readership of *PI* also reflected this specialization. Additionally, more policy journals began publication, many of which were narrower in their focus. On the whole, *The Public Interest* had the look and feel of a professional journal, with a clean design, a publisher, a sponsoring institution, a regular publication schedule, no advertisements, or any other extraneous material. There was no artwork, no graphics, no poetry, only a smoothness and innocuousness. To flip through an issue is to be bored. The articles themselves were not always boring, despite the inaugural editorial's promise to publish "dull" articles. However, the journal remained mostly unflappable. Its seriousness opposed the glamour of journals like *The New York Review of Books*. It cultivated a different audience, not the literati and the glitterati, but the policy wonk and the inside the beltway smooth operator.

Despite the academic backgrounds of many of the contributors, *PI* began firmly outside the academic milieu and for the most part, remained outside. Its founders avoided positions as professors in their early careers, working and making a living as editors and writers instead (Kristol 1995b). Bell, Kristol, and Glazer have all been named as members of the "New York Intellectuals," a description mainly used to define those individuals associated with the prominent New York intellectual journals, primarily *Partisan Review, politics, Commentary, Dissent*, and *The New York Review of Books*. Their cultural capital derived from those intellectual circles and magazines and later translated into a relatively significant force in the political arena.

While specialization may have increased as the journal "matured," an attention to larger questions continued. Their time spent at City College of New York, an

---

9 As Lilla remarks, "[t]he 'policy intellectual' writing for *The Public Interest* in 1975 was not the gentlemanly social scientist of 1965" (1985, pp. 70–71).

affordable public institution with an overwhelmingly Jewish student population, and their association with the early journals of the "New York Intellectuals" habituated the journal's editors to the study of big ideas. The sons of Jewish immigrants from working class homes, they came to know *Partisan Review* while university students. City College did not offer a rigorous education inside the classroom, these men recalled. So, they found their education elsewhere, largely through a culture of fierce intellectual discourse practiced in the college cafeteria at lunchtime and between classes (Bloom 1986).

Perhaps it was his introduction to *Partisan Review* that prompted Kristol, at the age of 23, to help found the small and short-lived magazine *Enquiry: A Journal of Independent Radical Thought* (Dorman 2001). Kristol went on to be an assistant editor at *Commentary*, a liberal Jewish publication at the time, then co-editor of *Encounter*[10] in London, and finally worked as an editor at Basic Books before co-founding *The Public Interest* at the age of 45. Bell held senior editorial positions at *The New Leader* and *Fortune*. After leaving his editorial position at *The Public Interest* in 1973, Bell went on to found *Correspondence*, a quarterly journal of ideas and cultural commentary. (Another friend from City College, Irving Howe, would found the journal *Dissent* in 1953.) In a certain way, then, these editors of *The Public Interest* were not only embarking upon a project of criticism but were also *the products* of criticism. They formed their political outlook and sense of critical purpose through a habituation to the practice of re-view.

Kristol's editorial career at *Commentary* in the 1940s contained the early hints of a conservative viewpoint that would become more visible in the late 1960s and early 1970s. For example, in a 1960 review of Friedrich Hayek's *Constitution of Liberty*,[11] Kristol echoed Hayek's criticism of the welfare state, asserting: "Above all, his book encourages us to take another look at our welfare state, which—lacking any general idea of 'welfare'—is coming more and more to resemble a monstrous pork-barrel" (1960, p. 354). Kristol also highlighted four of Hayek's tenets that later would become central to *The Public Interest*, namely 1) that our ignorance is greater than our knowledge, 2) that the more we know, the more we do not know, 3) that actions have unforeseeable consequences, and 4) that the senselessness of

---

10   In 1952, Kristol was given the opportunity to co-found *Encounter* in London. Supposedly without the editorial staff's knowledge, the CIA at least in part funded the journal through the Congress for Cultural Freedom in an effort that was a soft power offensive against the spread of communism. While in England, Kristol became friends with several British conservatives, of the Tory political party, such as Michael Oakeshott. He quickly found them to be like-minded and admired a conservative tradition that he thought was lacking in the US. At the end of his time with *Encounter*, Kristol returned to the US and for a short while worked for *The Reporter*.

11   Kristol would later emphasize the fact that he never read Hayek's *The Road to Serfdom* because "not for a moment did I believe that the United States was on any kind of road to serfdom" (2011c, p. 183).

coercing men to "build a better world" lies in the certainty that our children will detest this world (1960, p. 354).

What the City College group inherited from these older journals also influenced their editorial policies and practices.[12] On producing the journal, Kristol wrote: "I designed the magazine the way I had designed *Encounter*: by borrowing from the format of existing or previous magazines and changing things around a little. What was important was that, given our lack of staff, it should be as 'idiot proof' as possible" (Kristol 1995b, p. 30). At the outset, the editors decided upon a policy of non-remuneration to keep costs at bay. Also, they did not want to take money from their friend, Manshel. Until its closing in 2005, the journal continued largely to abide by this "principle." Lilla, who served as an executive editor in the 1980s, recalls earning a salary of around $11,000, which he described as "absolutely nothing" (Dorman 2001, p. 201). For the most part, the journal kept the operation small, as is the nature of journals with restricted audiences. In the winter of 1978, Elizabeth Kristol, Irving's daughter, became an assistant editor at the journal, making the journal a family affair. Her brother William later became a contributor. In 1995, he co-founded *The Weekly Standard*. His wife, Susan, also contributed an essay to *PI*. Irving's own wife, Gertrude Himmelfarb, a scholar of British conservatism who published widely, made several contributions to the journal and influenced Kristol's thinking.

Bell left his editorship at *The Public Interest* after Richard Nixon's election. Bell and Kristol fell out over the 1972 election, with Bell supporting George McGovern and Kristol supporting Nixon. Bell quietly resigned shortly after the election and was replaced by Glazer (Dorman, 2001). Although Bell continued to publish in the journal for a few more years, his reflective piece on the journal's twentieth anniversary was clearly critical of the journal's neoconservative and, what Bell described as, its "ideological" turn.[13] Describing the founding of *PI*, Kristol argued that at the time he was becoming increasingly skeptical of the Great Society and the liberal ideas behind it (1995b). He began to write op.-ed pieces for *The New Leader* expressing his skepticism, but he felt the urge to do something more, namely begin his own magazine. The next thought is striking. He writes that he and Bell thought the only existing conservative journal, the *National Review*, "was not to our tastes—at that time insufficiently analytical and 'intellectual,' too stridently hostile to the course of American politics ever since 1932" (1995b, p. 29). Kristol and Bell began *PI* in part because they could find no other outlet for the type of material they wished to publish. Here, in retrospect, the type of outlet Kristol finds lacking is a conservative one.

In 1988, *The Public Interest* published its first issue from Washington, D.C. After having spent more than 20 years in New York City, the publishing and arguably, intellectual, capital of the country, the journal moved to the state

---

12 Even *The Public Interest*'s office, once it had its own office, was set up to mirror the *Commentary* offices circa 1952 (D. Skinner 2005).

13 Bell made his final contribution to the journal in 1989.

capital. In the 1970s, Kristol had been offered an associate fellowship with the American Enterprise Institute. Kristol's relationship with AEI would continue to grow, and in 1987, he was offered a senior fellowship there. However, even prior to the move, as early as the late 1960s, the journal already described itself as a "Washington magazine." Or as Bell said, "We don't think of ourselves as a New York magazine. We're really a Washington and Cambridge magazine" (quoted in Goodman 1969, p. 72). The move brought them to the state's seat of power. It also helped blur the line between critics and the state, a hallmark of a journal that had some contributors who also held political and other governmental office. *The Public Interest* ceased publication in 2005.

Was there such a thing as a neoconservative movement developing in the 1960s?[14] And was *The Public Interest* at its center? Did a magazine really create a political change? Kristol himself was convinced that *The Public Interest* could make a difference and have an impact, no matter how low the circulation. He stated: "We had a circulation of a few hundred to begin with. That didn't bother us. With a circulation of a few hundred, you could change the world" (quoted in, Dorman 2001, p. 158). The circulation of the journal increased beyond "a few hundred"; however, it remained meager, perhaps topping out around 6,000. Still, copies made it into the right hands, such as President Nixon's (Steinfels 1979; Bronitsky 2013). Kristol argued that the journal acted as a focal point for what he described as a "neoconservative impulse" (1995a, p. 81). Yet, he continued, its impact was amplified because it was taken up and read by young intellectuals at other publications, like the *Wall Street Journal*, and then transmitted throughout the public sphere. The journal's influence likely peaked in the early 1980s when the Reagan administration's embrace of neoliberalism finally turned the page from Keynesianism and the welfare state to military Keynesianism and corporate welfare policies (Ehrman 1999). Indeed, the journal was the first to publish an article on the Laffer curve in 1975 (Allitt 2009). Associates of the journal also received government appointments, and the journal's influence on policymaking in D.C. gained notice in the press. That *The Public Interest* and its associates had influence can also be supported by the fact that most histories of the conservative or neoconservative movement in the latter half of the twentieth century include *The Public Interest* as a major player (Ehrman 1999; Nash 1976; Steinfels 1979).

---

14 In an article for *Newsweek* in 1976, Kristol laid out the main tenets of neoconservatism as it had developed. Neoconservatism 1) was not hostile to the idea of the welfare state but hostile to the Great Society version, 2) had great respect for the power of the market, 3) was respectful of traditional values and institutions, 4) affirmed the idea of equality but rejected egalitarianism, and 5) was critical of post-Vietnam isolationism and suspicious of detente. Kristol admitted that there was less consensus on this fifth proposition.

Negating "the Officially Available Nonsense": The Story of *Telos*

Telos began in May 1968 as a fledgling student journal of radical philosophy on the campus of the State University of New York (SUNY)—Buffalo. Paul Piccone, the founding editor, stated that "[i]t is no accident that one of the early subtitles of *Telos* was 'a journal definitely outside the mainstream of American philosophical thought'" (1988, p. 5). While the journal began as a forum for synthesizing philosophical thought, members of the editorial staff, notably Piccone, felt this purpose was insufficiently radical, and that the journal was "an amateurish microcosm of 'professional' philosophy," and inferior to numerous others (Staff 1970, p. 295).[15] By the second issue, Piccone was the only staff member remaining, and his vision for the journal included a different form of synthesis: namely, a merger of phenomenology with Western Marxism in an attempt to locate a new form of emancipatory politics that would "concretely negate the officially available nonsense" (Staff 1970, p. 295). Through *Telos*, Piccone also made clear his desire to introduce American readers to European and other foreign thinkers otherwise unnoticed in the United States. During the journal's early years, its focus would range from phenomenology to Frankfurt School critical theory to French existentialism and post-structuralism and onto Euro-communism, to name but a few avenues explored by authors in *Telos*.

In 1968, SUNY-Buffalo's philosophy department was the second largest in the country. However, the journal's founders described themselves as "intellectually starved graduate students" who "sought a radical alternative" (Staff 1970, p. 294). For the journal's founders, academia was not a productive setting for the type of philosophical and political thought that interested them. The journal's strategy to place itself outside academia would cause many of its editors and contributors to live double-lives. Many wrote for a journal that garnered little favor in academic circles, especially when it came to tenure review, but held jobs within academia that increasingly required professionalization (Breines 1988; Jacoby 1981/82). This strategy of avoiding a home within academia turned into a fear of institutionalization of any sort. Piccone suggests that the strategy saved the journal from conformity (Piccone 1988). The journal "chose" to remain on the margins. Choice or not, this non-institutionalization, in academia or elsewhere, helped keep the journal distinct from other intellectual currents and publications. Since *Telos* was a student journal without much support, production was a low-budget affair. These two facts combined to make the journal appear amateurish. Importantly, as with *The Public Interest*, *Telos'* foundational members were young, and many came from working-class and immigrant backgrounds. In both cases, it might be argued that this group's entry into the public sphere as re-viewers of the state represents one of the "successes" of the redistributionary American welfare state.

---

15 The first issue contained articles written by students at SUNY–Buffalo, the University of Oklahoma, and the University of Minnesota. The entire issue reached only 53 pages.

The journal's first editorial board consisted of five members and in the spirit of the age, appeared as a "collective." By Issue 3, Piccone was sole "Editor," alongside three associate editors, a review editor, and three staff members. With Issue 11 (Spring 1972), the total size of the *Telos* team numbered 24. However, this number fluctuated over time; Issue 12 listed only 17 members, five of whom also produced the journal. When the Toronto *Telos* group made its first appearance with Issue 22 (Winter 1974–5), staff had grown to 35.[16] Contributor and editorial member Tim Luke (2005) compiled an index of 74 editors, board members, and influential contributors associated with the journal over its life span. Interestingly, the vast majority were or are professional academics, many well-known, such as Andrew Arato, Seyla Benhabib, Russell Berman (the current editor), Susan Buck-Morss, Cornelius Castoriadis, Jean Cohen, Ferenc Feher, Agnes Heller, Axel Honneth, Russell Jacoby, Martin Jay, John Keane, Christopher Lasch, Mark Poster, Adolph L. Reed, Jr., and Richard Wolin. In early issues of the journal, the "Notes on Contributors" emphasized their ages and also displayed an irreverence that emphasized the journal's anti-professional intentions. Many contributors had ties to other journals that made *Telos* part of a broader transatlantic leftist intellectual milieu, including *Les Temps Modernes, Socialist Revolution, Radical America, Liberation, Studies on the Left, L'Esprit, Theory and Society*, and *Science and Society*. This said, even as early as Issue 21 (Fall 1974), the most common thing to appear in the "Notes on Contributors" was their faculty affiliations.

In Piccone's view, the early editions of *Telos* had sought out "forgotten and repressed texts that we had occasionally seen mentioned in passing or referred to in stray footnotes" (1988, p. 6). Whereas articles in most political science or sociology journals rarely consider their intellectual heritage, or only refer to works five or 10-years-old, *Telos* looked back 50 or 100 years to many texts that were Hegelian Marxist, Marxian, or anarchist, which had been out of favor for at least this long (Agger 2000). Piccone again: "[o]ur critique had to speak a language other than that of our opponents, and this necessitated the resurrection of otherwise forgotten philosophical traditions" (1988, p. 4). Further, many thinkers covered by the journal were individuals who had lived on the margins, having little political impact and small audiences. Robin Blackburn of the *New Left Review*, at an early *Telos* conference, asked why *Telos* was so interested in publishing these marginal figures. Paul Breines, *Telos'* book review editor, in retrospect answered: "the very lack of political success, the distance from actual power typical of these figures, their isolation, are in crucial respects the very things that drew us to them, their marginality serving as the ideal outpost for the activity of continual criticism" (Breines 1988, p. 41). Arguably, the political thinkers often found in the *New Left Review*, such as Georg Lukács, Antonio Gramsci, and Marx were also marginal figures in their times. Blackburn's comment then suggests some other definition of "marginal," as unpopular among the left that "counts."

---

16 The journal included a number of regional groups, such as the Toronto, Kansas, St. Louis, and Berkeley groups, who each contributed to the journal in various ways.

Telos' focus on marginal largely European theorists drew the journal further away from analyses of its home country, while attracting an international following (Adler 1988). For the most part, those involved with the journal believed that Western Marxism and European social thought, whether expressed by Karel Kosik, Enzo Paci, Jean Paul Sartre, or Michel Foucault amongst others, could offer more and better answers to the important political and philosophical questions. Europeans could also reflect on actual political questions of socialism or social democracy, as they existed in their home countries, whereas in the United States, those questions had little to no relation to an existing political reality that, implicitly it was asserted, would be improved if only it could accommodate even these "weak" or "compromise" positions.

While *Telos* found its voice in early issues, it would struggle with (or contest) its nature and purpose throughout its life span. In Issue 6, the journal stated that it fashioned itself after *Les Temps Modernes, Praxis*, and *New Left Review*, although the latter would become a favorite target of the journal in later issues. The journal's early editorial statements never made claims that the journal was Marxist or committed to advancing any political goals, no matter what the stripe.[17] Although never committed to fulfilling the revolutionary goals of overthrowing the capitalist class, the journal's first conference was dedicated to "The New Marxism" and its second conference to "Political Organization." Even at its most explicitly radical moments, *Telos*'s subtitle always spoke of the journal as one committed to "thought" or "theory," not politics. Rather than lay out a manifesto for action, the journal instead "proposed a systematic reexamination of the trajectory of radical thought during the last century …" (quoting Piccone, Raventos 2002, p. 136). *Telos* did not encourage political activities and, as "Moishe Gonzales"[18] argued, most of its editorial members were not politically active. "[A]s with almost all radical professors, almost no one in *Telos* engaged in any significant political activity" (Gonzales 1985). Not meant disparagingly, *Telos* practiced theory for theory's sake, and did not often attend to politics of an immediate nature. Rather, it maintained a critical distance and separated itself from other magazines and journals that commented upon or tried to influence current events in American political life. Indeed, attempts to make the journal more politically relevant had also, for some members, dumbed it down. Later forays into actual politics would raise levels of dissensus within the editorial board (Berman 1983; Frankel 1997).

The journal also distanced itself from the political movement that it appeared closest to, the New Left, which it viewed increasingly as a form of identity politics or as a rear guard action being fought from behind university walls. Indeed, *Telos* did not consider itself a journal of the New Left and maintained a critical distance from what

---

17 Still, an early article to appear in the journal was Herbert Aptheker's "Imperialism and Irrationalism" (1969, Issue 4). Aptheker was a prominent Communist intellectual blacklisted during the McCarthy era and a strong opponent of the Vietnam War.

18 In the tradition of Isaac Bickerstaff, "Moishe Gonzales" was an occasional pseudonym used by Piccone and Frank Adler.

remained of the movement(s). For the New Left, *Telos* acted as "a kind of theoretical *Listerine*: necessary, but not very pleasant, and to be spit out as soon as possible" (Raventos 2002, p. 134). Still, as the New Left movement disintegrated, Piccone labeled the journal a "political orphan," and asserted that it needed "to rethink its identity and to revise its project" (1988, p. 13). He later revised this assessment, redefining the journal's phenomenological project of providing an epistemological foundation for a "movement presenting itself as a radical alternative to the given" as having not collapsed but having been rendered "superfluous" (1994, p. 180). The journal's identity was therefore not dependent on the existence of the New Left, but in its current incarnation was irrelevant without it.

In the wake of the New Left, scholars and activists still considering themselves on the left but without an explicit political program began to consider the journal form itself as the new organizational means of "praxis" (Mattson 2002). The question of praxis was debated in *Telos*' pages, at its conferences, and in editorial correspondence. At the Antioch Conference in 1977, several argued that the journal needed to "escape the theoretical archaeology that has characterized *Telos*" (K. T. Group 1977, p. 191). This struggle with its theoretical relationship to current politics is reflected in changes made to the journal's subtitle, from "Marxist" to "radical" to "critical" and finally for one issue to "post critical," implying that even criticism was exhausted.[19] That *Telos*'s emerging anti-statism coincided with anti- or post-Marxism is also a question that contributors explored: was Marx's theoretical project necessarily the handmaiden of Stalinist authoritarianism. By the late 1970s, Piccone argued that the aim of the journal was to give Marxism, or "communism in theory," its "proper burial" (Piccone, at al. 1977). This desire made sense in light of transformations in the political economies of prominent states, such as the decline of Keynesianism in the United States and the United Kingdom, and especially as even communist states, like the Soviet Union and China, began to adopt more open responses to democracy and markets, respectively. This "burial of Marxism" may be a simplification of the journal's purpose, but it does accurately signal a shift for the journal from a critique based in political economy to one based in political theory, as I discuss further below (Nickel 2012).

While the post-New Left searched for some kind of direction, the intellectual, philosophical, and social scientific "mainstream" had identified the second generation of Frankfurt School critical theorists, most notably Habermas, as some kind of guide. And *Telos* also engaged with Habermas, and what Piccone would describe as the "Habermaniacs," throughout the 1970s and into the mid-1980s. Habermas appeared in the journal about a dozen times during this period, either as author or interview subject. Piccone later described this trajectory as

---

19 The subtitle then reverted to the previous designation "a quarterly journal of critical thought." Starting with issue 105 (1995), the journal ceased printing a subtitle, begging the question whether the journal had given up on trying to settle its identity. Online and in its advertisements, however, the journal has a new subtitle, "A Quarterly Journal of Politics, Philosophy, Critical Theory, Culture, and the Arts."

a "sacrifice." For Piccone, Habermas and the "linguistic turn" sacrificed what had been critical about the first generation of Frankfurt School thinkers—Theodor Adorno, Max Horkheimer, Herbert Marcuse—but did provide a temporary way station for those opposed to the industrial capitalist order. However, internal disputes began to surface more and more over the intellectual and/or political value of the linguistic turn that the German academic was said to have heralded. *Telos* devoted its 1984 conference to resolving these internal divisions, hoping that some theoretical resolution of this "pluralistic phase" could be achieved. Around the same time, the journal made its move from St. Louis to New York City. In the conference report, John Alt noted that "Piccone expressed hope, that with *Telos* relocating in New York, a major conceptual housecleaning would take place ..." (1985, p. 122). Writing as "Gonzales," Piccone noted that the internal consensus began to unravel as early as 1975 with the journal's (or Piccone's) abandonment of Western Marxism. It continued to unravel as the journal began to focus its attention on "more immediate political questions," dating back to 1982 and the journal's criticism of the European peace movement (1985, p. 165). Communication theory and Western Marxism would both ultimately be considered theoretical dead ends.

The end of the 1970s and the beginning of the 1980s was a crucial time for the journal. Piccone was refused tenure at Washington University in 1977 (Luke 2005). Shortly thereafter, a number of individuals important to the Left passed away: Herbert Marcuse, Rudi Dutschke, Jean Paul Sartre, Georges Haupt, Peter Ludz, Hans Gerth, and Nicos Poulantzas. Issue 44's introduction announced the "end of an age." The 1980 death of Alvin Gouldner, an office neighbor to *Telos* in St. Louis and sometime contributor and also founder of the journal *Theory and Society*, was announced two issues later.

It was during this period that *Telos* contributors began to develop the somewhat controversial concept of artificial negativity, which would come to dominate the journal's thinking. Piccone and Luke put forward the concept as an aid to understanding the continued vitality of capitalism and its co-option of intellectuals as members of the New Class. As the argument went, in the transition from entrepreneurial capitalism to monopoly capitalism, the "system" became too adept at domination eliminating all particularity and organic negativity (or criticism). This was a play off the conflict between "system" as one-dimensional society of state, economy, technology, and so forth and the "lifeworld" of the private sphere, civil society, and the periperhal, unrationalized domains beyond, beside, behind, or beneath the systemic forces or systemic structures. The New Class, comprised of liberal-left bureaucrats, activists, and intelligentsia, further "aided" the erasure of particularity and the homogenization of culture.[20] However,

---

20 Robert Antonio details how Piccone's theory of the New Class inverted Gouldner's vision of a potentially emancipatory group who operated through a culture of critical discourse. Its impact however, being historically contingent, depended on agency and circumstance. Piccone's version aligned more closely with the neoconservative view of the New Class, as professional reformers who led the state into areas it did not belong with all the attendant and

without negativity, the system cannot reproduce itself; capitalism being a beast that adapts to crises and criticism by correcting course and self-renewing. Therefore, monopoly or late capitalism began to artificially create various strains and currents of negativity to cure itself. In essence, the system lost its foil, "critical watchdogs" (Piccone, 1976, p. 104). The theory of artificial negativity made its "official" appearance in Issue 35, during the journal's tenth year of publication. Issue 35 (1978) contained Luke's "Culture and Politics in the Age of Artificial Negativity" and Piccone's "The Crisis of One-Dimensionality."

This concept would lead to investigations of work by Nazi sympathizer Carl Schmitt, figures associated with the contemporary European New Right, and to examine questions raised by the new populism and "postmodern" federalism. Throughout these intellectual journeys, the hopes of finding alternative forms of governance to an over-bureaucratized, governmentalized state remained paramount. Although this turn caused the journal to increasingly gain a reputation as "conservative" and "right-wing," it also allowed the journal to "rediscover America" and political theory (Ulmen 2008).

Robert Antonio adds that the journal's embrace of the artificial negativity thesis served as a boundary line between members of the *Telos* circle (2009). Whatever the reason for the split,[21] many people left the editorial board during the mid- to late 1980s, including Arato, Benhabib, Jose Casanova, Cohen, Habermas, Joel Kovel, Poster, and Joel Whitebook, all of them Piccone's "Habermaniacs," but for Poster, who never considered himself a *Telos* insider as he was wont to say. In 1994, Piccone observed:

> [T]he editorial board remains a hopelessly heterogeneous group still trying to come to some agreement concerning many crucial and not-so-crucial issues, such as precisely what constitutes this conservative involution, *who* has fallen victim to it, what the journal originally sought to accomplish, what it in fact has accomplished, and what it should be doing now and in the future (Piccone 1994)(p. 173).

Piccone suggested that the journal's "conservative turn" was a potential source of energy and creativity (Piccone 1994, p. 206). While *Telos* took pride in its transgressions over the years and used its functionality to carve out an identity, the journal's style and its affinity for the margin, and letting everyone else know that it prefers the margin, may give the impression that heterodox is not just a manner of critique but a way of being. What a past contributor called the "journal's

---

negative unforeseen consequences. Antonio also argues that Piccone used the "New Class" designation politically to mark boundaries between friends and enemies of the journal (2009).

21 The outcome of the 1985 "redemption debate," which centered around whether the journal should "abandon any lingering grandiose plans to change the world," a question put to the journal by recently added staff from East Europe, caused contributors and editors to leave (Piccone 1988, p. 21). Piccone pointed out that this redemption debate reflected a greater concern over radicalism in general, noting that the "conservative turn" in the journal reflected a similar process within American society (1988, p. 24).

notoriously hermetic style" distinguished *Telos* from other New Left publications that were more accessible, such as *Ramparts* or *Studies on the Left*, and could be more easily culled for slogans and statements for the movement (Breines 1988). To the charge that the journal has become "right-wing," one of its not-uncritical contributors replied in 1994, "[n]ow most of those who say this are just not reading the journal closely (or are reluctant to question old beliefs). But our style *invites* misinterpretations" (Ost 1994, p. 140). Whether the journal's alleged conservatism is a matter of style or something more is discussed further below.

Piccone passed away on July 12, 2004. At one time, Piccone had been a tenure-track professor in the sociology department at Washington University, St. Louis. He was turned down for tenure despite being unanimously approved by his department and having the outside recommendations of Daniel Bell, Marcuse, and Habermas, among others. A dean reviewing the matter remarked that Piccone's contribution "bears a problematic relation to the main currents of development in the social sciences" (quoted in Jacoby 1987, p. 138). Neither Piccone nor *Telos* ever sought to swim with the main currents of social science as determined by the flagship journals and departments that defined "main currents." As a result, both remained relatively marginal to these institutions. *Telos* continues to publish and is cited as a strong influence on the development and distribution of a North American critical theory (Nickel 2012).[22] However, it is more difficult to trace the impact of its view, if any, on the state in the US. Perhaps its greater influence has been to foster another generation of critics, having succeeded at its aim of helping to form more critical intellectuals.

Conserving the Welfare State? The "Sensible Revision" of *The Public Interest*'s Critique

In 1965, when *The Public Interest* began publication, a solid consensus existed on the contribution to nation building of the liberal-democratic, Keynesian welfare state. Of course, the consensus had its opponents, most notably from the movements of the New Right as well as the emergent New Left. Still, there was a notable center ground that clung to these ideas. Moynihan, a frequent contributor to *PI*, thought they should name the new journal, *Consensus*, after a favorite term of President Lyndon B. Johnson (Moynihan 1975). However, whatever degree of consensus still existed in the mid-1960s, new visions and di-visions quickly eroded it.

Glazer wrote on the journal's twentieth anniversary that when *The Public Interest* began publication, "[t]he business of the day was the completion of the welfare state, for which Christian Democratic or Social Democratic Europe provided a guide" (1985, p. 19). For Glazer, the welfare state would be completed through a process of social reform under the guidance of professionals from the social services, universities, and research organizations—in essence, the pool of people

---

22 Former members of *Telos* editorial circle would become active members of the journals *Praxis International* and then *Constellations*.

who would contribute to the journal. Technocratic experts and professionals would drive the completion of the welfare state, not mass-participation. This consensus defined the journal's avowed "non-ideological" position. To be against the state, or "anti-statist," was to be ideological, as were Presidential candidate Barry Goldwater and William F. Buckley's Jr.'s *National Review*. As Kristol wrote, "I deemed that kind of 'anti-statism' to be a species of political hysteria, and I felt its reaction to the New Deal excessive" (1995a, p. 83). Like Glazer, Kristol also had hopes that the project of *The Public Interest* would help improve, not dismantle, the welfare state: "we were meliorists, not opponents, and only measured critics" (Kristol 1995a, p. 85). The journal's founders believed that a non-ideological approach would allow for the "sensible revision" of state policies. Their view as critics held that the state could be amended or revised through a careful process that applied social scientific knowledge to policy problems as they existed.

What they would come to oppose was the overwhelming vision of the Great Society proponents who pursued such ideologically driven programs as a "War on Poverty," without fully and "scientifically" investigating the ramifications of such a "war." Kristol especially sought to rescue the welfare state from its European model and develop an American-style welfare state that would not "frustrate the spirit of enterprise" or "instill risk-aversiveness as a universal virtue" (2011a, p. 357).

According to *The Public Interest,* one of the major problems with the welfare state was "The Bureaucracy Problem" (Wilson 1967). Any attempt to fix it must be grounded on the principle that "[t]here are inherent limits to what can be accomplished by large hierarchical organizations" (p. 6). Further, the bureaucracy problem can only begin to be solved once "we decide what it is we are trying to accomplish" (p. 8). By linking the bureaucracy problem to the expansion of the state, and evoking the Royal we, the article set the stage for *The Public Interest* to serve as the vanguard of critique that challenged the purposes and processes of the welfare state.

This disillusionment or disappointment with the welfare state became the new consensus by the late 1960s. In the pages of *PI*, Peter F. Drucker (1969) expanded upon this disappointment to encompass a critique of government as a whole, writing that the enchantment with government ended the world over in the 1960s. Michael Harrington, who may have first referred to *The Public Interest* crowd as "neoconservatives,"[23] believed there was reason to be disappointed with

---

23 Harrington's use of the word "neoconservative" was not its first appearance in print. As Justin Vaïsse uncovered, Robert Bartley used the term "neo-conservative" in his 1972 article on the journal for the *Wall Street Journal*: "Casting about for a label, he considered several possibilities: "the *Public Interest* crowd" (too narrow), "the radical centrists" (too confusing), and "the neo-Whigs" (too imprecise)" (2010, pp. 74–5). Kristol had used it to describe himself, perhaps jokingly, in private correspondence as early as 1955 (Bronitsky 2013). After 1975, Kristol embraced the new description, perhaps recognizing its force, while other members of *The Public Interest*, like Glazer, Bell, and Moynihan, continued to reject the label.

the state. However, he also argued that different responses to the state were the result of different views, and the view belonging to the neoconservatives was unhistorical and abstract, ignoring the underlying "conservative power structure" of the welfare state (1973, p. 451). Importantly, and unlike *Telos, The Public Interest* was not anti-statist, even when vociferously criticizing Johnson's Great Society. Perhaps recognizing the truth of arguments propounded in the pages of *Telos* that the welfare state is good for capitalism, Kristol asserted that a tenet of neoconservatism was not hostility to the welfare state but only to its Great Society version (2011b).[24] It was this program of critique that would come to be known as "neoconservatism."

In 1972, Robert Bartley's article "Irving Kristol and Friends" appeared in the *Wall Street Journal*, signaling the emerging importance of the "neoconservative" impulse. The article gave them national exposure, and as Kristol recalls, "the editorials [in the *WSJ*] themselves began to reflect, in some degree, the mode of thinking to be found in *The Public Interest*—analytical, skeptical, and implicitly *ideological* in a way we did not ourselves at the time appreciate" (1995a, p. 32, emphasis added). Kristol himself began to write regularly for the *WSJ*. In one piece, he urged foundations to stop being reactive to the welfare state and start being proactive in regard to a conservative response. It was in reaction to that editorial, Kristol argued, that foundations, like the Smith Richardson, Olin, and Bradley Foundations, began to support the journal (2005, pp. 7–8). *The Public Interest* along with *Commentary* and the *Wall Street Journal* acted as "something like a national force, and politicians and editorial writers began to pay attention" (Kristol 1995a, p. 87). Kristol later described the three publications as a "*troika*," the Russian term for a team of three horses pulling a carriage, expressing faux-amazement that these publications, two with very small circulations, had the impact that they did (2005, p. 10).

Lilla (1985) has suggested that the journal's hopefulness for the *completion* of the welfare state was apparent only in the first five years of the journal. After 1970, the skeptical hopefulness increasingly gave way to disenchantment. On its tenth anniversary in 1975, *The Public Interest* published a special issue on the US bicentennial. The editors wrote, this issue is "distinctive in its focus on issues of political philosophy, as against our usual focus on questions of social policy. ... Whatever the costs or benefits of particular social policies, it is on fundamental issues of political philosophy that the American republic is likely to stand or fall"

---

24   *PI* later found an important role to be played by the state, namely as an inculcator of virtue, except it was not sure how that could be accomplished and offered few suggestions. *Telos* also took up the question of civic virtue through an engagement with Christopher Lasch's work. Lasch argued that liberalism assumes the state can dispense with civic virtue. However, unlike the members of *The Public Interest*, Lasch did not believe that civic virtue could be restored through the state, but rather it required a more populist or communitarian origin as he elaborated in *The True and Only Heaven: Progress and Its Critics* (2013 [1991]).

(Kristol and Glazer 1975, p. 3). The journal's shift from questions of policy to questions of philosophy had begun even earlier however. As Glazer (2005) noted in his retrospective essay, "Neoconservative From the Start," the journal quickly realized that questions of policy or "means" were very dependent on questions of values or "ends." To evaluate whether a social policy actually meliorated the public interest, one first needed to know what the public interest was. As early as 1971, Kristol wrote an editorial in which he noted a shift in public policy discussion from means to ends. His editorial gives the impression that the journal was merely reacting to outside change when it was the journal that played a great role in shaping public policy discussion.

> The shift is from argument over the selection of priorities to controversy over the choice of goals—a shift from means to ends, from economics to political philosophy ... It is hard to imagine a more important distinction—yet it has been blurred by the fact that so many people still talk of "reordering our priorities" when what they have in mind, more often than not unwittingly, is actually the redefinition of the purposes of our political life (Kristol 1971, p. 3).

For Kristol, at root is the question: "What *kind* of society should America be?" (1971, p. 4).

Bell later charged the journal with deriding the social sciences in favor of "common sense" (1985, p. 57). Bell argued that this change ran parallel with the journal's real ideological campaign, which for him was being waged against liberalism. In essence, *The Public Interest*'s critique of the state shifted from wanting the state to do better to wanting the state to do less, because they saw it not doing better by wanting allegedly always to do more. The journal became a mouthpiece for limiting the role of the state in domestic US policy. Contradicting Bell, Glazer (2005) explained that the journal's neoconservative tendencies appeared early, raising the question of whether the journal and its associates underwent a transformation (a "mugging" to use Kristol's term) or whether liberalism and neoconservatism are simply two sides of the same coin.

To further support the charge that the journal moved in the same direction since its beginning, one can point to events like Moynihan's address to the Americans for Democratic Action in 1967, in which he called for a "politics of stability" and an alliance with political conservatives (Nash 1976, p. 303). It appears the journal contained the elements necessary to its "neoconservative" emergence at the outset. There may have been some hesitation to reveal those true colors, but if there was, it did not last long. By the early 1970s, there could be little disputing the journal's political stripes, despite the various degrees to which its members wore them. Moynihan attributed this shift to the type of discourse prominent on the left at the time of the journal's founding. Liberals reacted to this "debasement of the standards of political discourse" by migrating to the right (1985, p. 126). He remarked that the journal's rightward shift was one of the great migrations in twentieth-century American politics. "The Republican Party and the conservative cause acquired an intellectual class ... . By 1980, Republicans 'had become, or were becoming, the party of ideas,'" representing a merging of conservatism with liberalism, an ideational ideology (1985, p. 112). In other words, American conservatism became capable of offering a re-view of the state grounded in theory or ideas.

Wilson, a frequent contributor to *PI*, in "'Policy Intellectuals' and Public Policy" (1981) noted that public policy was once again under the influence of ideas and intellectuals—the first great period of influence having been the 1960s. He rather facilely distinguished intellectuals from scholars by noting that the former often lacked evidence for their arguments. Scholars, conversely, are the persons who produce and test ideas under rules governing the quality of evidence. *The Public Interest* hoped to be a forum for scholars when it began, a place where policies could be rigorously tested and evaluated. However, Wilson found that not all scholars do their job well either due to scholarship's failures as a prognosticating tool, i.e., its inability to decide in advance which policies are beneficial to pursue. Such scholarship should be relegated to retrospective evaluations rather than prospective analyses. Wilson instead found a larger role in the policy process for the intellectual *as intellectual*, concluding that the true influence of intellectuals in the policy process is not knowledge, but *theory*. Wilson's article effectively traced the transition among *The Public Interest* crowd, from scholars (revisers) to intellectuals (re-viewers), or at least from realizing that as intellectuals (which perhaps they already were in 1965), they could more effectively influence the state and its policies.

Anticipating this belief in the greater power of intellectuals to influence politics, Kristol began in the mid-1970s to articulate a new political program for the Republican Party. In a *WSJ* article published in 1976, "The Republican Future," Kristol argued that Republicans needed to develop a clearer vision for the nation. "Every political party has its roots in some vision of an ideal nation," but the Republicans "tend to have only a blurred vision of a vague ideal" (p. 344). Instead, their party primarily functioned as negative "critics" of the Democratic Party without putting forward a positive program of their own. Kristol recommended that this positive program center on "the question of what a *conservative welfare state* would look like" (p. 346). He argued that the idea of a welfare state is consistent with conservative political philosophy, because in an urbanized, industrialized, highly mobile society, "people need governmental action of some kind if they are to cope with many of their problems" (p. 346). "The basic principle behind a conservative welfare state ought to be a simple one: Wherever possible, people should be allowed to keep their own money—rather than having it transferred (via taxes) to the state—on condition that they put it to certain defined uses" (p. 347).

Kristol then argued for a political platform that would not attempt to undo the welfare state in its entirety but instead repurpose it to create "conservatism (or Republicanism) with a human face." By that time, the majority thrust in the journal consisted of a conservative policy analysis—conservative in the sense that policy change should occur slowly, hesitantly, and without bringing about much change at all. The journal would consider later efforts by so-called "conservatives" to dismantle the welfare state to be radical or utopian (Teles 2000).

Despite Kristol's ardent support for neoconservatism, Glazer (2005) noted that *The Public Interest* continued to publish pieces favorable to liberalism and even socialism through the 1980s and even 1990s. However, the main force of the journal's neoconservative thrust as pushed by the increasingly ideological Kristol outweighed this open book policy. Glazer in part blames the journal's "rightward turn" on the journal's abandonment of special issues in the 1990s and its increasing dependence on what came in over the transom that was largely the product of conservative think tanks and foundations. As Glazer argued, "[m]any of these conservative ideas were indeed powerful. But, as they began to dominate the debate over policy, we should have done more to examine them critically" (2005, p. 16). In a sense, the journal's embrace of neoconservatism was a result of its failure to criticize and re-view, of getting close to, and in some cases, such as that of Moynihan, becoming those who actually wielded power.

Against the "State" at All Costs? *Telos* **and Criticism in Theory**

A similar charge would be directed at *Telos* after its rightward turn. However, the relationship between *Telos* and the seat of power in the US was of a fundamentally different nature. As Luke wrote on the occasion of the journal's 100th issue, "Despite the many zig-zags in the history of *Telos*, the journal remains consistent. Never convinced that the state is either just or rational, *Telos* has been emphatically anti-statist ... [and] has continually highlighted the irrational side of allegedly rational-bureaucratic state authorities" (1994, p. 106), even if from atop the "on-high" position of hermeneutical analysis.

This said, *Telos* contributor and former editorial board member, Scott McNall, in his reflection upon the journal, critiqued *Telos* for this approach, writing that "Hermeneutics is a stand-in for observation and the development of answers to the problem of alienation" (2011, p. 113). Piccone was even driven to remark in the early 1980s that, "[t]heory needs an objective political referent" (1983, p. 4).[25] This tension raises the question of whether the journal was actually engaged in a practice of re-view, or whether its theoretical focus only provided an array of "views" without sufficient connection to existing realities. McNall also accused *Telos* contributors of not being very good sociologists—again, suggesting too much distance between theorization and empiricism. Is this then something that separates the journal from its ancestors, notably the "great reviews," which were more closely connected to studying politics and political practice as such?

---

25   Piccone continued: "What is needed is a political *agency* which radical intellectuals would then theoretically articulate and represent. If new social movements didn't exist, they would have to be invented," to give politically marginalized intellectuals something to do because their social function was otherwise in crisis (1983, p. 3).

When *Telos* directed attention to political institutions and practices, it was often through an examination of foreign states. In the first 20 years of publication, articles examined politics in the USSR, Czechoslovakia, Germany (East and West), Yugoslavia, Poland, Spain, Greece, Afghanistan, Vietnam, Hungary, Japan, Iran, Algeria, Italy, Argentina, South Africa, Israel, Brazil, Albania, Romania, France, Austria, China, Guatemala, and Canada. While occasionally examining the United States, the journal did not formally announce its intention to analyze its home environment until 1977, and did so with some fanfare: "Our exile into European theory may be nearing an end!" (Piccone 1977, p. 3). However, sustained attention would not be paid to the United States for about another decade. Many of the articles that investigated conditions in other countries looked to Eastern Europe, prompting a contributor to argue that "*Telos* sees everything through the prisms of Eastern European dissidents" (Frankel 1983, p. 153). This focus on Eastern Europe also contributed to the journal's anti-statism, as it provided strong examples of the excesses of state bureaucracy and total administration. Piccone later considered this concern with Eastern Europe to be excessive as it took too seriously the ideas developed in political and intellectual contexts quite irrelevant to those in the United States (1988).

In the late 1970s and early 1980s, the journal translated much theoretical work by Italian scholar Norberto Bobbio.[26] His first article, "Is There a Marxist Theory of the State?" (1978a) made clear that there was no socialist theory of the state in Marx. For Bobbio, instead of trying to articulate such a theory, left intellectuals had scoured Marx's very limited writings on the subject and expanded a handful of theses into a political program that was a light sketch at best. Even though Bobbio's *Telos* contributions laid out the defects in the Left's politics and stressed the historical incompatibility of democracy and socialism, he remained optimistic. Socialism depended on democracy and while the slow workings of the democratic procedural method were somewhat (or very) inimical to the qualitative leap necessary to transform a capitalist society into a socialist one, the Left should not call for shortcuts. For Piccone and others at *Telos*, this was merely yet another dead end.[27]

The concept of artificial negativity, by this time more or less defining the telos of *Telos*, had also been introduced as a means for getting "Beyond Critical Theory,"

---

26 *Telos* published seven articles by Bobbio between 1978 and 1984, namely "Is There a Marxist Theory of the State?" (1978), "Are There Alternatives to Representative Democracy?" (1978), "Why Democracy?" (1978), "Marxism and Socialism" (1979), "Italy's Permanent Crisis" (1982), "Democracy and Invisible Government" (1982), and "The Future of Democracy" (1984).

27 It was this critical response to Bobbio's more or less meliorist contributions that helped steer the journal toward the controversial figure Carl Schmitt. Piccone and contributor Gary Ulmen especially embraced Schmitt in an attempt to find some political theory to move the journal forward ("Uses and Abuses of Carl Schmitt," Issue 122, 2002, p. 12).

and was touted as "the boldest and most exciting [concept] and, consequently, drew the most criticism" toward the journal (K. T. Group 1977, p. 190). With the artificial negativity thesis, *Telos* drew the ire of many on the left both within and beyond the US, and inside and outside the academy. Gouldner argued that it presupposed the one-dimensionality thesis of Marcuse and was "a critique without politics," or better, a critique that perhaps foreclosed the possibility of politics (p. 183). Barry Commoner went even farther calling Piccone "a threat to the Left," specifically to any future left whom "in their gullibility might be taken in by Piccone's account" (p. 183). Boris Frankel (1982) in the pages of *Thesis Eleven* described the theory as giving the "State" extreme omnipotence. For leftist critics of *Telos*, this was a theory that eliminated the possibility of a critical politics. Despite such criticisms, Piccone stood by the theory. At the Elizabethtown *Telos* Conference in February 1990, he contrasted artificial negativity to Habermas's "communication theory," which he argued had "generated a whole series of wrong forecasts concerning the direction of modern society during the past decade and a half," while "the projections made on the basis of the artificial negativity analysis have turned out much more accurate" (1989–90, pp. 116–7). While the concept may never have achieved the level of a major intellectual phenomenon, it is fair to say that the theory played a big role in the journal and perhaps foreclosed, and also opened, other investigations or theoretical avenues after its introduction. It is easy to argue that part of the motivating force behind the new theorization of the *possibility* of criticism that the artificial negativity thesis proposed was a re-evaluation of the journal's own purpose and existence.

The theory could also be considered a response to new forms of authority with no center. An early issue of *Telos* published a translated interview between Gilles Deleuze and Foucault titled "Intellectuals and Power." In the interview, Foucault argues that today's big unknown is who exercises authority: "Obviously, the theory of the State, and the traditional analysis of the State machinery does not exhaust all areas of exercise and functioning of authority" (Seem (trans.) 1973, p. 107). As a result, this problem of defining and locating authority, of the multiplicity of power, makes critique all the more difficult, because its object is dispersed or worse, invisible, or at least, obscured. This difficulty can then engender a form of pessimism, which some opponents of the theory of artificial negativity identify as its source. It can also be depoliticizing, a similar complaint made by the critics of post-structuralism. If power is everywhere, where should critique muster its forces?

Still, I contend that "artificial negativity" is not wholly pessimistic. Its main proponents, Piccone and Luke, still held out hope, however limited, for the creation of "organic negativity." Luke, in his 1983 piece, "Informationalism and Ecology," remarked that while most opposition and alternative organization was being manipulated from above, "these new localist citizens movements are also providing the structural possibilities [organic negativity] for realizing an ecologically sensible politics" (1983, p. 69). Similarly, in his last interview in the journal, and his second to last contribution to the journal before his death, Piccone explained:

> The only way out is to roll back the administrative apparatus to allow the natural gestation of "organic negativity"—autonomous individuality—thus reintroducing precisely that subjectivity essential for any self-sustaining social system. This state of affairs, however, exposes the predominant system to challenges it cannot deflect, resulting in radical qualitative changes (Raventos 2002, p. 134).

Despite this limited optimism, the idea that an "anonymous authoritarianism" "grounded in a modern welfare state that tends toward total administration" could only be combated by a turn to local, non-state forms of political organization (Luke 1983, p. 68) would dominate *Telos* pages for at least the next two decades, what the journal viewed as a continuous war of position between "system" and "lifeworld."

In addition to critiquing the welfare state through the theory of artificial negativity, as *Telos* began to cover US politics in the late 1970s, it also offered more targeted criticism of welfare state politics and emerging neoliberal policies. However, in contrast with *The Public Interest*, state expansion was seen as being at least in part fueled by the demands of corporate capitalism. For contributor Joan Roelofs, "[m]any 'Great Society' programs were based on pilot projects financed by the Ford Foundation" (1984–5, p. 72). The foundations were the means by which the Supreme Court, an elite institution, received and processed elite demands. Roelofs' earlier 1979 article, "The Warren Court and Corporate Capitalism," revealed the motivations behind the Court's judicial activism and social engineering. They were mechanisms by which to ensure elite control and channel demands from the masses into safe and mild reforms. The foundations aided this process and also in effect sponsored "artificial negativity," via patronage of universities, research institutes, and also "grassroots" organizations like Planned Parenthood and the Mexican-American Legal Defense and Education Fund. Roelofs' article on the influence of foundations on the Supreme Court highlighted the effect of *corporate* spending channeled through intermediaries on public policy. *The Public Interest*, meanwhile, often relied on foundation support for the publication of special issues. Certain key articles also received funding from such foundations. Roelofs' arguments borrowed from right-wing critiques of the state but demonstrated that an expanding welfare state was not in the interests of the poor and disenfranchised or any other minority group. Rather, the necessarily expanding state was a product of the demands of neoliberalism and the continued control of corporate capitalism. Roelofs argued in "The Warren Court" that the Court's 1937 turn from a protector of *laissez-faire* capitalism to a promoter of Progressivism was an adaptive change of means to accomplish the same end: to serve the interests of corporate capitalism, now by pacifying its critics.

In the early 1980s, *Telos* published an article by economist Hyman Minsky. The publication is notable because Minsky offered an unorthodox view of economic theory, which later entered more mainstream discussions as a result of the 2008 economic crisis; his "Financial Instability Hypothesis" provides a cogent explanation for its cause (Mihm 2009). Like Roelofs, Minsky argued that the "welfare state is good for capitalists" (1981–2, p. 51). Another article to appear in 1983 in *Telos* also analyzed the state of the economy and the policies of the state. John Kane and Ian Shapiro's article, "Stagflation and the New Right," re-viewed the economic policies of the New Right, more specifically, those of President Reagan and Prime Minister Thatcher (1983). Echoing a common refrain of *The Public Interest*, they argued that "[t]he power of governments to affect the economy consists all too often in the power to make things worse" (Kane and Shapiro 1983, p. 34). However, they claimed that the cause of inflation was not government policies but the monopoly power of business and/or the increasing concentration of capital since the 1950s, i.e., structural causes.

These are but a few examples of the investigations of liberalism and what was quickly becoming neoliberalism that occurred in *Telos*'s pages. Rather than turn to state policies of redistribution to solve problems of inequality, neoliberals advocated for "market mechanisms, high technology, international competitiveness, and economic growth to achieve these ends" (Siegel 1984, p. 171). Kristol described neoconservatism as the attempted merger of the philosophies of Adam Smith and Edmund Burke. Perhaps neoliberalism, or "Atari Democracy" as it was first described in the pages of *Telos*, embraced the market and the offerings of new technologies while eschewing the traditionalism that could potentially act as a fetter to new economic possibilities. Neoconservatism would reinvigorate the Republicans; Kristol claimed that it made the idea of American conservatism more appealing to voters (2011b). And neoliberalism would give the Democrats an alternative to Reaganomics. That the economic policies of each came largely to resemble one another is a topic for a different book. While *Telos* opposed the state, it also critiqued the non-state approach of neoliberalism, finding some sympathy with its faith in individuals, markets, and a reduced role for government, such as the journal's opposition to affirmative action, but not believing it to be *the* solution to what ailed the liberal welfare state (Luke 2011).

By the late 1980s, the journal had begun to try and think past conventional categories of Left and Right and to explore a new terrain. Key features on this new terrain were federalism and populism, which it was alleged could respond to the centralization of power that had been the legacy of the welfare state and which characterized the new neoliberal "governmentality." The initial special issue devoted to Schmitt exclaimed that *Telos* had undergone a large number of "theoretical false starts" over the almost 20 years of its existence, but had found the theme that would likely become the crucial one for the next decade: "To what extent is a democratic society possible in a context of over-specialization, increasing standardization of everyday life, and a drastic decline of social imagination?" (Piccone 1987, p. 3). This might arguably be regarded as the same question animating the journal over its life span. What is interesting in relation to my argument are the possible answers or solutions that the journal began to provide.

Beginning in the late 1980s, after "rediscovering" America through Schmitt, *Telos* began to embrace work by populist Christopher Lasch. Special issues on Schmitt in 1987, populism in 1988 and 1991, and federalism in 1991 and 1992 gave the journal the space to make these explorations. Only with federalism and populism could the journal envision a form of government that could be held accountable and in which organic, as opposed to artificial, negativity might emerge. As Luke remarked, "Much of the federal populism *Telos* is examining more closely in many of its recent issues is an attempt to think beyond the mechanical fusion of states and markets, which often sees abstract state power as a defender of popular class interests against predatory capital" (Luke 1994, p. 107).

Populist decentralization requires, however, local communities capable of governing themselves. *Telos* thus strove to distinguish "new" communitarian from "old" non-anti-statist populism, stressing the journal's ongoing anti-statist position (Piccone 1991). While the call for federalism brought *Telos* closer to an alliance with many conservatives, the journal's exhortations encouraged even more negative responses from the academic left. For Piccone especially, the New Class including academics hate populism, associating it with fascism and authoritarianism: "The problem with this association is that populism is usually a reaction against democratic deficits and is always much more democratic than any system based on representative democracy" (quoting Piccone, Raventos 2002, p. 147). Piccone went on to argue that the dominant New Class fears populism because it rejects the distinction between intellectuals and non-intellectuals. The New Class in fact was largely to blame for reducing "concrete individuals (with all their superstitions and defects) to abstract individuals manipulable by New Class social engineering which 'rationalizes' organic communities out of existence" (2008, p. 229). In many places, Piccone argued that the type of populism he advocated in the journal was not fascistic: "Communities have nothing to do with race and ethnicity, but with their particular histories, modes of interaction, institutional orders embodying common values, and a shared future" (1999, pp. 155–6). Given that *Telos* chose to explore populism and federalism through the lenses of French, German, and Italian right-wing theory and politics, while many others at the time such as Alasdair McIntyre and Charles Taylor had maintained leftist commitments to universalizing substantive equality, it is easy to see why the journal came under fire.

Following a special issue on Schmitt, *Telos* published a correspondence titled "Reading and Misreading Schmitt: An Exchange," between Jeffrey Herf, a historian of twentieth-century Germany with a focus on the Nazi period, and Piccone and Ulmen. In the correspondence, Herf stated that "[t]he issue devoted to Carl Schmitt is a sad event in the history of *Telos*," due to Schmitt's affiliations with Nazism (Herf, Piccone, and Ulmen 1987–8, p. 133).[28] Herf was not alone in this assessment. Why was *Telos* interested in publishing and analyzing such a controversial figure? As Piccone (1987) explained it, Schmitt and his friend/foe distinction and critique of liberalism, although limited, provided the journal with the political theory it was lacking. However, in *Telos*' defense, Piccone (1999) asserted that it did not embrace Schmitt without reservation. He noted that internally there was considerable opposition to the undertaking, mostly from the exiting Habermasians. Piccone's response to Herf was essentially that the journal chose to focus on Schmitt because *Telos* exists as a forum for such "repressed, ignored, or passed over" thinkers (1987–8, p. 140). The journal would continue to trot out this defense of anti-orthodoxy when it faced further criticism of its inclusion of other controversial groups and figures, such as the Lombardy League and Alain de Benoist.

I do not have the space available here to fully investigate *Telos*' engagement with Schmitt, federalism, populism, and other topics that have provoked controversy. Members, former and current, of the *Telos* circle have questioned the journal's use and analyses of these topics and themes. The journal remains a place where such unorthodox or radical ideas can be investigated. The criticism that cannot be ignored is whether *Telos* has not sufficiently critiqued these ideas, an echo of Glazer's argument about the lack of self-critique in relation to neoconservatism at *PI*. In other words, a journal devoted to criticism, described by one contributor as representation of "the pure *urge to criticize* somehow materialized in a journal format," gains a reputation as a forum that ruthlessly criticizes everything existing (D. Gross 1994, p. 110). If the journal then turns in new directions but does not continue that ruthless criticism, it could be thought to be deceiving its readers or at least depriving them of its re-viewing practice. As one contributor argues:

> *Telos* has in fact become a kind of policy journal. But it has done so only halfway. *Telos* is now routinely crammed with recommendations for the dismantling of all kinds of state programs that allegedly only help the interests of the New Class elite. At the same time, there is an almost complete absence of any systematic analysis of the real implications of such policy recommendations. The problem, in other words, is not that the journal has changed, but that it has not changed *enough* (Ost 1994, p. 138).

Interestingly, the journal's rightward shift was accompanied by (or a product of) its increasing attention to the US state and its domestic policies. Moreover, these investigations all amounted to a rather unconventional critique of welfare-style liberalism and its successor, neoliberalism. As Luke remarks: "The willingness

---

28 Although *Telos* was one of the first, if not the first, critical forums to engage with Schmitt in the US, other "leftist" thinkers would also explore his thought, including but not limited to, Gopal Balakrishnan, Slavoj Žižek, Chantal Mouffe, and Jacques Derrida (Wolfe 2004).

by *Telos* to grant the grim realities of neo-liberal hegemony, instead of longing for the romance of New Deal/Fair Deal/New Frontier/Great Society administration by the best and brightest beavering away within state bureaucracies, led many intellectuals to shun the journal for years" (2011, pp. 9–10).[29] He also noted that the journal did not always contest neoliberalism "programmatically," even while it pushed back against it. While it is easy to criticize these seemingly strange turns in a journal that began as a project to articulate an emancipatory politics by merging Continental phenomenology with Marxism and found its voice in the embrace of sub-fascist Schmittian ideology, the failure of progressive or left alternatives to neoliberalism to gain much traction may have made these strange turns more appealing.[30] One wonders though why intellectuals and journals seem discontented to stick with a vision, like the possibility of democratic socialism, through better and worse. And then one is reminded of the fear put forth by the *Westminster Review*. Its editors believed that wiser opinions must endure a slow process of transmission before they become the opinions of the many, and that a journal may not be the best means to achieve that goal. A journal may instead serve better as a place to engage with new ideas and new problems, something more like a laboratory where re-views are continually tested and new formulations are invented.

In a 1990 article in *Telos*, Simon Clarke argued that the New Left during the 1960s and 70s put forth a powerful critique of the state, equal to that generated by the Right. However, the New Left's critique had no coherent alternative to social democracy and state socialism like the Right's appeal to the market and "the lore of an idealized past" (1990, p. 71). The Left perceived the "crisis of social democracy" as a failure of realization rather than vision, a perspective that Clarke derides. But what if there are only a limited number of views? And what if the traditional views belonging to the Left and Right do continue to have meaning? Then the Left has no real alternative to social democracy or state socialism and maybe should not be so quick to abandon them. As Bobbio argued in *Telos*, there are no short cuts to "devoting one's work to the creation of a state apparatus which is both efficient and non-oppressive" (1978b, p. 43). Bobbio devoted his work to asking the question of whether a state can be both socialist and democratic. It is

---

29 Doug Kellner, a former contributor, lambasted the journal, writing: "*Telos* represents the collapse of a certain segment of the left intelligentsia that renounced its leftism and moved to totally reactionary positions, and in so doing drove away all the intelligent and creative progressives who once formed the best of *Telos*. All that is left are a few embittered and alienated pseudointellectuals who focus their 'critique' on their former comrades while Reagan and Bush have destroyed American democracy and now the Middle East" (quoting Kellner, Postel 1991, p. 19).

30 As Frankel comments: "The attraction of particularize right-wing populist movements in Europe, North America and Australia cannot be explained in isolation from the failure of Labor, Social Democratic, Euro-communist, Green and Center-Left parties to counter the effect of neoliberal policies during the past two decades" (1997, p. 92).

unfortunate that all too many on the Left have been quick to answer no. However, they may feel that sticking to a re-view that is increasingly marginalized risks a type of hermetic isolation.

For the members of *The Public Interest*, the journal became a place to voice the disappointment of their expectations for the welfare state. They were then able to channel this frustration into a new political view, neoconservatism, which would have a significant impact on late twentieth-century politics. *Telos* gave voice to disappointment with both politics and the theoretical analyses of such politics. Whether as a result of disappointment or due to their role as critics, both *The Public Interest*, a policy journal, and *Telos*, a theory journal, maintained some distance from politics—a greater distance for *Telos*, a lesser distance but still a distance for *The Public Interest*. Indeed, over time, *PI* shifted from a focus on policy questions to deeper concerns with political philosophy. Conversely, *Telos* also questioned the journal's purpose, abandoning its theoretical foundations in Western Marxism and becoming more interested in questions of policy.

I contend that, strangely, these divergent approaches to content produced the same form of re-view: the welfare state was exhausted or fatally flawed, the state intervened too much, and the meddling of intellectuals only made things worse. While the welfare state was being critiqued in letters, however, it was simultaneously being replaced in practice by policy neoliberalism, which withdrew state intervention in the economy at the same time as it depended upon it. Emerging neoliberal policies impacted not only how society and the state was ordered but also how they were viewed and re-viewed by these journals, calling into question whether society could be effectively and positively reordered by the state or its critics. Further, like the earliest members of the genre of political criticism, while the new formations of governance and the state influenced the trajectories of these journals and their views, the journals' practices of re-viewing also influenced new conceptions of the state and how it should govern.

Chapter 5
The Professionalization of Re-view? The New "Critical" Journals

This chapter discusses the "critical turn" within the world of disciplinary journals. It asks what happens to political criticism when it is confined to the university. I contend that the combining of challenges to disciplinary ways of knowing with a desire to make academic work more relevant to the "outside" world transformed the disciplines themselves. Disciplines such as geography, sociology, and political science became more open to a range of approaches to doing social scientific research, to a variety of "worthwhile" objects of study, opening up new fields, such as Black Studies, Cultural Studies, and Women's Studies. A diverse range of scholars with interests in researching hitherto ignored, tolerated, or even maligned topics emerged via publication in these journals as leaders in their fields. However, I find that criticism's purpose was at once extended and overshadowed. It not only aimed at how society should be governed, but also at the ability of a "public" (here academics) to determine how they should be governed within their disciplinary homes (Schostak and Schostak 2013). The chapter takes as its focus the critical moment of the split within the American Political Science Association of 1967. While seemingly less "critical" to wider society than the rise of the bourgeois public sphere, cementing of liberal-democracy, or war, my focus upon the split within the APSA is designed to draw attention to two issues. First is the continued institutionalization and further professionalization of the re-view function of the journal. Second is the bifurcation of the re-view function, already established in Chapters Three and Four, between radical opposition to the state's contingent ordering capacity and radical opposition to the state as a legitimate ordering institution per se.

Criticism and the "Postmodern" University

Telos's emergence in 1968 as a radical student philosophy journal seeking to "re-examine the nonsense that is passed as orthodoxy in [the] discipline" heralded the arrival of similar attempts in other disciplines (Staff 1969, pg. 132). Some of the new journals were also student-run, while others were composed mainly of younger faculty. That is those radicals who were also, or who had chosen to become, professional academics. These academics contested the insular nature of scholarship that, for them, too easily ignored the major oppositions to and entrenchment of traditional forms of power that were being put into action as the "outside" world was rocked by the new left and countercultural insurrections of the era. The new critical academics were also spurred on by beliefs that research was being deployed to further state goals, or to ends that appeared devious. Or, they resisted the tendency of the university as an institution to support the status quo. Indeed, it was scholarly discontent with the dominant approaches in academic disciplines from archaeology to zoology that mobilized many to launch new "critical" journals that opposed the "flagship" disciplinary journals. However, the new critical journals still existed within the academy. Criticism of the state, whether from the pages of a political science, sociology, geography, economics, or women's studies journal, was academic in its provenance. This raises the question of whether the new criticism was merely "academic," in other words, not of practical relevance but only of theoretical interest to other academics conducting similar research.

In the 1960s and 1970s, there was a migration, or "diaspora," of what could be called political criticism out from political science. This diaspora extended the reach of political criticism across the social sciences while at the same time, "political criticism" morphed, taking on new dimensions as political scientists' interests shifted from "politics" to "power" (Agger and Luke 2002). Together, these contestations critiqued the idea, which the historical forms of the disciplines reinforced, that politics only occurred in traditional political institutions or venues. Instead, almost all of the new critical journals, in the social sciences at least, sought out the workings of power in the home, the school, the workplace, and so on. This new attention to "power" as politics, or as "the political," expanded the scope of political criticism from criticism against the state to criticism against forms of domination wherever they might be found. At the same time, this "new" criticism perhaps introduced a greater distance between the critics and political practice, at least as conventionally understood. Some of these scholars were also activists and participated in social and political struggles outside the university. But many also confined their political critique to their scholarship. Academic work can influence politics and political practice, but the embrace of what would become known as postmodernism and post-structuralism within the disciplines also attenuated the relationship between the two.

The so-called postmodern turn shifted the site of political struggle away from state institutions but provided no specific alternative site upon which to engage with power. Following thinkers such as Foucault, power was widely regarded as ubiquitous and, importantly, not only repressive but also productive. In short, the Marxian political-economic critique of a "dominant ideology," propounded by the state in order to assist the capitalist classes in their efforts to exploit the working classes, gave way to a kind of intra-subjective critique of "the policeman inside all of our heads" (Foucault 1977 [1972]). While postmodernism valuably helped illuminate inequalities and hierarchies of knowledge, truth, and justice across social forms and also emphasized the ways in which knowledge constructs reality, the manner in which it dispersed "politics" was disorienting for political critique. Postmodern thinkers offered no systematic social or political theory focusing "instead on literary and philosophical topics in ways that require readers to infer their social and political intent" (Agger and Luke 2002, p. 181). Indeed, and somewhat ironically, the diffusion and in a certain sense dilution of political criticism was accompanied by a proliferation of the number of journals adopting the terms "critical" or "radical" in their titles. It is tempting to think that so much criticism would have left a degree of real political change in its wake.

Despite the "postmodern turn" and the desire of contributors to the new critical journals to disrupt domination and hierarchy wherever they may exist, many such projects found themselves over time all too subject to the very institutional pressures that they initially tried to resist, if not to entirely overcome. For example, in response to the desire to make political science more relevant and visible, the Caucus for a New Political Science was formed as an alternative to the American Political Science Association. However, even dissenting academic groups, like the Caucus, were to be reabsorbed within their disciplinary homes. With time, many of these groups succumbed to a degree of professionalization that perhaps inhibited their larger aspirations. As one of the doyens of the postmodern turn, Foucault argued at the time, the critical attitude does not reject governing altogether; it is not a call for anarchy. Rather, it demands an alternative to the current forms of governance (Foucault 2007). The question becomes how to maintain the critical attitude while also building alternative institutions.

Not everyone has the same ability to influence the state, to access "the" public, to shape the view of how society should be. Flagship disciplinary journals arguably have more "influence" or visibility, if only because many are distributed as "benefits" of membership within professional associations. Journals provide a forum for ideas to be produced and disseminated, and some reach "the" public more than others and some are content to cultivate their own publics. Those with funding or institutional backing may have greater success. Intellectuals who are critical of the state still need spaces or platforms from which to conduct that critique. Meanwhile, as many intra-disciplinary gains were made, an increasingly unequal world was emerging. In the era of "neoliberalism," academic work itself, along with full-time and relatively well-paid industrial work, was increasingly rendered precarious.

Spaces that welcome political criticism within academia also create their own strange contradictions. This is especially so at public universities that are in part, although decreasingly so, funded by the state. And, as the early new critics were well aware, academia is subject to unique "disciplinary" pressures and constraints. Even the most alternative space becomes a victim of processes of institutionalization. I contend that the new and now not so new critical journals provide sites, albeit often marginal ones, for critical disciplinary interventions that are largely missing from discussions in flagship journals. However, the need to craft institutions that operate within the same economy of the very journals and disciplinary discourses that they critique presents something of a paradox. "Critical" journals want to be visible in order to expand the reach of their interventions, and also to shore up the career prospects of the scholars who publish in their pages—a perhaps necessary evil in today's academic political economy, but to be visible, they must take on the professional trappings, such as regularized publication schedules, strong peer review, journal impact factors, and so on. These make up the disciplinary practices of the hegemonic institutions they often seek to remove or replace. To what degree then does this professionalization inhibit the very critique that animated their founding impulses? Can institutions remain critical even as they solidify, settle, and survive into old age? Additionally, how effective is "political" criticism when it has been transformed and dispersed across the disciplines, and when its main object of critique is no longer the state?

The Rejection of "State Intellectuals"

To reiterate, a motivating factor for those forming the new critical alternatives in the 1960s and 70s was the realization that intellectuals and scholarship were being co-opted, willingly or unwillingly, wittingly or unwittingly, by the state. In the 1910s Randolph Bourne and again in the 1960s Noam Chomsky had criticized intellectuals who chose to serve the state during times of war. In the 1960s, especially with the arrival of the Kennedy administration, a growing consensus held that more and more academics were joining the ranks of government and gaining access to state decision-makers. Critics on the right expressed anger over an impending liberal intellectual takeover of the state, while critics on the left chastised liberal intellectuals for propping up an increasingly unbearable status quo. That this opinion may not have accurately reflected reality[1] is less important than the fact that the consensus against the supposed wave of leftist intellectuals infiltrating the government and White House may have more clearly drawn the battle lines between intellectuals who identify with the state and those who are critical of it. The degree to which two intellectual camps can be distinguished—"conservers" and "critics" of the state, and extant power relations, statist or not—can, as I have suggested, be seen to become heightened at certain "critical moments."

This said, I do not regard the two camps as fixed; defenders of the state at one time may be opponents of the state at another, as the state itself transforms. And, the idea that two such camps exist may be more useful as a heuristic. Or, it may simply be accepted as a perspective on certain "consensus issues," such as in relation to growing academic power over the US state in the 1960s. Indeed, direct

---

1 Townsley's (2000) study of academic influence in government in the 1960s found that academics were recruited into government in large numbers as early as the years following World War II. While a number of high profile advisory positions were given to academics by the Kennedy and Johnson administrations, those positions quickly ended with the administrations. Social scientists, Townsley argues, were unsuccessful in any attempt "to institutionalize a place in the expert division of labor in the state" (pp. 754–5). Instead, what succeeded was the rise of an academic technocratic discourse, and those who engaged in it were able to secure positions of power and influence.

evidence of academic participation in some of the most problematic exercises of state power appeared in the late 1960s and into the 1970s. Revelations about the close ties between the security arm of the US government and academia were published in journals that rejected such links, such as *Ramparts* and *The New York Review of Books*. Reports that the CIA was actively funding a number of prominent journals, including *Encounter, New Leader, Partisan Review,* and *The Paris Review*, as well as a number of international journals, such as Germany's *Der Monat,* France's *Preuves*, and Japan's *Jiyu,* through the Congress of Cultural Freedom also emerged. Frances Stonor Saunders (2001) argued that the journals participated in a "propaganda war" on behalf of the CIA and that, but for CIA funding, these journals may not have stayed in print. CIA or defense funding of as varied projects as Harvard University's International Summer School, the AFL-CIO, Project Camelot, and the Himalayan Border Project was also disclosed around this time.

In April 1966, *Ramparts* published a whistleblower story about Michigan State University's Vietnam Project, which had been directly funded by the CIA. The project had been operating since the 1950s, and it involved the university in the training of Saigon police, stockpiling munitions, and writing the South Vietnamese constitution (Richardson 2009, 50). The story prompted the CIA to investigate *Ramparts* thus violating the National Security Act of 1947, which forbade the organization from spying on domestic soil. A year later, *Ramparts* broke the story of CIA sponsorship of the National Students Association. The Association funded university student groups to attend international meetings, with CIA funding aimed at countering similar Soviet-sponsored programs and recruiting foreign students (Richardson 2009).

In late 1970, *The New York Review of Books* article, "Anthropology on the Warpath in Thailand," detailed the involvement of a number of social scientists in Thai counter-insurgency activities. The article's authors, Joseph G. Jorgensen and Eric R. Wolf, were members of the Ethics Committee of the American Anthropological Association, which had been formed in 1967. The Association had condemned the Vietnam War in 1966, a step the American Political Science Association did not take, since it would have violated its bylaws.[2] The Student Mobilization Committee to End the War in Vietnam obtained and delivered to the Association a number of documents implicating various academics in war-related activities. One such project received more than $1,000,000 for a project in Thailand that argued, "One of the key problems in designing preventive counter-insurgency measures has been that we do not know which kinds of economic, social, and political action are the most effective in building national unity and in reducing vulnerability to insurgent appeal" (p. n/a). Commenting on the revelations held in the documents, Jorgensen and Wolf wrote:

---

2   It is perhaps too easy to point out the irony of an association devoted to the study of political science that forbids itself from rendering public opinions on political issues.

> The date themselves give a curious and chilling perspective on the uses of social science. Take, for instance, the first set of papers, which describe meetings of a Thailand Study Group made up of government officials, physical scientists, and members of what the minutes call the 'SS Community,' the community of social scientists. The meetings were organized at Falmouth, Massachusetts, in the summer of 1967, by the Institute for Defense Analysis, and designated a 'Jason Summer Study.' The IDA was organized in 1955 to coordinate war related work on the nation's campuses; its special Jason Division was set up to involve academics in the solution of military problems. The purpose of the Falmouth meetings was specifically to explore the usefulness of creating an 'SS' Jason, complementing the already existing Jason studies carried on by physical scientists (1970, p. n/a).

For Jorgensen and Wolf, the question of whether the government was soliciting the participation of academics, or whether academics were soliciting these opportunities from the government was central. They also noted that the work of anthropologists in the service of the state had a long history, with heavy involvement beginning at the close of World War II. To quote from them at length:

> During the cold war a new political alliance evolved, in which government officials, university personnel, and foundation executives became interchangeable. Area institutes and international studies programs proliferated. In many of our largest and most prestigious universities more traditional branches of learning were resynthesized with 'forward-looking' projects in economic development and political nation building. Nearly everywhere, anthropologists were drawn into the network of information gathering and processing; the demand was for their data, not for their values. The anthropologist was supposed to bring in the 'behavioral' information; others would use that information to formulate and execute public policy. Thus the curious *quid pro quo* which provides current working conditions for a great many anthropologists was established. The researcher would get the chance to carry on field work with a heady sense of engagement in a global welfare operation, punctuated by occasional participation in an international meeting, followed by a dry martini at the airport bar in Bangkok or Dar es Salaam. In exchange, others received the right to play with this data. Many signed their contracts, unwittingly or otherwise, in return for fellowships, research grants, and jobs. Others, more reticent, subcontracted (p. n/a).

Jorgensen and Wolf end their article by commenting on a "lone dissenter" who refused to make his research available, calling on his fellow academics "to help create radical political alternatives for the people among whom they work, people whose social integrity is already—and whose physical existence may soon be—at stake" (p. n/a).

This information and other similar reports[3] likely played a part in the critical and radical movements within academic disciplines that began in the 1960s and continued for the next few decades. These movements had a common desire to resist their disciplines' tendencies to serve those in power and maintain the status quo. They sought to reform these disciplinary aims. And some sought more radically to abolish their disciplines. In their attempts to return (or introduce) a spirit of criticism into their disciplinary homes, especially by setting up alternatives to the flagship journals, they also had to negotiate whether and how to institutionalize these alternatives. Meanwhile, the critical academics also had to work to avoid replicating the hierarchical structures and disciplinary norms that tamped down or eliminated critique among the mainstream. In a sense, they sought another way of governing (or of not being governed as such) that would provide the freedom and means to criticize the status quo, yet still preserve the academic positions and institutional resources necessary to make such work effective.

The "Critical" Reforms of the Disciplines

Beginning around the end of the Second World War, more and more intellectuals gravitated toward the safer environs of the university. This migration is well documented by Jacoby in *The Last Intellectuals: American Culture in the Age of Academe* (1987) and is probably not a new story. The aspect of this academification that interests me is the intellectual energy poured into radicalizing the disciplines themselves, energy that I suggest created an internal "critical turn" within the academy. Interestingly, this turn resembles or echoes the origins of the social sciences in the United States, which were largely spawned by reformist groups operating in the second half of the nineteenth century to abolish slavery, humanize industrial capitalism, or re-view a state that, for many, had simply run amok. These groups of amateur intellectuals were *actively* involved in social, economic, and political reform. They sought institutionalization through the university as a means of establishing authority and legitimacy for their aims. The social sciences then began as willful attempts to transform social and political environments. The "critical turn" beginning in the 1960s within the disciplines can be read as something of a return to the origins of the social sciences. However, by entering the university, alternative groups could not for long escape the disciplinary and professional constraints that university life places upon them. Such critical aims are then arguably always tempered by professionalization and institutionalization. It was indeed, "academic institutionalization and professionalization of the social sciences [that] were ... major factors in their deradicalization" (Gunnell, 1986, p. 153).

---

3 In 1974, *The New York Times* would reveal that the CIA was involved in a large domestic spying program known as Operation MHCHAOS.

The Sociology Liberation Movement founded the journal *Insurgent Sociologist* in 1969, now known as *Critical Sociology*. The Union for Radical Political Economics began the *Review of Radical Political Economics* in 1969, and the Union of Socialist Geographers founded *Antipode* also in 1969. In the United States, dissatisfied graduate philosophy students at SUNY-Buffalo founded *Telos* in 1968, while the Radical Philosophy group in the UK founded *Radical Philosophy* in 1972. The Mid-Atlantic Radical Historians' Organization began the MAHRO Newsletter in 1973, which grew to become the *Radical History Review*. The Caucus for a New Political Science (CNPS) formed in 1967. Members associated with the Caucus helped found *Politics & Society* in 1970 and in 1979 created the journal *New Political Science*, which remains the publication of CNPS. I very briefly discuss some of these alternative projects here to lend support to my argument for an "ideal type" of critical disciplinary turn. I then review the history of *New Political Science* at length to answer the question of whether institutionalization of criticism hampers its aims: to provide a critical re-view of the state and state-sponsored or supported injustice.

Initially appearing more like a newsletter, *Antipode*, in its editorial introduction to the first edition of this new radical journal of geography called for a more radical process of change that would be driven by a new breed of left-wing graduates. "The nascent New Left in geography can contribute to the cause in three fundamental ways": through 1) the design of a more equitable society, 2) the achievement of radical change, and 3) organizing for effective change within academic geography. The Union of Socialist Geographers who stood behind *Antipode* originally intended to push for organizational change within their discipline and political change without. By the early 1980s, the Union had become an official subsection of the Association of American Geographers, yet "the flow of articles to their journal, even the interest in it, flagged" (Jacoby 1987, p. 181). The journal now has joined the ranks of many of the other once marginal alternative disciplinary journals and since 1986 has been published by the commercial scholarly press, Blackwell (Jacoby 1987). However, unlike some other "critical" journals, it enjoys a relatively high impact factor, signaling its value within the academy.

Using a slightly different approach, the feminist journal *Signs* was founded in 1975 at the University of Chicago, and "consciously modeled [itself] on 'rigorous' academic journals" (Sanbonmatsu 2004, p. 85). Feminists occupied marginal positions within the academy, and the journal founders' decision to create an academic publication housed within an elite university's press likely gave the journal the imprimatur of serious thought. There are two ways that this serious quality can be made manifest (Chaves 2008). First, seriousness as a vehicle of thought allows the author to write more contemplatively, presumably better expressing her/himself. Second, seriousness as an indicator of authority prevails upon the audience to respect the author's words as representing truth. Then, to choose an academic journal as a vehicle of publication is to ease the burden of convincing the audience of your position. However, as one critic observes, the journal represented a "marked contrast with the impassioned discourse of

Frontiers and similar grassroots journals," perhaps a sacrifice of content for form (Sanbonmatsu 2004, p. 85).

The first issue of *Cultural Anthropology* appeared in February 1986, launched by the Society for Cultural Anthropology, newly formed within the American Anthropological Association. The impetus for the journal was a response to the perceived "sense of malaise since the decline in enthusiasm for a number of 1960s theoretical initiatives, including French structuralism, Marxism, and cognitive studies" (Marcus 1991, p. 122). It reflected a "general trend of fragmentation into specialized groups within the AAA during the 1970s and 1980s" (p. 122).

> But these "alternative" views recognize that they are firmly situated within the currents of the disciplinary mainstream. *Cultural Anthropology*, while making common cause with those in cultural studies and cultural criticism broadly conceived, nonetheless recognizes the importance of siting critique and exploration of other possibilities within the frame of given disciplinary traditions. Initiatives within disciplines are as important as those that apparently float free in self-styled interdisciplinary space (p. 124).

In fact, marginality in such an instance is illusory as these "carriers of the new are ultimately rooted in and connected dialectically to their originating disciplines" (p. 127).

As attempts at destabilizing the dominant traditions of their disciplines, these alternatives have had their productive moments. They represent a visible challenge to disciplinary norms, provide an outlet for divergent views, and seek to expand the interest in their disciplines. However, the inward turn that they represent marks a loss for political praxis, as few outside these disciplines read their journals, or could follow the arguments presented if they were to read them. These critical attempts at reform or renewal have multiplied the number of scholarly publications and may have even taken readers and writers away from the small, radical journals that once would have remained independent of the university.

Does Institutionalization Impair Critique?

What is interesting about these various critical movements of reform and revolution is how similar their trajectories are. One can create a sort of simplified model or ideal type.[4] A group of young professors and/or graduate students gets fed up with what counts as scholarship in their discipline. They believe that their discipline

---

4 There are of course many differences across these reform movements. For example, the Union for Socialist Geographers was almost entirely comprised of graduate students, while the Caucus for a New Political Science contained some more established academics (Jacoby 1987; Barrow 2008; Ong 1988; Burawoy 2005; Wisner, et al. 2012; Marcus 1991; Zald 2002).

should not just study the world but also change it for the better. Or alternatively, they argue that their discipline preserves the status quo and serves those in power when it should serve those with the least power. They decide to create a liberation movement or caucus or union to challenge the structures of authority within their discipline. Soon thereafter, they begin a journal that can serve as a forum and mouthpiece for the type of scholarship and world change they want to advance. The activists' energies are increasingly channeled into more intellectual endeavors. With time, the group's new organization becomes more solidified; its journal becomes more regularized. They succeed in bringing some change to their discipline. Perhaps they are more successful with this internal reform than with their activist aims. Once describing themselves as radical, socialist, or Marxist, most new groups now prefer the descriptor "critical." The journal is a key, if not *the* key, activity of the group. Their home discipline adopts a policy of accommodation rather than resistance. Their liberation movement becomes an organized section within the discipline's professional association. A major academic press now publishes the journal, a situation organized to help secure its editors' and contributors' professional positions. The journals increasingly succumb to "journal science" where academic scholarship is geared toward acquiring "professional points" (Agger 2000), maybe even asking contributors to cite earlier articles within the journal to increase "visibility." Importantly, today's graduate students and young professors have been born after the critical turn began.[5] And, they must be reminded that earlier generations were also disappointed by their professional disciplines.

This ideal type serves as an example or embodiment of Foucault's account of the critical attitude. For Foucault, criticism responded to the state's developing art of governing in the fifteenth and sixteenth centuries. Instead of accepting the state's way of governing, critics presented alternative visions of not being *quite so* governed or of not being governed *thusly* (2007, pp. 44–5). Similarly, in the latter half of the twentieth century, factions within academic disciplines also rejected their disciplines' mode of governing and created alternatives. While some of the movements may have begun or later acquired revolutionary aims, for most, the legacy of their work was disciplinary reform. The broad contours of academia still largely resemble what they were in the 1960s, even if room has been made for new fields of study and the "canons" have expanded to include once marginalized work. The various disciplines and fields can still be similarly mapped onto this structure. There continue to be more graduate students than there are academic jobs, demonstrating that intellectuals and scholars continue to seek an institutional home within the university. So, neither the university nor the disciplines have been thrown over for something else. These radical and critical turns began by mounting

---

5   I recognize that some disciplines and fields experienced "critical turns" much later than the 1960s. For example, Critical Management Studies arose in the 1990s. While every field and discipline now appears to have a critical journal, there still may be some that have not yet experienced a "critical turn."

an external critique, demanding not to be governed, but what has resulted is an internal critique directed at demands not to be governed *thusly*.

According to a title search within *Ulrich's Periodicals Directory*, there are now about 160 active journals that consider some facet of their work to be "critical." Of this number, about 140 began publication since 1968. There are also 13 journals with "radical" aims. All of these were launched after 1968. As a comparison, there are about 16,000 total journals listed within *Ulrich's* that meet the broader parameters of my search—active scholarly publications primarily within the Social Sciences and Humanities. Around 12,000 of those were founded since 1968.[6] Scanning the list of critical titles, there appears to be a critical journal for almost every discipline sub-field, including *Critical African Studies, Critical Anthropology, Critical Criminology, Critical Public Health, Critical Musicology, Critical Perspectives on Accounting*, and *Critical Studies on Terrorism*. What then explains this proliferation of critical journals and how are these critical journals different from the apparently "non-critical" journals in their fields? How is a critical perspective on accounting different from a non-critical perspective? Does every field with a critical journal imply that the rest of the field (a majority even) deploys a non-critical approach in its scholarship? Additionally, are the critical journals as widely read or as highly regarded as the non-critical titles? Or do they occupy the margin in their disciplines? Lastly, do these titles signal a democratization and/or diffusion of knowledge production and consumption within and outside the elite centers of their disciplines? Or are we experiencing a fragmentation of knowledge? (Rodgers 2012). In other words, maybe there is room for critical and alternative perspectives within each field but to be circulated within ever smaller and more distinct circles?

This proliferation of "critical" journals is reminiscent of the multiplication of texts with the word "critical" in their titles in the late seventeenth and early

---

6 I performed a title search within *Ulrich's* using the search term "critical." This returned results that included journals with the word "critical" in the title but also journals with the word "critical" in the description of the journal. I narrowed the periodicals search by only looking for "Journals" and "Magazines" that are classified as "Academic/Scholarly" and in English. This first search returned 385 results. I then narrowed it further by eliminating all publication formats except for "Print" and "Online." This returned 362 results. I then refined the search further by eliminating subject areas within mathematics, medicine and the hard sciences. The subject fields I retained included: "Social Science and Humanities"; "Arts and Literature"; "Government, Law, and Public Administration"; "Philosophy and Religion"; "Business and Economics"; "Education"; and, "Ethnic Studies, Gender, and Lifestyle." This returned 221 results. I then eliminated journals that were no longer actively publishing. Finally, I eliminated, by hand, any titles that appeared twice in "Print" and "Online" mediums to avoid redundancies. The final total was 142. The search is not without its flaws. *Ulrich's* may not contain listings for every journal publishing. More importantly, the descriptor "critical" may mean very different things across the 142 journals listed. I repeated this process with the search term "radical." There does not appear to be any overlap between the two lists.

eighteenth centuries. Koselleck (1988 [1959]) called "criticism" an eighteenth-century catchword. Spurred by the movement in natural philosophy toward pragmatic skepticism, traditional forms of authority, such as the authority of the ancients or the intellectual authority of the universities, were put into question. The spread of print encouraged this skepticism as new contestations of knowledge could circulate more broadly and easily. The embrace of pragmatic skepticism, or what could be deemed critical thinking, precipitated a "crisis of knowledge," or "a relatively short period of confusion or turbulence which leads to a transition from one intellectual structure to another" (Burke 2000, p. 203).

It is difficult to tell if the proliferation of academic journals which label themselves as "critical" will prompt a similar crisis of knowledge, whether they can sufficiently challenge or cast into doubt the mainstream way of doing academic work, or of what structures of authority mainstream academic work support or shores up. Many "critical" journals as detailed below have low visibility within and outside their fields. Further, the work they contain is probably best described as "skeptical," rather than coherently part of an identifiable political or social project. "Critical" and "radical" no longer necessarily mean "Marxist," or fit within any other grand narrative providing some direction for political and social transformation.

Table 5.1 gathers information on about 40 "critical" journals. It provides their Thomson Reuters impact factors and rank, as well as their start date and current publisher. I am not reproducing impact factors to validate this measure of a journal's worth.[7] Rather, it may be of interest to see which journals gained more visibility in their fields as measured by citation rates. Why for example do *Antipode* and *Politics & Society* have such high impact factors while the *Review of Radical Political Economics* has one that is very low? Is that because geography and political science are more receptive than economics to critical perspectives, or are *Antipode* and *Politics & Society* simply better journals because they have more resources or publish more cutting-edge scholarship, or are more often cited outside of their own journals? Or is there some other cause? While some of these "critical" journals do enjoy high impact factors, only one *Cultural Anthropology* comes close to rivaling the impact factor of a disciplinary flagship journal. For

---

7 As early as 1977, Jon Wiener pointed out the insidiousness of the seemingly innocuous *Social Sciences Citation Index*, stating that its purported purpose of identifying scholars "who have had a major impact on their fields," belies its true effects of disciplining the field, using the example of Marx to demonstrate that due to his lack of citations during a period, he must have had no impact on the social sciences. Further, Wiener highlights that certain journals had not been included in the *Index*, journals such as *Telos, Dissent, Monthly Review*, and *Radical America*. Wiener writes, "If a footnote to your work appears in *Commentary* or the *Public Interest*, you get counted; if it appears in *New Politics*, or *Social Policy*, or *Dissent*, you don't. Could it be that there is some logic behind these choices of the editor? Those who want their work to be indexed ought to ponder this question with particular care" (1977, p. 177).

my purposes, a disciplinary flagship journal ranks in the top three or five of its discipline. As a comparison, the *American Political Science Review*'s (*APSR*) impact factor is 3.05, meaning that on average each recent *APSR* article is cited 3.05 times, and it ranks number one in political science.

Table 5.1 Sample of "Critical" and "Radical" Journals and their "Impact"

Journal Title	Start Date	Current Publisher	Impact Factor	Rank*
Monthly Review	1949	Monthly Review Foundation	0.458	90/149 in Political Science
Dissent	1954	Foundation for the Study of Independent and Social Ideas	0.457	91/149 in Political Science 25/38 in Social Issues
New Left Review	1960	New Left Review Ltd.	1.538	20/149 in Political Science 13/89 in Social Sciences, Interdisciplinary
Critical Asian Studies	1968	Routledge	0.420	29/66 in Area Studies
Telos	1968	Telos Press Publishing	0.062	145/149 in Political Science 133/138 in Sociology
Antipode	1969	Wiley-Blackwell	2.150	10/73 in Geography
Critical Sociology[1]	1969	Sage	n/a	n/a
New Literary History	1969	Johns Hopkins University Press	n/a	n/a
Review of Radical Political Economics	1969	Sage	0.328	256/321 in Economics
Politics & Society	1970	Sage	2.188	9/138 in Sociology 4/38 in Social Issues 7/149 in Political Science
Radical Philosophy	1972	Radical Philosophy, Ltd.	0.488	33/47 in Ethics 19/38 in Women's Studies
Critique	1973	Routledge	n/a	n/a

Journal Title	Start Date	Current Publisher	Impact Factor	Rank*
New German Critique	1973	Duke University Press	n/a	n/a
Radical History Review	1973	Duke University Press	n/a	n/a
Critical Inquiry	1974	University of Chicago Press	0.948	4/35 in Cultural Studies
Critical Policy Studies	1974	Routledge	n/a	n/a
Critique of Anthropology	1974	Sage	0.475	51/81 in Anthropology
Signs	1975	University of Chicago Press	0.458	20/38 in Women's Studies
October	1976	MIT Press	n/a	n/a
New Political Science	1979	Routledge	n/a	n/a
Social Text	1979	Duke University Press	n/a	n/a
Critical Arts	1980	University of KwaZulu-Natal	0.316	17/35 in Cultural Studies
Thesis Eleven	1980	Sage	n/a	n/a
Critical Social Policy	1981	Sage	1.241	10/38 in Social Issues 19/89 in Social Sciences, Interdisciplinary
Critical Studies in Media Communication[2]	1984	Routledge	0.288	61/72 in Communication
Cultural Critique	1985	University of Minnesota Press	0.140	25/35 in Cultural Studies
Cultural Anthropology	1986	Wiley-Blackwell	2.950	3/81 in Anthropology
Critical Review: a journal of politics and society	1987	Routledge	0.625	49/89 in Social Sciences, Interdisciplinary
Critical Criminology[3]	1989	Springer-Netherlands	n/a	n/a
Constellations[4]	1994	Wiley-Blackwell	n/a	n/a
Organization	1994	Sage	1.671	52/168 in Management
Historical Materialism	1997	Brill Academic Publishers	0.661	66/149 in Political Science

Journal Title	Start Date	Current Publisher	Impact Factor	Rank*
Critical Social Work	2000	University of Windsor	n/a	n/a
Critical Psychology	2002	Palgrave	n/a	n/a
Journal for Critical Education Policy Studies	2003	Institute for Education Policy Studies	n/a	n/a
Critical Perspectives on International Business	2005	Emerald Group	n/a	n/a
Critical Literacy	2007	University of Nottingham	n/a	n/a
DataCrítica: International Journal of Critical Statistics	2007	University of Puerto Rico, Mayaguez	n/a	n/a
Critical Studies on Terrorism	2008	Routledge	n/a	n/a
International Journal of Critical Indigenous Studies	2008	Indigenous Studies Research Network QUT	n/a	n/a
The International Journal of Critical Pedagogy	2008	UNC-Greensboro	n/a	n/a
International Journal of Critical Accounting	2009	Inderscience Publishing	n/a	n/a
The Journal of Critical Globalisation Studies	2009	University of London	n/a	n/a

* Source of Impact Factor and Rank: 2011 Journal Citation Reports ® (Thomson Reuters, 2012)

Notes: [1] Formerly titled *Insurgent Sociologist*. [2] Formerly titled *Critical Studies in Mass Communication*. [3] Formerly titled *Journal of Human Justice*. [4] Published previously as *Praxis* (1965–81) and *Praxis International* (1981–94).

Instituting *New* (Critical) *Political Science*

While the number of critical journals seems ever increasing, the question remains as to whether the institutionalization of a critical project hampers its very aims. As Martin Parker and Robyn Thomas, the editors of the critical management studies journal, *Organization*, point out, a journal's "very institutionalization might produce structures which work to reproduce power and not to question it" (2011, p. 423). As a "self-instituting institution of criticism," does the journal's institutionalization begin to take priority over its criticism? I use the example of *New Political Science* to explore this question further.

In 1857, Francis Lieber became the first person to hold the title of professor of political science in the United States when he was appointed at Columbia University. However, it was not until 1880 that the Faculty of Political Science at Columbia was founded. Six years later, Columbia's faculty founded the *Political Science Quarterly*, which became the first scholarly journal of the new discipline. In 1903, the American Political Science Association (APSA) was formed, launching a cognate publication, the *APSR*. It was not until some 60 years later that APSA faced a significant organizational challenge.[8]

As with the other critical journals, an intra-disciplinary contest arose when many members of APSA joined the political turmoil of the 1960s. The critical upstarts challenged the established notions of what political science should study and how. Unrest centered on perceived failures on the part of political science to consider the many political changes that were underway at the time. More so, the apolitical "scientific" standard of which the discipline was so proud was an irony not lost on many younger academics. As Jacoby (1987) notes, during the tumult of the 1960s, the three main political science journals only published one article on Southeast Asia out of 924 pieces. Similarly, *APSR* published only one study on poverty and three on urban crises.

Charles E. Lindblom (1997), a former president of APSA, noted that political scientists, like all social scientists, in the 1940s and 1950s served the elites more often than the masses.

> [M]ost political scientists, in accepting grants and contracts or choosing research topics, left no evidence of having reflected on the issue: I do not recall that I have ever read a research prospectus that did so, although I am confident that some research proposals coming from the Left do so. Some political scientists who worked in or for government or on government grants simply assumed, I would guess, that democratic governments serve the people, as though the

---

8 APSA has faced several challenges from within (Barrow 2008). Challenges from other groups over the last half-century have also contributed to what APSA is today, arguably a more democratic and diverse or more fractured (depending on the viewpoint) discipline. Whether the discipline of political science is what it should be depends on whom you ask.

> mediating elites who set tasks or administered research funds could be counted on to pursue no interests of their own (p. 249).

The behavioral revolution of the 1950s further turned political scientists' attention away from *what* to study, placing greater emphasis on *how* to study it (Lindblom 1997, p. 231). Similarly, Luke writes that "[t]he reduction of politics to psychosocial behavioral events, rational choice acts, or ungrounded discursive textuality permits the discipline of other structures, markets, or rhetorics to circulate as productive power behind/below/beyond the liberal humanist anthropology unconsciously accepted as normal by most political scientists" (1999, p. 347).

Such inattention to what some thought should be the actual object of study for a discipline calling itself "political science" contributed to the formation of the Caucus for a New Political Science in 1967. Its animating impulses were opposition to the Vietnam War, a push for more internal democracy within APSA, the desire for a more diverse journal than *APSR*, and a call for a more pluralistic or diverse study of politics. However, the early aims of the Caucus were not reformist but revolutionary, at least according to a collection of the Caucus papers published in 1970. In the introduction to that book, the editors argue that

> because the only political science permitted in America today is that defined and determined within the existing paradigm, and because only those 'responsible' critics who are content to remain within the established pluralistic mold are tolerated, we conclude that the only option now available to critics and reformers is an end to political science. This will entail a negative act but also a positive commitment. It will require, at the same time, denouncing the current paradigm and moving toward the creation, along with other radical caucuses, of what Andre Gunder Frank has called a social science that is *political*. This means the continuation of criticism and the analysis of where power exists in America, how it functions, and the elaboration of concrete ways to change the existing power relations (Surkin and Wolfe 1970, p. 7).

Early Caucus members included Peter Bachrach, Christian Bay, Thedore Lowi, Michael Parenti, Alan Wolfe, Sheldon Wolin, and Hans Morgenthau (Dryzek 2006, p. 490). The Caucus sought to contest APSA's obsession with "scientific" and "objective" research, and the dominant "behaviorism" that informed it by "taking sides" on, or at a minimum, paying sustained attention to, controversial political issues such as the Vietnam War, race, poverty, the environment, and feminism. Caucus members who were political theorists also sought to bring critique of liberal democracy in from the margins. The APSA responded by freezing out Caucus sponsored panels at the next annual meeting. In 1971, the outgoing editor of the *APSR*, Austin Ranney, took pains to ensure that his successor would not be a "caucus type" (Dryzek 2006, p. 491). Heinz Eulau in his 1972 APSA Presidential report stated, "we are not set up or organized for political action, or the propagation of political points of view" (p. 491).

Members associated with the Caucus began a new journal, *Politics & Society*, in 1970 as an alternative to the flagship political science journal, *APSR*. As Clyde Barrow (2008, p. 238) argues, the new journal "soon emerged as a leading outlet for political analyses informed by Marxist theory." However, the journal underwent a transformation in its third year with a reconstitution of its editorial board and began to drift away from CNPS aims. By the late 1970s, Caucus members had created a broadsheet very similar to the geographers' *Antipode*, which subsequently evolved into the official journal *New Political Science* (*NPS*) in 1979. The new journal, however, also signaled an official shift from "organizational" to "intellectual activism" (Barrow 2008, p. 238). In a note to readers of the first issue, editors announced that it "aims to be a forum for discussion of theory, pedagogical practice, and organizational developments." These aims were originally realized by dividing the journal's contents into separate sections—Essays, Socialist Pedagogy, and Organizing News. The first issue featured articles by well-known critical researchers and theorists, including Kellner, Marcuse, and Habermas, several articles on academic freedom, and a brief advocacy piece titled "'No' to Kissinger at Columbia."[9] The "Organizing News" section of the issue took up about 25 pages and ranged from reports of the Caucus and the latest APSA convention to pieces on Youngstown and the steel industry, Taiwanese spies on campus, and an anti-nukes calendar.

Journal management was divided between an Editorial Collective and an Editorial Board, which as in most institutionalized journals played a mostly passive role, and Correspondents located in foreign countries. The work of the journal from the early 1980s to the early 1990s was attributed largely to the Caucus's New York chapter.[10] This East Coast collective would be later joined in Issue 8 by a West Coast collective, based initially in Berkeley. The collectives merged and shrunk with Issue 12, signaling a shift to a more traditional editorial structure. The journal's masthead developed into a tripartite structure made up of Editors, an Editorial Board, and an Executive Committee. Double Issue 41/42 explained the different functions of each group.[11]

For much of its life, *NPS* has dedicated issues to particular themes, announcing them on its front cover (Table 5.2). When Nancy Love and Mark Mattern assumed the editorship of the journal in 2009, a more regularized once-a-year appearance of special issues began with each special issue appearing as the last issue of the year.

---

9 The first issue of the journal focused on the university including discussions and analysis of academic freedom, the fate of radicals in the university, and radical organizing efforts on campuses.

10 It included graduate students Florindo Volpacchio and Nicole Fermon, and CNPS Chair Carl Lankowski, who was then teaching at CUNY.

11 An early issue of the journal complained that the Editorial Board adopted too passive a role and could have supported the journal's efforts better. The Executive Committee was added to put more faculty members on the journal, as too much of the weight of the work was carried by graduate students, and the CNPS was not happy with the irregularity of the journal's publication schedule.

Table 5.2 *NPS* Themed Issues

Issue No.	Date	Theme
2/3	1979	The Socialist Academic Between Theory and Practice
4	1980	Sexuality and Capitalism
5/6	1981	Tactics and Ethics: What's Left?
7	1981	Rosie the Riveter: An Update
9/10	1982	Critical Theory and Bureaucracy
11	1983	Ecology and Politics
12	1983	Socialism in France
13	1984	Marxism and Theory
14	1985	Social Movements
15	1986	Between Literature and Politics
16/17	1989	Racism in Europe
18/19	1990	The Central American Maelstrom
24/25	1993	Germany's Identity Crisis
28/29	1994	What's Wrong with American Politics? And What to Do About It?
30/31	1994	Bodies and Nations
32	1995	Ecology
33/34	1995	After Thatcher: Special Issue on Contemporary British Politics
35	1996	Critical Approaches in International Politics
38/39	1997	The Promise of Multiculturalism: Education and Autonomy in the 21st Century
41/42	1997	The Politics of Cyberspace
20.4	1998	Latino Politics in the United States
21.2	1999	Liberation, Imagination and the Black Panther Party
21.4	1999	1989/1999: Ten Years After the Fall of Communism
22.1	2000	Violence and Politics
24.1	2002	U.S. Militarism in an Era of Globalization and Blowback
25.2	2003	Gwangju Uprising
26.3	2004	U.S. Foreign Policy
27.3	2005	Social Policymaking and Inequality in the Era of Globalization
30.4	2008	Alternative Globalizations: Challenges to Neoliberalism, Empire and Militarism
31.4	2009	The Changing Face of Political Ideologies in the Global Age
32.4	2010	Art after Empire: Creating the Political Economy of a New Democracy
33.4	2011	The Great Recession: Causes, Consequences, and Responses
34.4	2012	Right-Wing Populism and the Media
35.3	2013	Studying Politics Today: Critical Approaches to Political Science

Early editions of the journal not only reported on CNPS efforts within APSA but also on activism outside the disciplinary confines of political science. Additionally, advertisements for other radical journals, conferences on left alternatives, and even pedagogical tools like a poster for sale depicting "Social Stratification in the U.S." put the journal squarely within the network of North American Leftist intellectuals and activists.

Beyond trying to connect *NPS* intellectual efforts with activism, the Organizing News section also on occasion connected radical political scientists with radicals in other disciplines and fields. Double-issue 2/3 contained information on alternative efforts within sociology (East Coast Conference of Socialist Sociologists), public health (Socialist Caucus of the American Public Health Association), history (Radical Historian's Organization) and economics (Union for Radical Political Economics). The section also gave primers on important political issues of the day. For example, Issue 11 featured a report on "The Political Economy of U.S. Intervention in El Salvador." The Organizing News section became defunct after Issue 12 (1983), reappearing only one more time in double-issue 30/31, perhaps to mark the journal's 15th year of publication. Essays and reviews would come to dominate the journal as the sections on pedagogy and organizing/activism faded away and then disappeared altogether.

When the journal began, the Caucus was at something of a crossroads, deciding between a continued push for organizational leadership within APSA and a more independent and activist role beyond the formal disciplinary borders of the field. Since recent APSA elections had produced the lowest returns for CNPS candidates, the membership chose to put their efforts toward developing the CNPS as a counter-institution to the APSA. Victor Wallis' report, "The Caucus at a Turning Point," noted from the outset the trepidation accompanying this decision, which largely revolved around the expansion and increased financing of the journal project, and referred to the decision as a "leap of faith" (1979, p. 92). For Wallis, the journal would act as an alternative outlet to APSA and its organs. "The journal itself, in any case, will be our most tangible immediate challenge to APSA's hegemony; eventually, it will both facilitate and reflect the struggles at every level of the political science profession" (p. 92).

Throughout the 1970s, the journal's avowedly socialist intentions increasingly caused divisions within the Caucus itself. Carl Lankowski's CNPS Chairperson report to the membership in 1981 reflected on the debate within the Caucus over its role as the left wing of the APSA versus its more activist potential. Lankowski reported that the decision to publish *NPS* indicated movement in the latter direction, as the journal represented the Caucus's theoretical and organizational development. He also confirmed that all the finances and most of the energies of the reformers were put toward the journal. The reform movement within CNPS, which sought to undertake a more activist role for the Caucus, however "exposed the lack of resources, human and otherwise, necessary to develop the support and coordination for the success of these experiments" (1981, p. 98). Lankowski summarized that "clearly the strength of the journal depends on the strength of the Caucus" (p. 103). Just two issues later, John Rensenbrink posed a more optimistic view of the reform effort:

Three and a half years have passed since the "takeover" of the Caucus in September 1978 by a group composed mainly of graduate students and youthful professors in New York City. Their success is plain to see: a creditable journal, one that is steadily growing and improving in quality and sense of direction; and *two* Editorial Collectives, one on each end of the Continent (1982, p. 93).

The journal was the crown and, to an extent, the only jewel of the reform effort. As Rensenbrink noted, "The emphasis put on the Journal since 1978 has, relatively speaking, hurt the Caucus" (1982, p. 96).[12] Despite devoting most Caucus time and effort toward *NPS*, the journal struggled to publish on a regular schedule.[13]

After this publishing gap, the journal more and more resembled a traditional scholarly outlet. The introductions to each issue no longer appeared regularly. Issue 18/19 began the practice of offering a very brief "Preface," replacing the lengthier introductions that used to offer more in-depth overviews of each issue. After Taylor & Francis, through its Carfax and then Routledge groups, began to publish the journal, this opening from the editors became a "Snapshot." Longer introductions were reserved for special issues, which also became less frequent over time. With Issue 15, the journal's official subtitle changed from "quarterly journal of the Caucus for a New Political Science" to "A Journal of Politics and Culture."[14] *NPS* entered into a publishing contract with Carfax Publishing, Ltd, to begin with the March 1998 (Volume 20, No. 1) issue of the journal. Carfax was then acquired by Taylor & Francis. Taylor & Francis also acquired Routledge, and the journal became a Routledge Group publication in 2005 with Volume 27, Issue 1. The journal now operates within the political economy of academic journal publishing. An institutional subscription to *NPS* is listed at $509 for the print and online editions, while an individual subscription costs $120.[15] Individual subscriptions are also included with APSA membership in the NPS organized section.[16] *NPS* continues to be published and owned by the Caucus, not the APSA

---

12 The relationship between the journal and the Caucus continued to be a question for the organization as late as 2000, as revealed by meeting minutes. Perhaps the relationship is still not clear.

13 Despite calling itself a quarterly journal, *NPS* did well to publish biannually in its early years. In some years only one issue appeared, and no issues appeared in 1987 and 1988, when Fermon and Volpacchio were busily at work on their dissertations.

14 The 2011 Editor's Report for *NPS* reported that there were discussions to possibly change the name of CNPS and the journal, along with potential cover and design changes for *NPS* (Love and Mattern 2011).

15 These prices remain reasonable compared to other academic journals. For example, in 2013, an institutional subscription to *Antipode* is $1251, and an individual subscription is $93. *Politics & Society's* institutional subscription price is $924, and its individual price (print only) is $134. However, individual subscription rates remain out of reach for many non-academic readers who the journal may hope to reach.

16 This became the practice around 2006 after encouragement from the publisher. Prior, individual subscriptions were low and only about 10 percent of Caucus members

organized section NPS. This said, CNPS remains more of a counter-institution to the APSA, rather than an organ within it.

It is difficult to assess the impact of *NPS*. On the one hand, the journal has published the work of many different scholars and intellectuals, some better known than others. Names of note include Wendell Berry, Jacques Derrida, Maurice Blanchot, Etienne Balibar, and Jean Baudrillard. Further, and perhaps more importantly, it has remained a forum for the voices within CNPS. Additionally, many of the thematic issues have become books, and some, such as *The Politics of Cyberspace* reader have sold well (Ehrenberg 1999, p. 419). Moreover, the journal has had a long life span and continues to appear viable.

On the other hand, in a review of the history of CNPS, John Dryzek (2006) commented that the rest of the discipline largely ignores *NPS*.[17] Likely contributing to this state of affairs is the fact that the journal is not included in the *Social Sciences Citation Index* and *Journal Citations Report*. According to a 2009 *NPS* Editors' Report, the journal was denied inclusion in *SSCI*, because it is cited too infrequently. As the editors noted in the report, this is a circular argument, as inclusion might boost the frequency of citations. After the denial, the editors circulated a memo to the NPS membership encouraging them to cite the journal (Love and Mattern 2011). Comparatively, the former CNPS affiliated journal *Politics & Society* continues to be published, now by Sage. In 2011, it had an impact factor of 2.118 and ranked 7th out of 149 journals of political science. *NPS* is not among those 149 disciplinary journals. Additionally, the journal receives a small number of submissions as compared to a journal like *APSR* (Table 5.3).

Table 5.3 Comparison of Submission Numbers[18]

Journal	2006–07	2007–08	2008–09	2009–10	2010–11	2011–12
American Political Science Review	543	778	693	677	685	761
New Political Science	35	50	68	51	73	78

subscribed. Total subscriptions hovered around 200 throughout the 2000s and then reportedly doubled in 2010. Current subscription figures are unavailable.

17 Dryzek bases his criticism on the fact that the journal did not appear in a 2003 ranking of 115 journals in political science compiled by Garand and Giles (2003).

18 These figures are taken from the "Report of the Editors of the *American Political Science Review*," which are published each April in *PS: Political Science and Politics* and from the "*New Political Science* Editors' Report" presented to the NPS section membership each August at APSA's annual meeting. In 2001, the *NPS* editors' report acknowledged that more submissions seemed to be coming from non-members of the Caucus, a trend that continues.

Obviously, *NPS* does not have a big impact on the discipline of political science, but I am not sure if that was ever its intention. What may be more relevant to a discussion of *NPS*'s merit or value is whether it contributes to political change, whether it encourages critically-inclined scholars to adopt a more critical perspective, whether it invigorates its founding body CNPS, and whether it renews itself by continuing to question its own purposes. Those are more difficult measures to quantify and assess. I suppose we could begin by asking what would be lost without *NPS*. Would a forum for a certain type of scholarship be lost? Would a network of scholars and intellectuals dissolve? Would certain questions not be asked?

To return to the question asked at the beginning of this chapter: does institutionalization impair critique? The answer is that there are tradeoffs. Further, any journal whose publication record stretches into decades may find it more difficult to remain as critical and wary of the status quo as it could be. *NPS* has now been publishing for over 30 years. That is an accomplishment. However, it could be that a new critical revolution, whatever that may mean or be, and if still possible, needs to happen elsewhere. Maybe the critical attitude and long-lasting institutions are not symbiotic. Of course it remains a truism to say that the power of critique lies in its relationship to the presence of a revolutionary ambiance in wider society.

Still, journals, which sometimes outlive their founding impulses, are often the chosen forum for the practice of criticism. When Marx called for a "ruthless criticism of everything existing," he was making plans with Arnold Ruge for a new journal, the *Deutsch-Französische Jahrbücher*, which they began in Paris in 1843 (Marx 1978). Marx told Ruge in this letter that the trend of the new journal would be critical philosophy, which he defined as "self-clarification ... to be gained by the present time of its struggles and desires" (1978, p. 13). He argued that reform of consciousness could only occur by man recognizing his sins and declaring them for what they were, by realizing the distance between the ideal and idealized reality. Within that gap lay something closer to the truth than the dogma that Marx accused philosophers, like the Young Hegelians, of holding. So, criticism itself needed reform, and the pages of Marx's and Ruge's new journal would encourage the criticism of such one-sided critique. Perhaps the very brief life span of that journal—it stopped publishing in 1843 after putting out one double issue—is one answer to the question of whether critique can outlast institutionalization.

If the founding drives of most "critical" journal projects can be traced back in whatever now attenuated form to Marx's famous dictum to ruthlessly criticize, then what should the *institutionalized* form of a "ruthless criticism of everything existing" look like today? Social theorist Jacques Derrida provides a somewhat confounding answer to this question:

> To continue to take inspiration from a certain spirit of Marxism would be to keep faith with what has always made of Marxism in principle and first of all a *radical* critique, namely a procedure ready to undertake its self-critique. This critique

wants itself to be in principle and explicitly open to its own transformation, re-evaluation, self-reinterpretation (2006, pp. 110–11).

If they are serious about the "everything existing" part, then journals maybe need to resist the regularized routines of their material form—the very things that mark them as "professional." Otherwise, it may be difficult to open themselves to needed "transformation, re-evaluation, self-reinterpretation." Whether that can occur within the confines of the academy is another question. Further, shedding the trappings of professional scholarship may be liberating but could also open critique to some dubious bedfellows, as the Sokal hoax at *Social Text* discussed in the next chapter suggests.

Coda

In 2013, the US Congress limited National Science Foundation (NSF) funding for political science research to projects that promote national security or American economic interests. In other words, the state would only fund research that advanced the state. A Republican senator from Oklahoma who ideally sought to cut off all federal funding for political science research because, in his view, it produced no concrete benefits for society sponsored the changes to the NSF funding.[19] Total federal funding of social science research is relatively small; the government provides about $10,000,000 per year for political science projects, and most of this funding goes toward quantitative "behaviorist" research.[20] The NSF's total budget is around $7,000,000,000, with only about $250,000,000 directed toward social and behavioral science research. At the annual meeting of APSA held later that year, the majority response to the new restrictions and the push to eliminate funding altogether was an acknowledgement that as a discipline, political science was not successful in persuading the public of its value (McMurtie 2013). The Association subsequently formed a task force to improve its public image. If political science now needs to make its case to the public for its continued importance and relevance to public life, then this could act as a further constraint on more radical forms of political criticism.

Political science as a discipline is torn between the often conflicting desires to be a "science" and to serve American democracy (Smith 1997). Because political science is the social science concerned with power, it is the discipline not only best suited to studying it but also the discipline most likely to be shaped by structures of power that favor the status quo.

---

19 Another bill circulating in 2013, named the High Quality Research Act, would further limit federal funding to projects that "advance the national health, prosperity, or welfare" (McMurtie 2013).

20 This underscores the tension between National *Science* Foundation funding and what is essentially political *studies*, rather than political *science*.

> Hence political scientists should be concerned, more so than other scholars, to define an intellectual agenda that does not simply maintain and extend the political understandings favored by the powerful. Such an agenda should accept responsibility for subjecting those understandings to critical questioning, from every intellectually plausible point of view. It should be particularly concerned with discerning how far those understandings arise from and reinforce dominant power structures (Smith 1997, p. 276).

However, as I have argued in this chapter, criticism of power has dispersed throughout the disciplines. Political science is no longer *the* discipline concerned with the workings of power, even if in its "mainstream" variants power is taken as given. In its more diffuse form, political criticism, now aimed at multiple objects, rather than just the state, may find it more difficult rather than easier to resist the co-option of scholarship, or worse, its elimination, by the state. The risk being that critique of "power" gives up its ability to see power at all. Perhaps, refocusing on state power could allow the discipline to regain some of its disciplinary authority. At the same time, "critique" would also be inserted, or reinserted, into the discipline, rather than existing in sometimes far-flung outposts.

Chapter 6
The Present Disconnect Between View and Re-view

In this chapter, I focus upon three journals begun in the late 1970s and early 1980s that sought in different ways to achieve a particular set of aims. I define these aims in engagement with political theorist Sheldon Wolin's seminal work on what he saw as the potential of "theory" to contribute to changing the world. The three journals are Wolin's own short-lived *democracy*, the Australian journal *Thesis Eleven*, and the American *Social Text*. Examining the experiences of these journals allows me to describe the trends transforming political criticism from what was practiced by the "great reviews," to new forms of criticism distinguished by anti-liberalism or anti-statism. The critical moment of the postmodern turn, taking place almost wholly within the academy and furthermore within the humanities and social sciences in the English speaking world from the 1980s and into the late 1990s, took place as professional academics became concerned to voice their perceptions that those holding power within the state were increasingly beholden to the demands of capitalism, rather than those of democracy. Ironically, and following work by commentators such as Eagleton (1996), Perry Anderson (1998), Peter Dews (1987), and others, I find that the postmodern turn hosts a certain deradicalization and aestheticization of critique. My accounts of these journals are not comprehensive, and I do not mean to reduce these journals to the trends that Eagleton, Anderson, and Dews capably delineate. They are more than that, and their stories are more complex than what I can engage with here. However, as I have done so far, I take their stories to serve as "ideal types" in support of my argument that the review's founding impulse to re-view the state, by the late twentieth century, no longer served as the founding impulse for new journals, even though publications such as *democracy*, *Thesis Eleven* and *Social Text* ostensibly practiced political criticism. These journals kept the form of the review while they transformed its practice.

"Theory" as a Form of Political Criticism

Issue 25 of the *London and Westminster Review*,[1] which appeared in 1836, contained a short essay, titled "Theory and Practice." The dialogue in Socratic

---

1 In 1836, John Stuart Mill merged the *Westminster* with the recently created *London Review* (1834). The *London and Westminster Review*, itself undergoing several

form was aimed at Members of Parliament who used "practice" as a way to denigrate "theory." "Theory" was built on flights of fancy, while "practice," or being "practical," was the only legitimate way to inform governance. They traded in "practice" to resist any calls for change that would deprive them of the interests they had accrued through the (practice of some) abuse "theory" sought to reform. "Whenever a great man gets up and with a commanding voice and manner says, 'Away with such and such a scheme of improvement! We will have no theories! Give us practice!' The *hear hims* are more fervent than on almost any other occasion" (P.Q. 1836, p. 132).

As the author of the dialogue, "P.Q.," explained, "philosophy" was once the target of conservative resistance to change. "Philosophy" revealed the abuses of influence and power carried out by the clergy of the Church of England. Once the public began to be "prying" and take notice of these abuses or of philosophy's ability to reveal them, then "the cry against philosophy was raised" (p. 132). But it was difficult for the opponents of philosophy to maintain their opposition as the general value of philosophy's criticism became widely held. So they shifted tactics to oppose practice to theorizing.

> The cry of practice against theory began to be used when the force of the cry against philosophy began to grow feeble, and it grew rife as the cry against philosophy died away ... There is never anything which needs amendment in the state, but there are numbers of men who see it is their interest to fight against the amendment; because they make their profit out of the abuse. All this disposition to pry into abuses was imputed to philosophy. If philosophy, that is, the disposition to inquire, could be successfully cried down, men would be quiet; and those good things which good men has so long enjoyed at the expense of others, would rest in peace (1836, p. 132).

While the majority of the dialogue was concerned with showing the necessary imbrications of theory within practice, its overall purpose appeared to be to legitimate or validate the role played by a journal such as the *London and Westminster Review*.

As its author "P.Q." argued, "theory consists in drawing up a theorem for the guidance of the future from the observation of the past" (p. 128). Similarly, all rational practice is founded on observation of the past, and when these observations are generalized and articulated in language, they become theorems. So, there is no practice without theory. The more general and comprehensive the theory, the more valuable. Philosophy's remit then was to render theories as comprehensive as possible. "Theories are of importance, therefore, in proportion as the sequences of which they are the expression have much or little influence on human life" (p. 130). However, the degree to which theory is decried, or contested as invaluable, is more in proportion to the extent it seeks to undermine the status quo. In other

---

transformations, continued publication until 1914 (Nesbitt 1966, p. 163–4).

words, for the *Westminster* author, theory as a form of political criticism, or review, is not value free; the importance of its influence is measured in how well it combats the state's orders of governing that shelter abuses of power. As Wolin would, 130 years later, argue,

> Because history suggests that all political societies have both endured and employed violence, cruelty, injustice, and known the defeat of human aspirations, it is not surprising that the theorist's concern for *res publicae* and the commonweal has issued in theories which, for the most part, have been critical and, in the literal sense, radical (1969, p. 1079).

Political theory as described by the *London and Westminster Review* and by Wolin is, when at its best, a form of radical political criticism. However, Wolin's argument for transformative political criticism was also a defensive posture. As I describe it in Chapter Five, the practice of political criticism was by the 1960s becoming increasingly absorbed into academic political theory as a consequence of more and more intellectuals finding a home within the university. While academic political theory became institutionalized, it also became more insular. "Theory" was detached from politics and became a thing unto itself, dispersed across disciplinary fields and with an ever-multiplying number of objects upon which to aim its critique. Simultaneously, as I put it in Chapter Four, with the onset of neoliberalism, the state too was becoming increasingly diffuse and no longer an easily graspable object of criticism as the distributive welfare state was displaced by neoliberalism. Moreover, anti-statism on both the left and right displaced concern away from the state to other institutions, all perceived "politically" to be sources of authority and domination. In a sense, the state was regarded as a lost cause, and no longer worth critics' time and attention. The critical practice of re-viewing the state became something of an historical relic, even while new journals molded themselves to the shape of the earlier "great reviews."

The Failures of Political Criticism

When Wolin wrote his 1969 article, "Political Theory as a Vocation" in the *American Political Science Review*, he sought to return theory to this role. The dispersion of theory and its increasing separation from political science within the academy alongside its growing distance from everyday life contributed to a perception that political theory no longer held much relevance for politics or provided much useful guidance for ordering society. In a 1995 issue of the journal, *Political Theory*, Jeffrey C. Isaac provocatively asked how political theorists had failed to take notice of the world changing events of 1989. He examined over the period 1989 to 1993 the leading journals of the field, including *Polity*, *American Political Science Review*, *Philosophy and Public Affairs*, and *Political Theory*, and found less than a handful of articles on the fall of Communism in Central Europe and the Soviet Union.² Isaac referred to *The Nation*, *Dissent*, and *Social Research*, where pieces on the end of the Cold War were regularly published. One could easily add *Telos* to that list. Some essays, Isaac recognized, were even written by political theorists.³ Yet he saw a divide being maintained between academic scholarship and the more journalistic field of opinion magazines, especially regarding what counts toward tenure. Moreover, the criticism offered by academic political theory no longer offered a re-view of the state if the critical state transformations of 1989 were being largely ignored.

Wolin's article called for the return of the "epic theorist" who would promulgate "epic theories" as a response to what he would later describe as the "undertheorization" of political studies. He pointed to a number of "unpolitical theories," such as systems theories, communication theories, and structural-functional theories, and argued that they failed to offer any "significant choice or critical analysis of the quality, direction, or fate of public life" (Wolin 1969, p. 1063). At best, these theories offered mild reforms of a generally accepted political system unlike the re-view made possible by political theories "which would seriously question and reflect upon the qualities of the system as a whole" (p. 1069). The "unpolitical" theorist was more concerned with problems within theory rather than problems outside theory. "Epic theorists" are those that are "preoccupied with a particular magnitude of problems created by actual events or states of affairs in the world rather than with problems related to deficiencies in theoretical knowledge" (p. 1079).

Wolin argued that important political theories had been responses to political crises, where critical decisions about the re-ordering of political and social life are necessitated by the "derangement" caused by "errors in arrangements, in decisions, and in beliefs" (p. 1080). Political criticism and crisis were bound up with one another, and political criticism of the meaningful sort was aimed at re-viewing theoretical rather than technical problems, at resolving errors in arrangements, decision, and beliefs at the level of the system. Drawing upon Plato's criticism of Athenian democracy, Wolin depicted a form of critique concerned with the "*systematically* mistaken," rather than particular bad policies or actions but instead how those policies and actions are the products of a problematic ordering of society (p. 1080). For Wolin, the impulse to get at the "systematically mistaken"

---

2   The "premier journal of American political theory," *Political Theory*, published only one article out of 108 between 1989 and 1993 that dealt with the subject (Isaac 1995, p. 637). The *APSR* published only 30 theory articles during that period and none on 1989.

3   William Connolly responded to Isaac's piece and challenged his nod to "public intellectual journals," arguing that while they might include political theory by pragmatists such as Isaac, they often excluded theorists such as Derrida, Foucault, Judith Butler, Luce Irigaray, among others. Connolly wondered if "[p]erhaps the conception of politics governing these journals is too flat to appreciate *the extrastatist movements* in which this disparate gang is involved" (p. 654, emphasis added).

"determines why a political theory takes the form of a symbolic picture of an ordered whole" (p. 1080).

Wolin's 1969 article was responding to changes in the discipline in the US that began in the 1920s with the introduction of positivism and culminated in the "behavioral revolution" of the 1950s. He later explained that the article was in response to "a widely acknowledged crisis in American politics centered in the Vietnam War" (2000, p. 13). He accused political science of being complicit with this "derangement" as it failed to reveal what was "systematically mistaken" in American politics at that time, instead "being so focused on methodological applications as to be unaware that it was merely producing a simulacrum of the existing political order" (p. 14).

In the same year that Wolin's article appeared, a study tracing the influence of intellectuals and their publications was underway. Charles Kadushin's *The American Intellectual Elite* sought to identify the leading intellectuals in the United States and the journals they read and published within.[4] In 1969, the professors, writers, and editors surveyed named the following journals as the "leading American intellectual journals" of general interest: *The New York Review of Books, The New York Times Book Review, The New Yorker, New Republic, Commentary, Harper's, Partisan Review, Saturday Review, The Nation, The Atlantic, Daedalus, Ramparts, Yale Review, Dissent, The American Scholar, The Hudson Review, The Village Voice, The Progressive, Foreign Affairs*, and *The Public Interest* (2005 [1974], p. 18).[5] From this list, Kadushin located the top intellectuals who published within them and then asked those intellectuals which publications they read most often. The one read by the highest number of "elite intellectuals" was *The New York Times Magazine*, which was not a "leading American intellectual journal," but over 80 percent of the elite intellectuals reported reading it regularly. The publication with the lowest response was the left magazine *Progressive*, which only 10 percent of elite intellectuals read. Kadushin's study found that the journals with the highest proportion of political content, the *Progressive, Dissent*, and *The Reporter*,[6] were not among the most influential publications, the implication being that top intellectuals were not as interested in politics.

---

4 A preview chapter of Kadushin's book, "Who are the Elite Intellectuals?" perhaps unsurprisingly appeared as an article in *The Public Interest* in 1972. The list included Daniel Bell, the leading intellectual, Irving Kristol, and Daniel Patrick Moynihan, in the top 20, with Nathan Glazer and James Q. Wilson also making it into the 90 named. The book was first published in 1974.

5 Kadushin then used this list of journals to locate the 90 leading intellectuals who published within them. The methodology of his study was somewhat circular.

6 *The Progressive* is a left-leaning magazine that began publication in 1909 as *La Follette's Weekly* before changing names in 1929 and continues to publish. *Dissent* began as a democratic socialist journal in 1954 and also continues to publish. *The Reporter* was a liberal magazine that began in 1949 and interestingly ceased publication in 1968, the year before Kadushin's study was published.

Kadushin argued that the "chief method chosen by contemporary intellectuals for the dissemination of their ideas is the intellectual journal" (2005 [1974], p. 342). However, he also noted that the "world of intellectuals' journals is rapidly changing," with the increasing disappearance of intellectual circles and networks that supported them. He was not sure if the unraveling of denser networks was the result of mass society, the absorption of intellectuals into the "geographically dispersed university structure," or a transition phase. While the cause remained unclear, the unraveling continued, and Kadushin asked in a 2005 preface to a new edition "do such journals really matter as much today?" (p. xxi). The three journals that I next consider in reverse chronology came into being during this time of rapid change. Wolin's *democracy* only survived two years, while *Thesis Eleven* and *Social Text* have had long life spans but have weathered storms and undergone transformations. After providing a review of their trajectories, I return to Kadushin's question but also ask not only whether they matter but also whether they are needed today.

Wolin's *democracy*

In 1980, Larry Spence,[7] in "Political Theory as a Vacation," wondered why political theorists spent so much time looking to the past but almost never directly engaged with the present. In political science and its considered subfield, political theory, scholars were largely ignoring the present and instead consecrating the canon of political theorists long dead. In a sense, political theory had become a field devoted to literary studies. Ironically, the field of literary studies within many university English departments was becoming the domain of "theory." Much of the negative response to the quantification of scholarship manifested itself in a "theoretical turn," which arguably was carried to the same extremes as its positivist other. While "theory," which was largely French theory at the time imported into campuses beginning in the late 1960s and becoming fully realized in the 1970s and 1980s, had strong ties to the question of "the political," the farther it was practiced, the less political it became.

Spence argued that Wolin's call for epic theory has been echoed but at the same time, it has been accompanied by an increasing sense of failure. "For while books and articles too numerous to mention have asserted that we live in a time of crisis that requires the imagination of heroic political thinkers, no such thinkers have appeared" (1980, p. 697). At the same time, the call for epic or heroic theory was itself damaging. Because, as Spence argued, theories as guides to ordering political life must be put into practice, and they are put into practice by people. In other

---

7   A member of the New Left on the Berkeley campus, Larry Spence then questioned the role of the university, or "multiversity," calling it "the anteroom of the power structure and of monopoly capitalism, where managerial cadre are recruited and young men on the make are made" (Breines 1982, p. 24).

words, theory does not bring the world into being on its own. And putting theory into practice requires that theory be subject to revision as the facts it encounters in the political communities it seeks to reorder may call into question some aspects or all of that theory. When political theory is viewed as something heroic or epic that lives more in the past than the present, then it is put on a pedestal that distances it from the polis it seeks to address. Political theorists who curate that past are then considered as separate from the communities they seek to guide, and "their knowledge is privileged beyond dispute and beyond improvement" (p. 708). Spence concluded "Political theory has been too long on an intellectual resort beach with overvalued pastimes and ill-tempered defenses of privilege. It is time we all went home and got down to more important work" (p. 710).

A year later Wolin began the journal *democracy*, which he later viewed as "providing an example for people in political theory for how you might make it relevant" (quoted in Hauptmann 2001, p. 4).[8] Wolin attempted to reconnect theory to politics and political communities outside the university when he began the journal in 1981.[9] However, more immediate concerns may have played a larger role in the journal's founding, namely the election of Ronald Reagan, the beginnings of new ways of governing, which would come to be known as "neoliberalism," and the desire to challenge the "value-free" ideology of policy critique found in *The Public Interest*. Its lowercase title was homage to Dwight Macdonald's journal *politics*, which published from 1944 to 1949 (Xenos 2001). *democracy* continued a lineage of radical journals in the United States that had indigenous roots in thinkers such as Thomas Jefferson and John Dewey and later C. Wright Mills, Paul Goodman, and William Appleman Williams and looked more to the "radical Republican" tradition of politics and participatory democracy than Marxism (Mattson 2002). The lineage included journals such as the *Seven Arts, politics, Liberation, Dissent, Studies on the Left*, and *New University Thought*.

In *democracy*'s opening editorial, Wolin wrote that the reasons for beginning the journal and giving it the title *democracy* was "the steady transformation of America into an anti-democratic society" (1981, p. 3). As a result, democracy itself was forced into opposition, and the journal subtitled "A Journal of Political Renewal and Radical Change" would play a conservative but also hopefully transformative role: "the crucial challenge to radical democracy is to be as zealous in preventing things of great value to democracy from passing into oblivion as in bringing into the world new political forms of action, participation, and being

---

8 Wolin also later said of his experience with the journal that "[Before working on *democracy*], I'd never really joined in my own mind the question of the relationship between participatory politics which had been my experience at Berkeley and elsewhere in the 60s and early 70s with the sort of actual structure of American politics as it was taking shape in terms of the national government and national politics" (quoted in Hauptmann 2001, p. 4).

9 Interestingly, he did not make as much effort to connect theorists to politics as the number of theorists who published in the journal or sat on its editorial board was small (Hauptmann 2001).

together in the world" (p. 4). The journal's aim was to "encourage the development of an historical and theoretical understanding around the concrete problems of the present" largely through a process of remembrance (p. 4). The journal spoke to "radicals," who were apparently the journal's intended audience, but it promised no political program for radicals to follow.

> We cannot offer recipes or specific policies, but we can bring a critical approach that will illumine what is at stake for the future of democracy in current debates; how specific problems have come to have their present form; and what kinds of broad alternatives, consistent with democracy, are possible (p. 4).

The journal published just 12 issues before folding in 1983. However, it enjoyed a relatively large audience with a circulation that peaked at 10,000 copies before plateauing at 8,000—a very respectable figure compared to the 6,000 subscribers of *The Public Interest* (Miller 2010, p. 266).

democracy largely resembled *The Public Interest*, plain and scholarly. It contained articles, "explorations," review essays, and a section titled "Classics of Democracy" that revisited past texts to recover democratic traditions. There was no extraneous material. Its cover carried the title split in two, "demos" and "cracy," to emphasize the people's rule. Each issue carried a theme—the first was "The Current Crisis" and the second "Democracy's State."

Its editorial board included Joyce Appleby, Jerry Berman, Lawrence Goodwyn, William Kornhauser, Christopher Lasch, David Noble, and Hanna Pitkin, the only traditional political theorist to sit on the board. The rest were mainly historians and sociologists. Lasch played a large role at *Salmagundi*[10] beginning in the mid-1970s and in the 1980s would become a prominent member of the *Telos* circle—journals both open to his heterodox views. After Wolin contacted him in 1979 and asked him to join the journal project, Lasch replied: "This is the most encouraging news I've had in a long time." He also wrote that he had "pretty much reached the end of what it seems possible to do in political and intellectual isolation." He looked forward to the journal's "undogmatic and unsectarian analysis of the contemporary crisis" (quoted in Miller 2010, p. 251). Lasch's article in the first issue, "Democracy and the 'Crisis of Confidence,'" spoke of a United States in "a state of permanent crisis," a situation ripe for the "epic theory" Wolin earlier called for.

Wolin served as the journal's editor, while Nicholas Xenos was managing editor. The journal's publisher Max Palevsky operated the journal from his Common Good Foundation, which he had used to fund the candidacies of a number of notable politicians, such as 1972 presidential candidate George McGovern and Los Angeles mayor Tom Bradley. He made his money in computers, having

---

10 Robert Boyers founded *Salmagundi*, a "quarterly of the humanities and social sciences," in 1965 as a journal that would speak to a more general than academic audience. It has been published at Skidmore College since 1969.

founded Scientific Data Systems, which he later sold to Xerox, and also was a primary funder of Intel. Palevsky previously provided critical early funding for then foundering *Rolling Stone* magazine in 1970, but his connection to the magazine was not long lived. In 1990, he provided major funding to begin *The American Prospect*, a liberal magazine still in publication.

Palevsky and Wolin had different views of what they wanted the journal to be. Palevsky envisioned an antidote to *The Public Interest*, which would eventually serve as an arm of a liberal think tank, which he hoped to form. Wolin was less interested "in the business of offering precise remedies" and created a journal that leaned more toward critical theoretical reflection than policy prescriptions (quoted in Hauptmann 2001, p. 3). Apparently, Palevsky was unsatisfied with this plan or became more interested in other forums to advance his political goals. The journal ended when Palevsky decided he no longer wished to fund it (Hauptmann 2001). However, Wolin had been disappointed with the journal; the contributions to it did not achieve the vision he had for the project. Wolin wrote that the journal failed to attract the caliber of contributors the editorial board wanted. Further, most contributors were academics, "which means of course that we're dealing most of the time with functional illiterates" who "can't meet deadlines" (Wolin quoted in Miller 2010, p. 266). Still, the journal's ending was disappointing.

Gunnell offers one assessment of the journal that forms part of his larger argument regarding the alienation of academic political theory from politics. He concedes that *democracy* succeeded to some extent at overcoming this alienation since it did not "merely transform political issues into philosophical ones or treat them in terms of abstract hypothetical examples" (Gunnell 1986, p. 129). However, he argues that the journal failed to transcend "the confines of academic discourse" (p. 129).

> The real institutional distinctions and relationships between the academy and conventional politics in late-twentieth-century America, and their historical evolution, were elided. *Democracy*'s particular prejudice was the assumption that the particularities and ambiguities of political interests, movements, and structures could be bypassed in favor of an appeal to an undefined disembodied Hegelian public consciousness and that democracy could be pursued as an idea without an institutional and behavioral dimension. It was the belief, the academic prejudice, that, if political action can no longer be a transformational force in the contemporary age of rationalized structures, then political change can emerge through the force of ideas and education (p. 129).

The force of Gunnell's critique of *democracy* would doom many journal projects invested in using theory to inform their understanding of politics. If a journal was unwilling to offer specific political actions that its readership could undertake, then it would also be guilty of confusing political practice and political education or revelation.

The other option for a journal would be to practice a form of political journalism like what may appear in intellectual magazines like *The New Yorker* or overtly political magazines like *The Nation*. The long form journalism available in *The New Yorker* often provides engaging accounts of important and concerning political issues, but the magazine does not offer solutions and does not provide a coherent vision of how politics and society could be better ordered. The shorter form journalism in *The Nation* may provide a clearer picture of the magazine's overall political position, and the magazine is not shy about telling its readers what needs to be done. However, the weekly magazine is necessarily of the moment, and it cannot engage in the deeper and sustained reflection perhaps necessary to foster "wiser critical opinions." Gunnell's critique of *democracy* leaves open the question of whether and what kind of journal-ism a political project should undertake, especially when the journal is not tied to any particular political party but rather operates as something like a party.

Gunnell's arguments against *democracy* are perhaps too bound up in the question of connecting theory and practice. And perhaps this question has occupied too much attention from theorists and many other radical critics of the state. Maybe what deserves greater consideration is how theoretical positions on politics undermine the very visions of the world they hope to achieve. In *democracy*'s last issue, an article by George Shulman titled "The Pastoral Idyll of *democracy*" (1983) reviewed the journal and critiqued its form of radicalism as anti-modern and anti-statist. The journal sought to remedy the increasing distance between theory/theorists and politics, especially concerning the degree to which that distance was caused by theory's retreat into university life. But also increasing that distance was the absence of a political agent or of political will to realize the left's aims. The view of the state was that it had been captured by corporate capitalism, so it was no longer a possible ally for any democratic or egalitarian reordering of society. Moreover, the left, after the election of Reagan, became further disenfranchised, having little to no purchase on the state. Some of the response on the left was then "anti-statist" or at least "a-statist," seeking alternatives that fostered political organizing and participation at local levels. The majority perspective within the journal fostered a localist and thus anti-statist perspective. As Lasch wrote, *democracy* was "just about the only journal on the left that showed much interest in the small-is-beautiful tradition on the left (if it is even correct to identity it as a left-wing tradition)" (Miller 2010, p. 266).[11]

As Shulman argued, the journal's pastoral inclination celebrates populist republicanism whose "vision of the good life always moves us in two directions: from 'the city' toward 'nature,' and from the present toward the past" (1983, p. 43). Grounded in early American republicanism, this pastoral view is necessarily against the state. The majority voice in the journal "avoids considering the actual meaning of local control, sidesteps the primal stain on localism in America, and

---

11 Arguably Lasch would find another such journal as *Telos* developed its populist and federalist themes over the 1980s and 90s.

thereby avoids a major justification of state intervention into community life" (p. 50).¹² If localism is idolized, then economic, political, and racial inequalities may persist.

> Granting the limitations of localism would return democrats to the basic dilemma of social change and political power, specifically, how to promote systematic and radical social change while preserving and extending democratic participation. Democrats might then reexamine the consoling certainty that the state *must* be a devil, that large scale power can *only* be antipolitical and undemocratic. We need not embrace Leviathan and endorse Lenin to consider that the republican critique of the bureaucratic state has blinded us to the positive uses of the state (for social justice, racial equality, and civil rights) and deterred us from exploring how we might transform and use the powers we now demonize (p. 51).

The journal's hopes of realizing democracy without the aid of the state seem somewhat naive, but it is a naiveté made to appear as common sense for radical projects on the left due to its continued repetition in publications like *democracy*. It feels now like something of a dead end, as I suggest in the following section, Marxism would come to appear for those involved in Australian journal *Thesis Eleven*. The question is whether the left's critical support of participatory politics and its radical critique of capitalism can exist without rejecting the possibility that existing institutions, such as the state, which may hinder participatory politics and advance capitalism, may not *necessarily* need to always do either.

Thesis Eleven

In 2007, *Thesis Eleven* editors, Peter Beilharz and Trevor Hogan, agreed to give a talk about the journal to the School for Social and Cultural Studies at the University of Victoria, Wellington. They sat down with a (very) small group of students and

---

12 Shulman notes as an exception the two-part article by Phillip Green titled "In Defense of the State" to appear in the journal's second and third issues. Green's article focuses on the new individualism of thinkers and politicians like Milton Friedman, Robert Nozick, Ronald Reagan, and Margaret Thatcher. While concerned more with anti-statism on the right, Green worries that this has come to take on a "partially democratic character" and impliedly poses problems for the left (1983, p. 6). Green still is no champion of the state and wants to "confront the argument of these new individualists in order to distinguish between that part of it that simply serves as a mask for privilege, and that part of it that truly does locate obstacles that the pseudodemocratic, uncontrolled state apparatus has placed in the way of genuinely democratic self-government" (p. 7). However, the state as the only successful opponent of capitalism's worst excesses is something of a necessary evil. As he concludes in the article's second part, "the state, though indefensible, yet has to be defended" (p. 67).

faculty to discuss the journal, how it began, its history, and current projects. I was one of those students.

As its title suggests, the journal had Marxist origins. The eleventh thesis from Marx's "Theses on Feuerbach" reads: "The philosophers have only *interpreted* the world in various ways; the point, however, is to *change* it." The editorial statement of the first issue of *Thesis Eleven* in 1980 stated that

> Marxism as a theory and as a movement is in crisis. Radical theory has become completely undiscriminating. In the movements and parties there are blockages, perhaps decay, but little advance. In the turn of Anglo-American Marxism away from the project of importing Continental theory there is a danger that theory will be allowed to lapse altogether. There is a need for a new "theoretical" journal attaching a specifically political understanding to "theory" (1980, p. 2).

The journal argued that theory was losing its political potency. The editors aimed to create a new kind of "theoretical" journal. Arguably, they were criticizing other journals devoted to theory that failed to connect theory with praxis. The editors of this journal saw what they regarded as a severe divide between those who practice politics and those who theorize politics. One can argue whether or not this was an accurate perception. What is important is that the individuals behind *Thesis Eleven* responded to this crisis of theory by beginning a journal. As did other journal projects such as *Social Text*, discussed below, they also created a press *as* party, rather than a party press, and *in lieu of* a party—that no longer functioned or could no longer exist—they intended that their *press* enter service in the cause of both working to construct and right politics. "The intention of *Thesis Eleven* is to provide the framework in which these themes, problematics and struggles might be unified as politics" (1980, p. 2).

The editorial continued with a discussion of the relationship between Marxists and the workers' movement. It then discussed the fragmentation of Marxism into many knowledges, "knowledge is not only separated from practice, but also internally compartmentalized" (p. 2). The journal argued that a central theme accompanying its emphasis on politics would be "everyday life" and its necessary corollary, "the cultural specificity of marxisms." It recognized that it was not alone in its aims. The editorial named projects such as the British *Hegemony* group, the recently founded *Social Text* in the United States—with the caveat that its manifesto, if less its content, expresses positions close to *Thesis Eleven*, the new openness within *New Left Review*, as well as Perry Anderson's *Arguments Within English Marxism*, and the "radical rethinking evident in the three volume *Issues in Marxist Philosophy*." It stressed that what was valued in these projects was their openness to debate and not assertion. The journal wanted to investigate the contradictions and differences within theory, not simply formulate a politics based upon a dogmatic understanding of Marxism.

While much of the editorial seemed to counterpoise theory to politics, the editors did not understand them as part of a dichotomy, as passive versus active, or thinking versus the absence of thought, or whatever other simplified conventional understanding is often brought conceptually to these terms. Still, they recognized a distance between them. Even if ideas might have a force within themselves, that force was not being sufficiently articulated in politics. "The point is not that theory needs to be obliterated, only that it needs to be constituted politically. We invite you to participate as writers and as readers in the spirit of the eleventh thesis" (p. 4). The editors believed that within the pages of a journal they could make gains in politically constituting theory.

At the same time, they appeared to at least implicitly, or subconsciously, recognize the contradictions or limits of their project as they invited readers and writers to participate with them in "the spirit of the eleventh thesis" (p. 4). Why not instead ask readers and writers to participate in carrying out the eleventh thesis and change the world? If they recognized that the theoretical and political investigations of a journal, and hopefully the reconciliation of those often-divergent practices, could be part of the Marxist project to change the world, they also seemed to recognize that a journal could not be politics *tout court*. Maybe I am reading too much into what they meant by joining them in "the spirit of the eleventh thesis."

However, I feel that what the journal's editors said in that New Zealand meeting almost 30 years after this editorial was written gives weight to the approach to politics, journals, and intellectuals that I develop in these pages. Indeed, during the discussion, one person asked the editors, what the political purpose of the journal was. In essence, the question was, what is the political power of your journal? Beilharz and Hogan gave the person who had posed the question a funny look and answered that that was of no real concern to them (Peter and Trevor) or something to that effect. In other words, the journal's aim was not to carry out any political program. They were operating a journal and a center for cultural sociology. They organized international conferences, focusing on Southeast Asia. SAGE, a large academic publisher, now publishes their journal. When you look up the journal on SAGE's website, the journal's description reads

> *Thesis Eleven* encourages the development of social theory across the social sciences and liberal arts. The journal is international and interdisciplinary with a central focus on theories of society, culture, and politics and the understanding of modernity.

There is no mention of Marxism or a desire to reconcile theory with politics, much less any stated intention to change the world. Farther down the page, the description continues with an analysis of the journal's contents.

> *Thesis Eleven* publishes theories and theorists, surveys, critiques, debates and interpretations. The journal also brings together articles on place, region, or problems in the world today, encouraging civilizational analysis and work on alternative modernities from fascism and communism to Japan and Southeast

Asia. Marxist in origin, postmarxist by necessity, the journal is vitally concerned with change *as well as with tradition* (emphasis added).

Here, the journal acknowledges its Marxist roots, which are quickly identified as historical only. What made the journal *necessarily* post-Marxist is not acknowledged. This implies that if you are reading the journal then you already know. In other words, the transition from Marxism to post-Marxism can be regarded common knowledge, or a store of "common sense," among social or critical theorists. That transition no longer requires investigation; it is a moot point.[13]

Even more interesting is the suggestion that while the journal still remains "vitally" committed to change, it also values tradition. The word "tradition" is most commonly associated with a conservative outlook. Associated with tradition are the ideas of conserving or preserving. Its dictionary definition is "the transmission of customs or beliefs from generation to generation, or the fact of being passed on in this way." Tradition is derived from the Latin *tradere* meaning "deliver, betray," from *trans* meaning "across" and *dare* meaning "give." Traditions then are preserved because they are carried forward or given across time.

In its conservative understanding, tradition implies a holding onto, or a keeping back. It is the antithesis of moving forward or progress. Yet, as its etymology suggests, for tradition to be maintained, there must also be a forward movement, something must be passed on to the next generation. As Marxism became post-Marxism, for *Thesis Eleven* and many others, the old theoretical framework was left in the past as a new framework or multiple frameworks took its place. The desired change in the world could no longer be based on this old reading of a multivocal theoretical framework. Instead of being a change maker, Marxism, once radical, became a dusty tradition, one no longer worth passing forward. To return to Marxism now for many becomes a conservative position, a rehabilitation of tradition.

Thesis Eleven's title may have become a relic of its past. At the meeting, the editors said the title had been, at least in part, homage to a deceased friend. He had suggested the title, and when he passed away, they decided to use it. On its face, the journal's history reads like a narrative of de-radicalization, a once Marxist journal intent on changing the world turned a commercially published critical theory journal that values both change and tradition. Still, the journal cannot really be blamed; perhaps its conservation of some degree of radical critique is the best that can be done during times when there is no or limited purchase for those ideas on given realities. But finding moments of purchase or recognizing opportunities

---

13 These statements may also get you past gatekeepers, such as university deans and librarians, which may then allow you to publish more critical or Marxist/Marxian material. Earlier examples of such self-censoring include Max Horkheimer's substitution of "critical theory" as code for Marxism while in the United States and Antonio Gramsci's elimination of words like Marx and "class" from his prison writings. (Horkheimer and Adorno 2002); (Gramsci 1971).

Social Text

Social Text first appeared in 1979. Its original editors were Stanley Aronowitz, John Brenkman, and Frederic Jameson, but a number of other scholars constituted its editorial collective. On the occasion of its one hundredth issue, its editors, Brent Hayes Edwards and Anna McCarthy, remarked on the fact that none of the original members of the first collective are still involved with the journal, which perhaps testifies to disillusionment with the journal's original aims. Its founding was a product of relationships formed around the Marxist Literary Group. Aronowitz and Jameson wanted to grow this Marxist intellectual movement and when they met to discuss the possibility in 1975, they discussed the curious argument then "circulating on the intellectual Left that politics was no longer organized around political parties, but instead around journals" (Edwards and McCarthy 2009, p. 4). Brenkman joined the two men, and they announced the journal's founding in 1977 during the Modern Language Association's convention in Chicago while at a reception in Gayatri Chakravorty Spivak's apartment. The journal would operate independently, affiliated neither with a university nor an academic publisher. In 1992, the journal agreed to be published by Duke University Press, which remains its publisher.

The "Prospectus" included within the journal's first issue, stated the following:

> This is to announce the publication of a new journal devoted to problems in theory, particularly in the area of culture and ideological practices. These are areas shared by the social sciences, philosophy, and the humanities; *Social Text* is designed to offer a place in which theories developed in the various specialized disciplines can be made available for wider discussion. The framework of the journal is Marxist in the broadest sense of the term (p. 3).[14]

The journal's subtitle was "Theory, Culture, Ideology." The prospectus also promised attention to a large number of themes: "Everyday Life and Revolutionary Praxis," "The Proliferation of Theories,"[15] "Symbolic Investments of the Political," "The Texts of History," "Ideology and Narrative," "Mass Culture and

---

14 As Brenkman would reflect on the journal's hundredth issue: "Why at the moment that *Social Text* was founded did Marx seem so relevant and liberalism so bankrupt, whereas today—a scant thirty years later—Marxism might reasonably be thought to be dead, while the fundamental elements of liberalism are in need of vigorous defense?" (2009, p. 205).

15 The journal expressed its intention to seriously engage with "the various new theories which have come into being following the breakup of classical liberalism in the various disciplines" (p. 4). It seems somewhat odd to refer to liberalism breaking up inside

the Avant-Garde," "Marxism and the State," and "'Consumer Society' and the World System."

As Brenkman recalls, most of the scholars to get involved with the journal had backgrounds in literary studies, and *Social Text* intended to include fiction and poetry within its pages alongside essays that engaged more "political" questions (2009, p. 207).[16] The journal saw itself as "a hybrid between a political review or journal and a literary magazine" in the tradition of the "little magazine." This raised questions for the journal including whether the creative writing needed to have a political line and how creative writing fit within the broader mission of the journal to explore theory, culture, and ideology. As Edwards later reflected,

> [T]he inclusion of fiction and poetry must raise questions about the scope and definition of the term *theory* (as in the first sentence of the "Prospectus" announcing the founding of a journal devoted to "problems in theory").[17] "Theory" is not only a matter of conceptual precision and rhetorical force, in other words, but also inherently a matter of writerly practice. And if poetry and fiction—not to mention the unique and sundry short pieces that the journal would publish under the rubric "Unequal Developments"—could all be subsumed under the rubric, then perhaps one should not presuppose that theory composes a genre onto itself, with its own standards of evidence, protocols of reception, and formal predilections (2009, p. 181).

In these terms, "theory" is divorced from political or social concerns, and is instead a form of *literary* inquiry, albeit one that may not "compose a genre unto itself." According to Edwards and McCarthy, "the three founding editors shared a vision of a journal that would attend to the broadest range of inquiry into the understanding of culture across academic fields, striving for clarity at a level of abstraction to be named '*theory*'" (p. 6, emphasis added). "Theory" then appeared to be the journal's main concern and at least in 1996, during what became known as the Sokal hoax, also perhaps its undoing. Treating "theory" as a thing in itself only contributed to its aestheticization and hence depoliticization.

In order to understand the Sokal hoax in the context of my broader argument, it is important to recognize that *Social Text*'s editors were responding to what they saw as the ossified and reactionary practice of the scientific peer review process. As a self-styled radical departure from the regime of peer review, grounded as it was in the hegemonic discourse of the positivist and empiricist Enlightenment, the

---

the disciplines rather than the disciplines reacting to liberalism's breakdown in political life. This underscores the distance between the "new theories" and politics.

16   The creative writing and also short essays that were more experimental or perhaps less "scholarly" constituted a section of the journal titled "Unequal Developments."

17   To some, "problems *in theory*" (emphasis added) might read as if the journal was devoting itself to theoretical problems, i.e., problems that might or could exist but did not actually exist as far as they knew, rather than problems within "theory."

editors of *Social Text* chose to practice a form of editorial control that forewent the peer review process for vetting by the editorial collective itself. As members of its editorial collective commented in a retrospective of their one hundredth issue,

> Peer review might once have served the purpose of ensuring professional autonomy, but the politics of late-twentieth-century disciplinarity demanded that the peer-review editorial system trade blindness for oversight. This profoundly altered the contract of professionalism, linking judgment over the validity of knowledge to its determinate forms of production (manifest as tenured lines bestowed with academic freedom). As the university's aims and methods increasingly find justification not in the model of a public good of enlightened citizenship, but rather in the realm of 'value-added,' protocols of empirical evaluation become the technology par excellence of higher administration, fueled by the ratings-driven demands of incessant comparison. To this condition, the collective held out a modest and partial antidote (2009).

The Sokal hoax sought to point out the deficiencies of such a process. However, most non-academic journals have practiced such collective review or single review by an editor-in-chief, and many have managed to publish successfully and with respect for many years. As members of the collective would later surmise, it was perhaps not the editorial practices of the collective review that allowed the Sokal hoax to occur but rather the increasing professionalization of the journal sparked by the affiliation with Duke University Press in 1992 that loosened the collective's bonds and impliedly made its members less interested in the journal as an engaged political project and more as a calculated means to professional success. In other words, less attention would be paid to evaluating "theoretical innovation," which required a level of inquiry not afforded by competing professional demands.

In 1996, the physicist Alan Sokal submitted for review and had accepted for publication in *Social Text* his article, "Transgressing the Boundaries: Toward a Transformative Hermeneutics of Quantum Gravity." It appeared in a special issue devoted to the "Science Wars." As submitted, Sokal's pastiche of the currently in vogue French poststructuralist "theory" set out to prove that quantum gravity had "profound political implications," for social scientific thought. After it appeared, Sokal published his rationale for the caper in another journal *Lingua Franca*. There he stated,

> My article is a theoretical essay based entirely on publicly available sources, all of which I have meticulously footnoted. All works cited are real, and all quotations are rigorously accurate; none are invented. Now, it's true that the author doesn't believe his own argument. But why should that matter? The editors' duty as scholars is to judge the validity and interest of ideas, without regard for their provenance. (That is why many scholarly journals practice blind refereeing) (1996, p. n/a).

Sokal wanted to reveal the shortcomings of *Social Text*'s content—its "self-indulgent nonsense," its "epistemic relativism," its "subjectivist thinking"—by castigating the laxity of *Social Text*'s review process. The journal's intellectual standards were not up to snuff. And worse, the decision to publish was based more on ideological affiliation than intellectual rigor.

> The results of my little experiment demonstrate, at the very least, that some fashionable sectors of the American academic Left have been getting intellectually lazy. The editors of *Social Text* liked my article because they liked its conclusion: that "the content and methodology of postmodern science provide powerful intellectual support for the progressive political project." They apparently felt no need to analyze the quality of the evidence, the cogency of the arguments, or even the relevance of the arguments to the purported conclusion (1996, p. n/a).

However, I contend that what the publication of Sokal's article pointed to was less a problem of editorial control or political preferences and more a matter of an engagement with postmodern "theory" that saw value in theory, in and of itself, as a vehicle for professional advancement. This context made it all too easy for scholars to lose sight of the political, social, and economic realities that their "theory" was intended to explain. If new theories could be slapped together by signaling the right names and including the right rhetoric and then pass editorial review without having actually said anything or worse having said something controvertibly wrong or nonsensical, then what usefulness did this overwhelming attention to "theory" actually provide? I am not arguing that all the theoretical offerings published in *Social Text* over its almost 35 years of existence contain nothing of value. Rather, I am arguing that the journal has contributed to a perspective, largely but not exclusively held amongst left-leaning academics in the English speaking world, that theoretical exegesis can exist in a vacuum and both count as political intervention and "research," that is, as a means for advancing one's career in the academy. Theoretical exercises may not be meritless, but they should not be mistaken for political criticism. They are more likely to obscure the re-view of the state and the prevailing political order than clarify it.

Critique and the Return of "Crisis"

While the 1980s were the era of the post-New Left, they were also the era of the rise of a new conservatism that was, in part, impelled by the relative success of the right-leaning *Public Interest*. By the mid- to late- 1990s, the so-called "end of history" and blowback from the Sokal hoax combined to ensure that the possibility of some new theoretical frame emerging to unify support for leftist political practice was remote. Postmodernism had itself dismissed the potency of unifying grand narratives, and the collapse of the Soviet Union and East Germany extinguished the living examples of the most powerful of such grand narratives. Political theory critical of capitalism, neoliberalism, and neoconservatism became fragmented and diverse. In 2000, Wolin revisited his earlier article on political theory as a vocation. Thirty years later, the threats to theory had changed. Now Wolin wrote of a situation of "overtheorization" in the context of an absent public sphere. Instead of calling for political theory, Wolin invoked or recalled theory, more as remembrance or as "a response to a certain kind of loss" (p. 5).

> [I]s the concept of a calling still plausible, even urgent, in the context of pseudo-democracy, not as a personal choice or as institutional certification but as a public commitment for a time when the idea of publics has pretty much been superseded by that of constituencies or dissolved into various identities based on race, gender, or sexual preference? (p. 5).

As for "overtheorization," Wolin pointed to the "impressive or alarming" number of theorists to be found across the disciplines, the large number of theory journals, and the increase in theoretical books and articles (p. 8). Theory is not the only thing in overproduction; Wolin also argued that politics is being overproduced both by academics and also "by think tanks, pollsters and survey researchers, and pundits" (p. 9). "In this world both theory and politics are ubiquitous and indeterminate" (p. 9). As a result, what is "common" to a polity has been lost, or lost sight of. Wolin wondered if diversity has put too great a strain on the political.[18]

What seems to drive Wolin's rethinking of the possibility of political theory is the changed meaning of "critical." In 1969, the concept of "critique" had related more directly to "crisis" as the urgency of the situation required critical intervention: "the world shows increasing signs of coming apart" (1969, p. 1081).[19] By 2000, "critique" and "critical" were more closely related to "critic," the figure of the armchair theorist, contemplative, judging from afar, as spectator rather than participant.

> It is theoretic theory rather than political theory. And even though it makes references to real-world controversies, its engagement is with the conditions, or the politics, of the theoretical that it seeks to settle rather than with the political that is being contested over who get what and who gets included. It is postpolitical (p. 15).

---

18 This reaction to diversity would also form the basis of Shulman's critique of Wolin's journal *democracy*, discussed above.

19 Wolin continued: "our political systems are sputtering, our communication networks invaded by cacophony. American society has reached a point where its cities are uninhabitable, its youth disaffected, its races at war with each other, and its hope, its treasure, and the lives of its young men dribbled away in interminable foreign ventures. Our whole world threatens to become anomalous. Yet amidst this chaos official political science exudes a complacency which almost beggars description" (1969, p. 1,081).

Wolin wondered if the actual condition of society was converging toward that of theory itself by preferencing disorder over order, decenteredness over centeredness, and so on. He noted the common affinity (a commonality?) between conservatives and postmodernists in their hankering for some kind of anti-state social condition, "except that conservatives know what some postmodernists have forgotten, that multiple centers mean multiple masters" (p. 15). In a world now dominated by change, one can no longer point to a crisis, or turning point, because turning points are normalized or routine, and as a result crisis is absent. The system appears "crisis-proof" (p. 16).

According to Wolin, substantive democracy is antithetical to an ever-changing world, a utopia that contains its own dystopia, and one where the present concentration of power faces no oppositional political will or the political culture that would foster such will. Wolin ended pessimistically with little hope for either democracy or political theory, the latter too has become subject to rapid change and with no turning point to latch onto, it has become increasingly ineffective.

> It would be nice to end on an uplifting note and invoke political theory to come to the aid of democracy, but besides being fatuous that call may be too late in the day. During the few decades that have elapsed since my original essay the academic intellectual has undergone a dizzying series of intellectual permutations—Marxism, critical theory, poststructuralism, deconstructionism, neopragmatism, etc. The theorist, in other words, has replicated the pace of technological change (p. 21).

The proliferation of "theory" journals, such as *Social Text*, and the diaspora of theory into multiple disciplines (Agger and Luke 2002), as I suggest in Chapter Five, have created a "permanent revolution," but one of theory, rather than of political change. This said, I use the remainder of this chapter to argue that "crisis" seems to have returned to the forefront of politics, and that this is creating an opportunity for new forms of re-view to emerge, breathing new life into the journal as review.

After 9/11, the economic crash of 2008, and with scientific evidence that the ecosphere's climate is being altered dramatically and dangerously by human actions within it, it is difficult to argue that societies no longer confront political dilemmas. The emergence of journals like leftist *n+1* in 2004, progressive *Democracy: A Journal of Ideas* in 2006, or socialist *Jacobin: a Magazine of Culture and Polemic* in 2011 suggests that the critical impulse has re-emerged, and in forms perhaps more attuned to crisis, rather than engaging merely in criticism with no political referent. All three journals exist in both print and electronic formats. For example, the most well-known of the new crop of journals is *n+1*, its first issue titled "Negation." While including essays on bulking up in the National Basketball Association and a diatribe against exercise, it also contained somewhat scathing critiques of the neocon magazine *The Weekly Standard*, the literary section of *The New Republic*, and of Dave Eggers' *McSweeney's* and *The Believer* magazines. In its "Politics" section, short essays appeared on George W. Bush, Abu Ghraib, and Palestine. The journal was unafraid to have an opinion. *n+1*'s "Editorial Statement" began:

> We are living in an era of demented self-censorship ... But try saying that the act we call "war" would more properly be termed a massacre, and that the state we call "occupation" would more properly be termed a war; that the conspiracy theories, here and abroad, which have not yet been proved true by Seymour Hersh or the General Accounting Office are probably, nonetheless, true; or that the political freedoms so cherished and, really, so necessary, are also the mask of a more pervasive, insidious repression—try saying all this, or any of it, and see how far you get. Then try saying it in a complex way, at some length, expressing as you do so an actual human personality (2004, p. n/a).

Resisting such "self-censorship," the journal publishes a section titled "The Intellectual Situation" at the front of each issue. There the editors anonymously re-view the important political and cultural topics of the day.

At least several of *n+1*'s founding editors—Keith Gessen, Mark Greif, Chad Harbach, Benjamin Kunkel, Allison Lorentzen, and Marco Roth—could perhaps now be considered "public intellectuals," as they regularly publish in various other media like *The New York Review of Books*, the *London Review of Books*, *The New Yorker*, *The American Prospect*, *The Atlantic*, the *Nation*, and *Dissent*, or have published acclaimed novels. Some are now academics and book editors. Kunkel fashioned himself a Marxist public intellectual with the publication of a collection of essays titled *Utopia or Bust: A Guide to the Present Crisis* in 2014. The book, as marketed, hopes to translate academic critical thought for the "politically committed or simply curious" outside the university with chapters on the theory of David Harvey, Frederic Jameson, Robert Brenner, David Graeber, Slavoj Žižek, and Boris Groys. The *New Left Review*'s book line, Verso Books, and *Jacobin*, co-published the collection. Another editor, Gessen, was arrested in New York during the Occupy Wall Street protest movement.

The new *Democracy* bears some resemblance to the unrelated short-lived *democracy* but also to *The Public Interest*, although with different politics. It is a middle-aged Washington, D.C. journal that closely re-views many of the same policy issues—taxes, poverty, immigration, crime—that *The Public Interest* took up but from a left-leaning perspective. Echoing the *Westminster*'s doubts about the review form but transported into a new media age, *Democracy*'s opening editorial read:

> What could be more anachronistic—in the media culture and political climate of 2006—than the founding of a quarterly journal of ideas? ... But we believe that, to regenerate the strength of the progressive movement, big ideas are vitally important. And *Democracy* represents our bet—and the bet of our supporters—that they will matter (Baer and Cherny 2006, p. 1).

The journal offers specific policy prescriptions, such as advocating a sovereign wealth fund, creating 40 hour "work weeks" for inmates as a step toward reforming the criminal justice system, the addition of a value-added tax, and automatic voter registration, to name but a few.

Jacobin is the youngest of the new magazines in life span and editorial composition. *Jacobin*'s introduction subverts the hopefulness of *Democracy*'s vision but still seeks an audience for a critical view.

> Publications with tiny audiences have a knack for mighty pronouncements. A grandiloquent opening, some platitudes about resurrecting intellectual discourse followed by issue after issue of the same old shit. We can admire the confidence of our peers, but there is something pathological about this trend. These delusions stem from a well-warranted sense of impotence. The intellectual was born out of, and thrived throughout, the twentieth century, but left a mixed legacy ... Perhaps the death of the public intellectual is deserved. And yet, *Jacobin* was founded on the premise that there still is an audience for critical commentary ... Sober analysis of the present and criticisms of the Left does not mean accommodation to the status quo (Sunkara 2011, p. 1).

Begun by a then 21 year old college student, Bhaskar Sunkara, the journal's first issue was a large 8 1/2 by 11" glossy with a cover price of $5.99. Its appearance seemed to contradict its message: an attempt to revitalize class struggle, or more pointedly, class warfare, on behalf of the Left. Under the title of each essay in its first issue's Table of Contents, the magazine emphasized its focus on politics by describing each piece as "on the politics of _____," with the blank filled by the particular essay's general content—work, resistance, occupation, lesser "evilism," identity, being alone, resentment, "orientalism," and fear. In its fifth issue published in Winter 2012, which followed the Occupy Wall Street demonstrations the previous fall, Sunkara's impassioned editorial seemed fueled by a more visible Left. Although he concedes that the Occupy protestors might not pick up the mantle of "class struggle," he argues that it is a phrase and political language that needs to be reclaimed and asserted. He critiques constituents of the movement who label themselves "post-political."

> A "post-political movement" of people who recognize they have the power to create change? It's an obvious contradiction. If one side is pushing austerity and the other is countering with calls for income redistribution and public goods, a high-stakes class struggle is being waged. Far from post-political, this is a reassertion of democratic politics at its purest (2011, p. 2).

Now with a book series published in partnership with Verso Books and Random House,[20] the ongoing development of a nationwide series of reading groups, a strong social media presence, with over 40,000 Facebook "fans," and a print readership of about 6,000 with another 300,000 web audience members a month, the socialist magazine is perhaps making radical critique "popular" again.

All three publications may find their audiences limited to social science academics and other members of the highly educated class. And, it is difficult to know how far these journals travel outside such circles. However, with the academically trained and other highly educated groups increasingly joining the ranks of "the precariat,"[21] an audience may yet be primed to demand the kinds of broad political change that the new, new Left journals are promoting. Or, at least, they may constitute a group poised to publicize further the radical re-views represented in their pages. Still, the practice of political criticism, especially the radical variety, may never again be in a position to regain the force it may have once had in the age of the "great reviews." Further, as political philosopher Raymond Geuss (2010a, p. 185) argues, it is the very presence of extreme crises that make the old bourgeois forms of political criticism superfluous, as the leisure time for such "systematic ratiocination" is no longer available. As radical social criticism has largely continued to operate within those old forms, it too is "a very expensive luxury good" (p. 185). New journals then are caught between the competing demands to act in response to immediate problems and to provide the space and time for critical reflection. Perhaps their employment of new social media and other digital technologies in conjunction with the traditional review form will better enable them to do both.

---

20 Interestingly, Verso is the imprint of the New Left Review collective while media corporation Bertelsmann owns Random House.

21 In 1969, 78.3 percent of faculty positions were tenure track, while only 21.7 percent were non-tenure track. In 2009, those numbers were almost reversed, with 66.5 percent of faculty ineligible for tenure and only 33.5 percent in tenure track positions (Kezar and Maxey 2013).

Conclusion
The Future of Re-view?

What then is the future of re-view in new digital environments that transform both how the state governs and how critics can intervene in that governance? To return to *Telos*, the journal now maintains an on-line presence with a website sponsored by Telos Press that includes: TELOSscope, a blog with multiple authorship, which readers can respond to with comments of their own; TELOSthreads, an indexing service that clusters articles around various topics such as "Liberalism," "Schmitt," and "Critical Theory"; Telos Online, which provides an electronic archive of its articles that can be searched by a variety of filters such as author, issue number, keyword, and so forth; and, a catalog of Telos Press's publications, among other features. The journal has also made forays into social networking sites like Facebook (it currently has 1,367 "likes"), Twitter, YouTube, and LinkedIn.

The TELOSscope blog now creates more interaction between journal and audience. Readers can become writers as they post comments (reactions) to the blog posts written by *Telos* contributors. The journal digitized may also now be able to cross into other fields that it previously was excluded from, perhaps simply because it was unknown to them. The journal's new on-line subtitle lends credence to this idea, calling itself now, "A Quarterly Journal of Politics, Philosophy, Critical Theory, Culture, and the Arts," as opposed to its earlier subtitles such as "A Marxist Quarterly," "A Journal of Revolutionary Thought," or "A Journal of Radical Thought." The web presence and social networking could also be an effort to reach out to a younger generation as the journal's original founders and contributors reach their sixties and seventies. Without younger readers and contributors, the journal would eventually age out and fade away.

The very existence of a website for the journal may allow it to reach more readers than it otherwise would, but how do all these new media extensions of the journal affect the journal's project? Someone's energies, whether owner's, editors', and/or contributors', are going into the creation and maintenance of these electronic manifestations of the journal rather than into the construction of the print journal itself. Further, these attempts to publicize journals through electronic means, whether by *Telos*, *Jacobin*, or any other critical journal now digitized, seem to be buying into the dominant trends of capitalism's digital economies, such as hyperspeed, brevity, superficiality, and the communities of congratulation that many on-line forms of re-viewing are becoming, rather than criticizing them. Still, the digital environment is likely what allowed *Jacobin* to accelerate from a relatively unknown upstart in 2011 to an on-line presence with 43,046 Facebook "likes," dwarfing *Telos*' numbers, and to gain mentions in *The New York Times*,

Rolling Stone, and *The Nation*. Whether the journal's "fame" will be lasting or ephemeral remains to be seen.

When the *Edinburgh Review* came into being, the times were ripe in Scotland for a liberal organ, and the presence of thinkers and writers like Thomas Malthus, David Ricardo, James Mill, Lord Byron, William Wordsworth, and William Hazlitt, among numerous others, provided the journal with a wealth of ideas to transmit to a starved public. In many ways, the influence of the *Review* was a product of its circumstances (Weir 1852). Looking back, a critic could say that "The establishment of the *Edinburgh Review*, as all the world knows, was the beginning of a new era in the history, not only of Scottish, but also of British politics" (Masson 1856, p. 439). It is unlikely that any review from the last 150 years would merit such a pronouncement. What journal today would be heralded as the *Edinburgh Review* was? Maybe, however, the circumstances have become or are becoming ripe again for the critical re-view. Whether the review form of the journal is still the right home for the re-viewing practice is open to question. Maybe critical surveillance of the state can better take place through other means?

There are now many examples of actors who are using "information" in various ways to work as new digital "critics" of the state. They include hackers, leakers, citizen journalists, and surveyors of satellite imagery. By trying to bring the state *and* other forms of authority into view, they also renew the possibility of criticism. These "critics" of invisible authority both make that authority visible and offer counter-information that challenges the state's and market's increasingly interwoven "official" view. They accomplish this through various systems of what can be defined as "surveillance," or keeping watch or guard. Their "surveillance" activities are directed against states, both democratic and authoritarian, and against corporations, rendering both sites of power more accountable to the public. They exercise a necessary form of vigilance in societies hoping to achieve anything approaching real democracy. The review form of journal may still have a place amongst these various surveillant actors. And no single actor, or form of re-view, can ever satisfy the critical demands of overseeing and challenging the state's ordering of society and the economy.

When a new journal, especially one whose aim is political intervention, is founded, its editors often announce its arrival by identifying some lack (of thinking, being, reading, writing) that their journal will remedy. Their publication, or political project, seeks to fill some absence in the intellectual field, and their opening editorials (or plans, since not all these projects reach fruition) assert this intention forcefully. There is no other journal than ours to address this issue, and this absence necessitates our existence. The new more diffuse forms of re-view mounted by hackers, leakers, citizen journalists, and surveyors of satellite imagery present the same case, albeit in a manner suited to the times. Journals have new allies and outlets, and new mediums for the task of re-viewing the prevailing view. The desire for change is necessarily ongoing.

Bibliography

1824. "Miscellaneous Notices." *The North American Review* no. 18 (April):407–26.
1834. "Tory Views and Machinations." *The Edinburgh Review* no. 68 (118):457–468.
1845. "Introductory." *The American Review: A Whig Journal of Politics, Literature, Art and Science* no. 1 (1):1–4.
1874. "Autobiography of John Stuart Mill." *The New Englander* no. 129 (October):605–22.
1916. "Editorials." *The Seven Arts* no. 1 (1):52–6.
1917a. "American Independence and the War—A Supplement." *The Seven Arts* no. 1 (6):1–9.
1917b. "Enemies Within: 'Seven Arts' Magazine Says 'Democracy Is a Wornout Ideal; Patriotism Is Just a Form of Anger.'" *New York Tribune*, August 17, 7.
1980. "Editorial." *Thesis Eleven* no. 1 (1):2–6.
Addison, Joseph, and Richard Steele. 1803. *The British Classics, Vol. I, Containing the First Volume of the Tatler*. London: A. O. Stansbury.
Adler, Frank. 1988. "*Telos*, 1968 and Now." *Telos* no. 75 (Spring):52–5.
Agger, Ben. 2000. *Public Sociology: From Social Facts to Literary Acts*. Lanham, Md.: Rowman & Littlefield Publishers.
Agger, Ben, and Tim Luke. 2002. "Politics in Postmodernity: The Diaspora of Politics and the Homelessness of Political and Social Theory." *Theoretical Directions in Political Sociology for the 21st Century* no. 11:159–95.
Allitt, Patrick. 2009. *The Conservatives: Ideas and Personalities Throughout American History*. New Haven, CT: Yale University Press.
Alt, John. 1985. "Radical and Conservative Critique: A Conference Report." *Telos* no. 63 (Spring):121–38.
Anderson, Benedict. 1983. *Imagined Communities: Reflections on the Origin and Spread of Nationalism*. London: Verso Editions/New Left Books.
Anderson, Perry. 1998. *The Origins of Postmodernity*. London: Verso Books.
Antonio, Robert J. 2009. Absolutizing the Particular. *Fast Capitalism* 5.1: n/a, http://www.fastcapitalism.com.
Armor, David J. 1972. "The Evidence on Busing." *The Public Interest* no. 28 (Summer):90–126.
Ash, Timothy Garton. 2013. "From the Lighthouse: The World and the NYR After Fifty Years." *The New York Review of Books* no. 60 (17):51–3.
Atlas, James. 2006. The Ma and Pa of the Intelligentsia. *The New York Times Magazine*: n/a, http://www.nymag.com/news/media/21344.
Baer, Kenneth, and Andrei Cherny. 2006. "A Message to Our Readers." *Democracy: A Journal of Ideas* no. 1 (Summer):1–2.

Barrow, Clyde W. 2008. "The Intellectual Origins of New Political Science." *New Political Science* no. 30 (2):215–244.

Bell, Daniel. 1985. "The Revolt Against Modernity." *The Public Interest* no. 81 (Fall):42–63.

Bell, Daniel, and Irving Kristol. 1965. "What is the Public Interest?" *The Public Interest* no. 1 (Fall):3–5.

Berube, Maurice R., and Marilyn Gittell. 1970. "In Whose Interest is "The Public Interest"?" *Social Policy* no. 1 (1):5–9.

Blanchot, Maurice. 2010. *Political Writings, 1953–1993*. Translated by Zakir Paul. New York: Fordham University Press.

Bloom, Alexander. 1986. *Prodigal Sons: The New York Intellectuals & Their World*. New York: Oxford University Press.

Bobbio, Norberto. 1978a. "Is There a Marxist Theory of the State?" *Telos* no. 35:5–16.

Bobbio, Norberto. 1978b. "Why Democracy?" *Telos* no. 36:43–54.

Bobbio, Norberto. 1982. "Democracy and Invisible Government." *Telos* no. 52:41–55.

Bourdieu, Pierre. 1969. "Intellectual Field and Creative Project." *Social Science Information* no. 8 (2):89–119.

Bourdieu, Pierre. 1989. "The Corporatism of the Universal: The Role of Intellectuals in the Modern World." *Telos* no. 81 (Fall):99–110.

Bourdieu, Pierre. 1991. *Language and Symbolic Power*. Translated by John B. Thompson. Edited by John B. Thompson. Cambridge, Mass.: Harvard University Press.

Bourdieu, Pierre. 1998. *Acts of Resistance: Against the Tyranny of the Market*. Translated by Richard Nice. New York: The New Press.

Bourne, Randolph. 1917. "The War and the Intellectuals." *The Seven Arts* no. 2 (2):133–46.

Bourne, Randolph. 1919. "The State." In *Untimely Papers*, edited by James Oppenheim, 140–230. New York: B. W. Huebsch.

Bourne, Randolph. 2006 [1917]. "Twilight of Idols." In *The American Intellectual Tradition, Volume II: 1865 to the Present*, edited by David A. Hollinger and Charles Capper, 181–87. New York: Oxford University Press.

Breines, Paul. 1988. "Recalling Telos." *Telos* no. 75 (Spring):36–47.

Breines, Wini. 1982. *Community and Organization in the New Left: 1962–1968 – The Great Refusal*. New York: Praeger Publishers.

Brenkman, John. 2009. "Prospectus." *Social Text* no. 27 (3):205–09.

Briggs, Asa, and Peter Burke. 2009. *A Social History of the Media: From Gutenberg to the Internet*. 3rd ed. Cambridge, UK: Polity.

Bronitsky, Jonathan. 2014. "The Brooklyn Burkeans." *National Affairs* no. 18 (Winter):121–36.

Brown, Harcourt. 1972. "History and the Learned Journal." *Journal of the History of Ideas* no. 33 (3):365–78.

Burawoy, Michael. 2005. "The Critical Turn to Public Sociology." *Critical Sociology* no. 31 (3):313–26.
Burke, Peter. 2000. *A Social History of Knowledge: From Gutenberg to Diderot*. Cambridge, UK: Polity.
Burke, Peter. 2012. *A Social History of Knowledge II: from the Encyclopaedia to Wikipedia*. Cambridge, UK: Polity.
Calhoun, Craig. 1992. *Habermas and the Public Sphere*. Cambridge, MA: The MIT Press.
Chaves, Elisabeth. 2008. "The War between *n+1* and *The Elegant Variation*, or When Production Overlooks Consumption in the Literary Political Economy." *Fast Capitalism* 4 (1), www.fastcapitalism.com.
Chiapello, Eve. 2013. "Capitalism and Its Criticisms." *New Spirits of Capitalism? Crises, Justifications and Dynamics*, edited by Paul du Gay and Glenn Morgan, 60–82. Oxford, UK: Oxford University Press.
Chomsky, Noam. 1967. "The Responsibility of Intellectuals." *The New York Review of Books* no. 8 (3):n/a.
Chomsky, Noam. 2011. "The Responsibility of Intellectuals, Redux." *Boston Review*: n/a, https://www.bostonreview.net/noam-chomsky-responsibility-of-intellectuals.
Clarke, Simon. 1990. "The Crisis of Fordism or the Crisis of Social-Democracy." *Telos* no. 83:71–98.
Collini, Stefan. 2006. *Absent Minds: Intellectuals in Britain*. Oxford, UK: Oxford University Press.
Collini, Stefan. 2010. "A Life in Politics: *New Left Review* at 50." *The Guardian* (February 13): n/a, http://www.guardian.co.uk/books/2010/feb/13/new-left-review-stefan-collini/.
Collini, Stefan, Donald Winch, and John Burrow. 1983. *That Noble Science of Politics: A Study in Nineteenth-Century Intellectual History*. Cambridge, UK: Cambridge University Press.
Collins, Randall. 1998. *The Sociology of Philosophies: a Global Theory of Intellectual Change*. Cambridge, MA: Belknap Press.
Connolly, William E. 1995. "The Uncertain Condition of the Critical Intellectual: A Response." *Political Theory* no. 23 (4):653–57.
Coser, Lewis A. 1997. *Men of Ideas: A Sociologist's View*. New York: Free Press Paperbacks, Simon & Schuster.
Cox, R. G. 1937a. "The Great Reviews (I)." *Scrutiny* no. VI (1):2–20.
Cox, R. G. 1937b. "The Great Reviews (II)." *Scrutiny* no. VI (2):155–75.
Cox, R. G. 1947. "The Critical Review To-Day." *Scrutiny* no. XIV (4):256–68.
Danner, Mark. 2013. In Conversation: Robert Silvers. *New York Magazine*, http://nymag.com/news/features/robert-silvers-2013-4.
de Certeau, Michel. 1984. *The Practice of Everyday Life*. Translated by Steven Rendall. Berkeley, CA: University of California Press.
Debray, Regis. 2000. *Transmitting Culture*. Translated by Eric Rauth. New York: Columbia University Press.

Dell, Floyd. 1919. "Randolph Bourne -obituary." *The New Republic* January 4:276.
Derrida, Jacques. 2006. *Spectres of Marx: The State of the Debt, the Work of Mourning, adn the New International*. London: Routledge Classics.
Dewey, John. 1916a. "Force, Violence and the Law." *The New Republic* no. 5:295–7.
Dewey, John. 1916b. "On Understanding the Mind of Germany." *The Atlantic* no. 117:251–62.
Dews, Peter. 1987. *Logics of Disintegration: Post-Structuralist Thought and the Claims of Critical Theory*. London: Verso.
Dorman, Joseph. 2001. *Arguing the World: The New York Intellectuals in their Own Words*. Chicago: University of Chicago Press.
Drucker, Peter F. 1969. "The Sickness of Government." *The Public Interest* no. 14 (Winter):3–23.
Dryzek, John S. 2006. "Revolutions Without Enemies: Key Transformations in Political Science." *American Political Science Review* no. 100 (4):487–92.
Eagleton, Terry. 1984. *The Function of Criticism: From the Spectator to Post-Structuralism*. London: Verso.
Eagleton, Terry. 1996. *The Illusions of Postmodernism*. London: Blackwell Publishing.
Edwards, Brent Hayes. 2009. "Poetry." *Social Text* no. 27 (3):177–81.
Edwards, Brent Hayes, and Anna McCarthy. 2009. "Introduction." *Social Text* no. 27 (3):1–24.
Edwards, Jason. 2007. *The Radical Attitude and Modern Political Theory*. Houndmills, Basingstoke, Hampshire, UK: Palgrave Macmillan.
Ehrenberg, John. 1999. "History of the Caucus for a New Political Science." *New Political Science* no. 21 (3):417–20.
Ehrman, John. 1999. "*Commentary*, the *Public Interest*, and the Problem of Jewish Conservatism." *American Jewish History* no. 87 (2 and 3):159–81.
Eisenstein, Elizabeth L. 1979. *The Printing Press as an Agent of Change: Communications and Cultural Transformations in Early-Modern Europe*. Cambridge, UK: Cambridge University Press.
Epstein, Barbara, and Robert Silvers. 1963. "To the Reader." *The New York Review of Books* no. 1 (1):n/a.
Febvre, Lucien, and Henri-Jean Martin. 2010 [1958]. *The Coming of the Book: The Impact of Printing, 1450–1800*. Translated by David Gerard. Edited by Geoffrey Nowell-Smith and David Wootton, *Verso World History Series*. London: Verso.
Fekete, John. 1981/82. "*Telos* at 50." *Telos* no. 50 (Winter):161–71.
Fender, Stephen. 1986. "The New York Review of Books." *The Yearbook of English Studies* no. 16 (Literary Periodicals Special Number):188–202.
Ferguson, Kathy E. 2010. "Anarchist Counterpublics." *New Political Science* no. 32 (2):193–214.
Fontana, Biancamaria. 1985. *Rethinking the Politics of Commercial Society: the Edinburgh Review 1802–1832*. Cambridge, UK: Cambridge University Press.

Foucault, Michel. 1977 [1972]. "Preface." *Anti-Oedipus: Capitalism and Schizophrenia*, edited by Gilles Deleuze and Felix Guattari, xi-xiv. London: Athlone Press.
Foucault, Michel. 1979. *Discipline and Punish: The Birth of the Prison*. Translated by Alan Sheridan. New York: Vintage Books.
Foucault, Michel. 2007. "What is Critique?" *The Politics of Truth*, edited by Sylvere Lotringer, 41–81. Cambridge, MA: Semiotext(e).
Foucault, Michel. 2009 [1978]. *Security, Territory, Population: Lectures at the College de France 1977–1978*. Translated by Graham Burchell. Edited by Francois Ewald, Alessandro Fontana and Arnold I. Davidson, *Lectures at the College de France*. New York: Picador.
Fox, William J. 1824. "Men and Things in 1823." *Westminster Review* no. 1:1–17.
Frankel, Boris. 1982. "Identifying Dominant Misconceptions of States." *Thesis Eleven* no. 4 (1):97–123.
Frankel, Boris. 1983. "The View from Australia." *Telos* no. 56 (Summer):149–55.
Frankel, Boris. 1997. "Confronting Neoliberal Regimes: The Post-Marxist Embrace of Populism and Realpolitik." *New Left Review* no. I (226):57–92.
Geuss, Raymond. 2010a. "On Bourgeois Philosophy and the Concept of 'Criticism.'" *Politics and the Imagination*, 167–85. Princeton, NJ: Princeton University Press.
Geuss, Raymond. 2010b. "Political Judgment in Its Historical Context." *Politics and the Imagination*, 1–16. Princeton, NJ: Princeton University Press.
Gitlin, Todd. 1993. *The Sixties: Years of Hope, Days of Rage*. New York, NY: Bantam.
Glazer, Nathan. 1985. "Interests and Passions." *The Public Interest* no. 81 (Fall):17–30.
Glazer, Nathan. 2005. "Neoconservative from the Start." *The Public Interest* no. 159 (Spring):12–17.
Gonzales, Moishe. 1985. "Theoretical Amnesia." *Telos* no. 65 (Fall):163–70.
Goodman, Dena. 1989. *Criticism in Action: Enlightenment Experiments in Political Writing*. Ithaca, NY: Cornell University Press.
Goodman, Walter. 1969. "On the (N.Y.) Literary Left." *The Antioch Review* no. 29 (1):67–75.
Grafton, Anthony. 2009. *Worlds Made by Words: Scholarship and Community in the Modern West*. Cambridge, MA: Harvard University Press.
Gramsci, Antonio. 1971. *Selections from the Prison Notebooks of Antonio Gramsci*. Translated by Quintin Hoare and Geoffrey Nowell Smith. New York: International Publishers.
Gross, David. 1994. "Where is *Telos* Going?" *Telos* no. 101 (Fall):110–116.
Gross, John. 1969. *The Rise and Fall of the Man of Letters: A Study of the Idiosyncratic and the Humane in Modern Literature*. New York: The Macmillan Company.

Grote, Harriet. 1970 [1866]. *The Philosophical Radicals of 1832, Comprising the Life of Sir William Molesworth and Some Incidents Connected with the Reform Movement from 1832 to 1842*. New York: Burt Franklin.

Group, Kansas *Telos*. 1977. "The Antioch *Telos* Conference." *Telos* no. 32 (Summer):188–92.

Gunnell, John G. 1986. *Between Philosophy and Politics: The Alienation of Political Theory*. Amherst, MA: The University of Massachusetts Press.

Habermas, Jurgen. 1991 [1962]. *The Structural Transformation of the Public Sphere: An Inquiry into a Category of Bourgeois Society*. Translated by Thomas Burger. Cambridge, MA: The MIT Press.

Hageman, Amy M., Vicky Arnold, and Steve G. Sutton. 2009. "Starving the Beast: Using Tax Policy and Governmental Budgeting to Drive Social Policy." *Accounting and the Public Interest* no. 9:10–38.

Harrington, Michael. 1973. "The Welfare State and Its Neoconservative Critics." *Dissent* no. Fall:435–54.

Harrison, Henry. 1891. "Defoe's Political Career: Its Influence on English History." *The Westminster Review* no. 135 (5):512–23.

Hauptmann, Emily. 2001. "'Our Highest Aim': *Democracy* and the Public Role of the Political Theorist." In *Midwest Political Science Association Meeting*. Chicago, IL.

Herf, Jeffrey, Paul Piccone, and Gary L. Ulmen. 1987–8. "Reading and Misreading Schmitt: An Exchange." *Telos* no. 74 (Winter):133–40.

Hobbes, Thomas. 1991 [1642]. *Leviathan*. Cambridge, UK: Cambridge University Press.

Horkheimer, Max. 1972. "Traditional and Critical Theory." In *Critical Theory: Selected Essays*, 188–243. New York: Herder and Herder.

Horkheimer, Max, and Theodor W. Adorno. 2002. *Dialectic of Enlightenment: Philosophical Fragments*. Translated by Edmund Jephcott. Edited by Gunzlein Schmid Noerr, *Cultural Memory in the Present*. Stanford, CA: Stanford University Press.

Innis, Harold A. 1942. "The Newspaper in Economic Development." *The Journal of Economic History* no. 2 (Dec.):1–33.

Innis, Harold A. 1946. *Political Economy in the Modern State*. Toronto, ON: Ryerson.

Innis, Harold A. 2006 [1943]. "The Crisis in Public Opinion." *Canadian Journal of Communication* no. 31:307–24.

Isaac, Jeffrey C. 1995. "The Strange Silence of Political Theory." *Political Theory* no. 23 (4):636–52.

Jacobs, Ronald N., and Eleanor Townsley. 2011. *The Space of Opinion: Media Intellectuals and the Public Sphere*. New York: Oxford University Press.

Jacoby, Russell. 1981–2. "Symposium: The Role of the Intellectual in the 1980s." *Telos* no. 50 (Winter):115–60.

Jacoby, Russell. 1987. *The Last Intellectuals: American Culture in the Age of Academe*. New York: Basic Books.

Kadushin, Charles. 2005. *The American Intellectual Elite*. 2nd ed. New Brunswick, NJ: Transaction Publishers.

Kafka, Ben. 2012. *The Demon of Writing: Powers and Failures of Paperwork*. New York, NY: Zone Books.

Kane, John, and Ian Shapiro. 1983. "Stagflation and the New Right." *Telos* no. 56 (Summer):5–39.

Kezar, Adrianna, and Daniel Maxey. 2013. "The Changing Academic Workforce." *Trusteeship* no. 21 (3):n/a.

Kingsley, W. L. (pub.). 1843. "Prolegomena." *New Englander* no. 1:4–8.

Knight, Charles A. 2009. *A Political Biography of Richard Steele*. London: Pickering & Chatto Ltd.

Koselleck, Reinhart. 1988 [1959]. *Critique and Crisis: Enlightenment and the Pathogenesis of Modern Society*. Cambridge, MA: MIT Press.

Kraft, Joseph M. 1965. "Understanding the Vietcong." *The New York Review of Books* no. 4 (6):n/a.

Kristol, Irving. 1960. "Last of the Whigs." *Commentary* no.?? (April):353–4.

Kristol, Irving. 1971. "From Priorities to Goals." *The Public Interest* no. 24 (Summer):3–4.

Kristol, Irving. 1995a. "American Conservatism, 1945–95." *The Public Interest* no. 121 (Fall):80–91.

Kristol, Irving. 1995b. *Neoconservatism: the Autobiography of an Idea*. New York: Free Press.

Kristol, Irving. 2005. "Forty Good Years." *The Public Interest* no. 159 (Spring):5–11.

Kristol, Irving. 2011a. "My Public Interest." In *The Neoconservative Persuasion, Selected Essays, 1942–2009*, edited by Gertrude Himmelfarb, 356-358. New York: Basic Books.

Kristol, Irving. 2011b. "The Neoconservative Persuasion." In *The Neoconservative Persuasion, Selected Essays, 1942–2009*, edited by Gertrude Himmelfarb, 190–94. New York: Basic Books.

Kristol, Irving. 2011c. "The Right Stuff." In *The Neoconservative Persuasion, Selected Essays, 1942-2009*, edited by Gertrude Himmelfarb, 180-189. New York: Basic Books.

Kristol, Irving, and Nathan Glazer. 1975. "Preface." *The Public Interest* no. 41 (Fall):3.

Lankowski, Carl. 1981. "Report to the Membership, 1981: Goals and Strategies for the 1980s." *New Political Science* no. 2 (1–2):98–110.

Lasch, Christopher. 2013 [1991]. *The True and Only Heaven: Progress and Its Critics*. New York: W. W. Norton & Company.

Lilla, Mark. 1985. "What is the Civic Interest?" *The Public Interest* no. 81 (Fall):64–81.

Lindblom, Charles E. 1997. "Political Science in the 1940s and 1950s." *Daedalus* no. 126 (1):225–52.

Lippmann, Walter. 2006. "Selection from *Drift and Mastery*." In *The American Intellectual Tradition, Volume II: 1865 to the Present*, edited by David A. Hollinger and Charles Capper, 165–9. New York: Oxford University Press.

Lopate, Phillip. 1995. *The Art of the Personal Essay: An Anthology from the Classical Era to the Present*. New York: Anchor Books.

Love, Nancy, and Mark Mattern. 2011. *New Political Science* Editors' Report for the Period September 1, 2010 to August 31, 2011.

Loveman, Mara. 2005. "The Modern State and the Primitive Accumulation of Symbolic Power." *American Journal of Sociology* no. 110 (6):1,651–83.

Luke, Timothy W. 1983. "Informationalism and Ecology." *Telos* no. 56:59–73.

Luke, Timothy W. 1994. "Toward a North American Critical Theory." *Telos* no. 101 (Fall):101–8.

Luke, Timothy W. 1999. "The Discipline as Disciplinary Normalization: Networks of Research." *New Political Science* no. 21 (3):345–63.

Luke, Timothy W. 2005. The Trek with *Telos*: A Rememberance of Paul Piccone (January 19, 1940–July 12, 2004). *Fast Capitalism* 1.2, www.fastcapitalism.com.

Luke, Timothy W. 2011. "The 'Americanization' of Critical Theory: Legacies of Paul Piccone and *Telos*." In *A Journal of No Illusions: Telos, Paul Piccone, adn the Americanization of Critical Theory*, edited by Timothy W. Luke and Ben Agger, 1–22. New York: Telos Press Publishing.

Macdonald, Dwight. 1974 [1945]. "The Responsibility of Peoples" In *The Responsibility of Peoples and Other Essays in Political Criticism*, 9–45. Westport, CT: Greenwood Press.

Mackie, Erin. 1998. *The Commerce of Everyday Life: Selections from The Tatler and The Spectator*. Boston, MA: Bedford/St. Martin's.

Marcus, George E. 1991. "American Academic Journal Editing in the Great Bourgeois Cultural Revolution of Late 20th-Century Postmodernity: The Case of Cultural Anthropology." *Cultural Anthropology* no. 6 (1):121–27.

Marx, Karl. 1978. "For a Ruthless Criticism of Everything Existing." In *The Marx-Engels Reader, 2nd ed.*, edited by Robert C. Tucker, 12–15. New York: W. W. Norton & Co.

Mason, H. A. 1938. "'The New Republic' and the Ideal Weekly." *Scrutiny* no. VII (3):250–260.

Masson, David. 1856. "Edinburgh Fifty Years Ago." *The Westminster Review* no. 66 (130):407–42.

Mattson, Kevin. 2002. *Intellectuals in Action: The Origins of the New Left and Radical Liberalism, 1945–1970*. University Park, PA: The Pennsylvania State University Press.

McCutcheon, Roger Philip. 1923. "John Houghton, a Seventeenth-Century Editor and Book-Reviewer." *Modern Philology* no. 20 (3):255–60.

McMurtie, Beth. 2013. "Political Scientists Acknowledge Need to Make Stronger Case for Their Field." *The Chronicle of Higher Education* Sept. 3:n/a.

McNall, Scott G. 2011. "The Good, the Bad and the Ugly: A Retrospective on *Telos*." In *A Journal of No Illusions: Telos, Paul Piccone, and the Americanization of Critical Theory*, edited by Timothy W. Luke and Ben Agger, 102–14. New York: Telos Press Publishing.

Mihm, Stephen. 2009. "Why Capitalism Fails." *The Boston Globe* (September 13): n/a, http://www.boston.com/bostonglobe/ideas/articles/2009/09/13/why_capitalism_fails/?page=full.

Mill, James. 1824. "Periodical Literature." *Westminster Review* no. 1:206–68.

Miller, Eric. 2010. *Hope in a Scattering Time: A Life of Christopher Lasch*. Grand Rapids, MI: William B. Eerdmans Publishing Company.

Mitchell, Timothy. 1988. *Colonising Egypt*. Berkeley, CA: University of California Press.

Mitchell, William J. T. 1982. "'Critical Inquiry' and the Ideology of Pluralism." *Critical Inquiry* no. 8 (4):609–18.

Mitchell, William J. T. 2004. "Medium Theory: Preface to the 2003 'Critical Inquiry' Symposium." *Critical Inquiry* no. 30 (2):324–35.

Moynihan, Daniel P. 1965. "The Professionalization of Reform." *The Public Interest* no. 1 (Fall):6–16.

Moynihan, Daniel P. 1975. "Introduction: The American Experiment." *The Public Interest* no. 41 (Fall):4–8.

Moynihan, Daniel P. 1985. "The Paranoid Style in American Politics Revisited." *The Public Interest* no. 81 (Fall):107–27.

Moynihan, Daniel P. 1995. "The Professionalization of Reform II." *The Public Interest* no. 121 (Fall):23–41.

Mulhern, Francis. 1981. "'Teachers, Writers, Celebrities': Intelligentsias and Their Histories." *New Left Review* I (126):43–59.

Nash, George H. 1976. *The Conservative Intellectual Movement in America*. New York: Intercollegiate Studies Institute.

Nesbitt, George L. 1966. *Benthamite Reviewing: The First Twelve Years of The Westminster Review 1824–1836*. New York: AMS Press, Inc.

Nickel, Patricia Mooney. 2012. *North American Critical Theory After Postmodernism: Contemporary Dialogues*. New York: Palgrave Macmillan.

Nobile, Philip. 1974. *Intellectual Skywriting: Literary Politics and The New York Review of Books*. New York: Charterhouse.

Ong, B. Nelson. 1988. "Radicals Reflect: The First Twenty Years of the Caucus for a New Political Science." *Academic Questions* no. 1 (3):55–9.

Oppenheim, James. 1930. "The Story of the *Seven Arts*." *American Mercury* June:156–64.

Oppenheimer, Mark. 2008. "Where Have All the Intellectuals Gone?" *The Chronicle of Higher Education*, B14.

Ost, David. 1994. "Search for Balance." *Telos* no. 101 (Fall):137–54.

Parker, Martin, and Robyn Thomas. 2011. "What Is a Critical Journal?" *Organization* no. 18 (4):419–27.

Payne, William L. 1951. *The Best of Defoe's Review: An Anthology*. New York: Columbia University Press.

Pettigrew, Thomas F., Elizabeth L. Useem, Clarence Normand, and Marshall S. Smith. 1973. "Busing: a Review of "The Evidence."" *The Public Interest* no. 30 (Winter):88–118.

Piccone, Paul. 1976. "From Tragedy to Farce: The Return of Critical Theory." *New German Critique* no. 7 (Winter):91–104.

Piccone, Paul. 1977. "Introduction." *Telos* no. 31 (Spring):3–4.

Piccone, Paul. 1983. "Introduction." *Telos* no. 56 (Summer):3–4.

Piccone, Paul. 1987. "Introduction." *Telos* no. 71 (Spring):3–4.

Piccone, Paul. 1988. "20 Years of Telos." *Telos* no. 75 (Spring):3–25.

Piccone, Paul. 1994. "From the New Left to New Populism." *Telos* no. 101 (Fall):173–208.

Piccone, Paul. 1999. "elements Interview." *Telos* no. 117 (Summer):133–66.

Piccone, Paul. 2008. "Populism vs. the New Class." In *Confronting the Crisis: Writings of Paul Piccone*, edited by Gary Ulmen, 197–230. New York: Telos Press Publishing.

Piccone, Paul, James Schmidt, Robert D'Amico, Bart Grahl, Ferenc Feher, and Paul Breines. 1977. "Internal Polemics." *Telos* no. 31 (Spring):178–97.

Postel, Danny. 1991. "A Splintered Journal Pokes into Its Own Contradictions." *In These Times*, 18–19.

Raventos, Jorge. 2002. "From the New Left to Postmodern Populism: An Interview with Paul Piccone." *Telos* (122):133–51.

Rensenbrink, John. 1982. "CNPS and NPS: Pitfalls and Prospects." *New Political Science* no. 2 (4):93–8.

Richardson, Peter. 2009. *A Bomb in Every Issue: How the Short, Unruly Life of Ramparts Magazine Changed America*. New York: The New Press.

Rodgers, Daniel T. 2012. *The Age of Fracture*. Cambridge, UK: Belknap.

Roelofs, Joan. 1979. "The Warren Court and Corporate Capitalism." *Telos* no. 39 (Spring):94–112.

Roelofs, Joan. 1984–5. "Foundations and the Supreme Court." *Telos* no. 62 (Winter):59–87.

Said, Edward. 2002. "The Public Role of Writers and Intellectuals." In *The Public Intellectual*, edited by Helen Small, 19–39. Oxford, UK: Blackwell Publishers.

Sanbonmatsu, John. 2004. *The Postmodern Prince: Critical Theory, Left Strategy, and the Making of a New Political Subject*. New York: Monthly Review Press.

Schmidt, Roman. 2010. "Utopian Failing: Two Magazine Projects." *Eurozine* (December 3):1–7.

Schostak, John, and Jill Schostak. 2013. *Writing Research Critically: Developing the Power to Make a Difference*. London: Routledge.

Scialabba, George. 2009. *What Are Intellectuals Good For? Essays & Reviews*. Boston, MA: Pressed Wafer.

Scott, James. 1998. *Seeing Like a State: How Certain Schemes to Improve the Human Condition Have Failed*. New Haven, CT: Yale University Press.

Secord, Arthur Wellesley. 1965. *Defoe's Review, Reproduced from the Original Editions, with an Introduction and Bibliographical Notes*. 2nd ed. Vol. 1. New York: AMS Press, Inc.

Seem (trans.), Mark. 1973. "The Intellectuals and Power: A Discussion between Michel Foucault and Gilles Deleuze." *Telos* no. 16:103–9.

Sennett, Richard. 1976. *The Fall of Public Man*. Cambridge, UK: Cambridge University Press.

Shapiro, Gary. 2004. "'New' New York Intellectuals." *The New York Sun*, July 26, 14.

Shattock, Joanne. 1980. "Spheres of Influence: The Quarterlies and Their Readers." *The Yearbook of English Studies* no. 10 (I):95.

Shattock, Joanne. 1989. *Politics and Reviewers: The Edinburgh and The Quarterly in the early Victorian Age*. London: Leicester University Press.

Sherman, Scott. 2004. "The Rebirth of the New York Review of Books." *The Nation*.

Shulman, George. 1983. "The Pastoral Idyll of democracy." *democracy* no. 3 (4):43–54.

Siegel, Fred. 1984. "Emil Oestereicher (1936–83), Notes on Neo-Liberalism." *Telos* no. 59:171–4.

Siskin, Clifford. 1998. *The Work of Writing: Literature and Social Change in Britain, 1700–1830*. Baltimore, MD: The Johns Hopkins University Press.

Skinner, David. 2005. "Farewell to 'The Public Interest.'" *The Weekly Standard* 10 (30): n/a, http://www.weeklystandard.com/Content/Public/Articles/000/000/005/497hprai.asp?pg=2.

Skinner, Quentin. 1989. "The State." In *Political Innovation and Conceptual Change*, edited by Terence Ball, James Farr and Russell L. Hanson, 90–131. Cambridge, UK: Cambridge University Press.

Smith, Rogers M. 1997. "Still Blowing in the Wind: The American Quest for a Democratic, Scientific Political Science." *Daedalus* no. 126 (1):253–87.

Smolenski, John. 2005. "'Incorporated ... Into a Body Politics': Clubs, Print, and the Gendering of the Civic Subject in Eighteenth-Century Pennsylvania." In *Periodical Literature in Eighteenth-Century America*, edited by Mark L. Kamrath and Sharon M. Harris, 47–73. Knoxville, TN: The University of Tennessee Press.

Sokal, Alan. 1996. "A Physicist Experiments with Cultural Studies." *Lingua Franca* May/June:n/a.

Spence, Larry D. 1980. "Political Theory as a Vacation." *Polity* no. 12 (4):697–710.

Staff, *Telos*. 1969. "Graduate Student Journals: Predicaments, Prospects, and Pitfalls." *Telos* no. 2 (Fall):132–7.

Staff, *Telos*. 1970. "First *Telos* International Conference." *Telos* no. 6 (Fall):294.

Steiner, George, and Noam Chomsky. 1967. "'The Responsibility of Intellectuals': An Exchange." *The New York Review of Books* no. 8 (5):n/a.

Steinfels, Peter. 1979. *The Neoconservatives*. New York: Simon & Schuster.

Stone, I. F. 1964. "The Wrong War." *The New York Review of Books* no. 3 (9):n/a.

Stonor Saunders, Frances. 2001. *The Cultural Cold War: The CIA and the World of Arts and Letters*. New York: The New Press.

Sunkara, Bhaskar. 2011. "Editor's Note: Introducing *Jacobin* ..." *Jacobin* no. 1 (Winter):1.

Surkin, Marvin, and Alan Wolfe. 1970. *An End to Political Science: The Caucus Papers*. New York: Basic Books.

Teles, Steven M. 2000. "Paradoxes of Welfare-State Conservatism." *The Public Interest* no. 141 (Fall):17–40.

Thompson, Denys. 1935. "A Hundred Years of the Higher Journalism." *Scrutiny* no. IV (1):25–34.

Townsley, Eleanor. 2000. "A History of Intellectuals and the Demise of the New Class: Academics and the U.S. Government in the 1960s." *Theory and Society* no. 29:739–84.

Ulmen, Gary. 2008. *Confronting the Crisis: Writings of Paul Piccone*. New York: Telos Press Publishing.

Vaïsse, Justin. 2010. *Neoconservatism: The Biography of a Movement*. Translated by Arthur Goldhammer. Cambridge, MA: The Belknap Press of Harvard University Press.

Wallis, Victor. 1979. "The Caucus at a Turning Point." *New Political Science* no. 1 (1):89–92.

Ward, A. W., and A. R. Waller. 2000. *The Cambridge History of English and American Literature: An Encyclopedia in Eighteen Volumes*. New York: Bartleby.com.

Warner, Michael. 2002. "Publics and Counterpublics." *Public Culture* no. 14 (1):49–90.

Weir, William. 1852. "Lord Jeffrey and the Edinburgh Review." *The Westminster Review* no. 58 (113):95–110.

Wiener, Jon. 1977. "The Footnote Fetish." *Telos* no. 31 (Spring):172–7.

Williams, Jeffrey J. 2009. "The Rise of the Theory Journal." *New Literary History* no. 40 (4):683–702.

Wilson, James Q. 1967. "The Bureaucracy Problem." *The Public Interest* no. 6 (Winter):3–9.

Wilson, James Q. 1973. "On Pettigrew and Armor: an Afterword." *The Public Interest* no. 30 (Winter):132–4.

Wilson, James Q. 1981. "'Policy Intellectuals'" and Public Policy." *The Public Interest* no. 64 (Summer):31–46.

Wolfe, Alan. 2004. "A Fascist Philosopher Helps Us Understand Contemporary Politics." *The Chronicle of Higher Education* 50 (30): B16, http://chronicle.com/free/v50/i30/30b01601.htm.

Wolin, Sheldon S. 1969. "Political Theory as a Vocation." *American Political Science Review* no. 63:1,062–82.

Wolin, Sheldon S. 1981. "Why democracy?" *democracy* no. 1 (1):3–5.

Wolin, Sheldon S. 2000. "Political Theory: From Vocation to Invocation." In *Vocations of Political Theory*, edited by Jason A. Frank, and John Tambornino. Minneapolis: University of Minneapolis Press.

Wolin, Sheldon S. 2004. *Politics and Vision: Continuity and Innovation in Western Political Thought*. Expanded ed. Princeton, NJ: Princeton University Press.

Xenos, Nicholas. 2001. "Momentary Democracy." In *Democracy and Vision: Sheldon Wolin and the Vicissitudes of the Political*, edited by A. Botwinick and W. E. Connolly, 25–38. Princeton, N.J.: Princeton University Press.

Zald, Mayer N. 2002. "Spinning Disciplines: Critical Management Studies in the Context of the Transformation of Management Education." *Organization* no. 9 (3):365–85.

Index

Addison, Joseph 11, 19, 21–6
advice books 12–13
American Magazine: A Monthly View of the Political State of the British Colonies 1, 16
American Political Science Association 105, 120–26, 128; *see also* political science
American Political Science Review 117, 133
American Review 36
American Revolution 62, 72
anti-statism 2, 8, 87, 91–2, 95–6, 100, 131, 133, 140–41, 150
Antipode 112, 116–17, 122, 125

Bell, Daniel 68–9, 76–7, 79–83, 90–91, 93
Bentham, Jeremy 35, 44
Blanchot, Maurice 4, 126
Bobbio, Norberto 9, 96, 102
Bourdieu, Pierre 3, 6–7, 9, 34
Bourne, Randolph 55–64, 67–70, 72, 108
    "The State" 62–3
    "The War and the Intellectuals" 57–8
    "Twilight of Idols" 60

Caucus for a New Political Science 8, 107, 112–13, 121, 125
censor 26–7, 33
    etymology 26–7
censorship of periodicals 7, 13, 28
Chomsky, Noam 61, 64, 66–73, 108
    "The Responsibility of Intellectuals" 64, 66–70
    "The Responsibility of Intellectuals, Redux" 70–71
coffeehouse 14–15, 17, 19, 21–2, 26, 32
crisis 4, 58, 64, 72, 95, 102, 134–6, 138, 142
    crisis of knowledge 116
    return of 8, 148–53
critical attitude 13, 59, 107, 114, 127

Critical Inquiry 10, 71–3, 118
critical moment 7, 31, 42, 55, 72, 75, 131; *see also* crisis
critical practice 2–3, 11–13, 31, 133; *see also* view and re-view
critical theory 7, 64, 72, 84, 87, 90, 96, 123, 150, 155
critical turn 105, 111, 114
criticism
    digital criticism 156
    political criticism
        aestheticization of 8, 131, 146
        deradicalization of 8, 111, 131, 144
        diaspora of 106, 150
        genre of 12, 16, 103
    professionalization of 72, 77–8, 105, 107–8, 128, 148
    radical criticism 5
        as luxury good 153
        "ruthless criticism of everything existing" 101, 127
    reformist criticism 13
    "self-instituting institutions of criticism" 44, 120
critique, *see* criticism
Cultural Anthropology 113, 116

Defoe, Daniel 1, 11, 16–18, 26, 28–9, 38
    nonconformist 17, 21
democracy 131, 136–41, 149, 151; *see also* Wolin, Sheldon
    anti-statism 131, 140–41
    pastoralism 140
Democracy: A Journal of Ideas 150–53
Democratic Review 36
democratization of knowledge 43
Deutsch-Französische Jahrbücher 127
Dewey, John 57–60, 137
    "para-nationalism" 60
Diderot, Denis 4, 13

Supplément 13
doxa 9
  doxosophers 9

early periodicals 13
  Coranto 13
  Diurnall 13
  licensing 13, 15
  newspaper 7, 19, 32, 35–7
  privilege 14
  Relations 13
  stamp tax 19, 28, 36
Edinburgh Review, or Critical Journal 1, 31–41, 43–52, 156
  circulation 35, 37, 47
  partisanship 38–40, 46
  political focus 37–9
  popularization of political economy 47–8, 51
  Whiggism 25, 27, 35, 37, 39–40, 44–6, 48, 50, 91
Encounter 69, 81–2, 109
English Revolution 12
Epstein, Barbara 64–5

fictional persona 23, 27; *see also Spectator, The; Tatler, The*
  Bickerstaff, Isaac 20, 23, 27, 33, 86
  Spectator 24–5, 33
Foucault, Michel 3, 5–6, 11, 34, 86, 97, 106–7, 114, 134
French Revolution 37, 47

Geuss, Raymond 4, 153
Glazer, Nathan 79–80, 82, 90–91, 93, 95, 101, 135
Goodman, Dena 12
"great reviews" 1, 7, 24, 55, 59, 65, 72, 95, 131, 133, 153; *see also Edinburgh Review; Quarterly, The; Westminster Review*
  anonymous reviews 33
  as exemplars 52
  corporate personality 33–4
  creation of a critical milieu 37
  intellectual standards 44–5
  partisanship 18, 26, 39–41, 46, 48
  party allegiance 39–40

Habermas, Jürgen 4–5, 11–12, 14–16, 18, 22
  involvement with *Telos* 87–90
Hobbes, Thomas 4, 12
Horkheimer, Max 9, 88, 144

intellectual
  irresponsible intellectual 58, 68–9
  public intellectual 55, 151–2
  responsible intellectual 58, 67, 69, 71

Jacobin 150–52, 155
Jeffrey, Francis 35, 39, 41, 46
Journal des Sçavans 14
journals 1–4, 6–15
  academic journal 14, 112
  CIA funding of 69, 109
  critical journal 31, 47, 114–15, 155
  disciplinary journal 105–7, 116–17, 126
  impact factor 116–19, 126
  intellectual journal 53, 135–6
  journal of opinion 17, 28
  jurnal 6
  party journal 36
  policy journal 69, 101, 103
  scholarly journal 71, 120
  theory journal 103, 144

Koselleck, Reinhart 4–5, 27, 45, 116
Krise und Kritik 4
Kristol, Irving 69, 75–7, 79–83, 91–5, 99, 135

Lasch, Christopher 85, 92, 100, 138, 140
  involvement with *democracy* 138, 140
  involvement with *Telos* 85, 100
London and Westminster Review 40, 45, 131, 133
  "Theory and Practice" 131–3
London Review of Books 1, 26, 151

Macdonald, Dwight 61, 64, 67, 69, 137
  "The Responsibility of Peoples" 61, 67, 69
Manshel, Warren Demian 79, 82
Masses, The 18, 42, 57, 59, 98, 120
Mill, James 43–6, 49
Mill, John Stuart 35, 39–41, 43–4, 47, 131
Minsky, Hyman 98–9
mirror for princes, *see* advice books

Mitchell, W. J. T. 10, 71–2
Montesquieu, Charles-Louis de Secondat 12–13
  Lettres persanes 12
Moynihan, Daniel Patrick 75, 77–79, 90–91, 93, 95, 135
  "The Professionalization of Reform" 77–8

n+1 52–3, 150–51
New Class 11, 79, 88–89, 100
New Englander 33–4, 48
New Left Review 3, 53, 85–6, 117, 142, 151, 153
New Political Science 70, 112, 120, 122–7
New Republic, The 58–60, 70, 135, 150
New York Review of Books, The 1, 75, 80, 109, 135, 151
  Chomsky's association 61, 64, 66–73, 108
  Stone, I. F. 65–6, 139, 156
North American Review 41

overconsumption of news ("news-addiction") 21, 22

Palevsky, Max 138–9
Partisan Review 52–3, 60, 70, 80–81, 109, 135
Philosophical Transactions of the Royal Society 14
Piccone, Paul 84–90, 95–101
political science 116–17, 133, 135–6, 149; *see also* American Political Science Association
  behavioral revolution 121, 135
  discipline of 105–6, 120–21, 126–9, 135
Political Science Quarterly 120
politics 61, 137
Politics & Society 112, 116, 122, 125–6
postmodern turn 106–7, 131
Public Interest, The 3, 7, 69, 75–85, 87, 97–9, 101, 103, 116, 135, 137–9, 148, 151
  criticism of welfare state 83, 90–92, 98
  founding 79
  influence on neoconservative movement 83, 94–5
  limits of policy intervention 78
  move to Washington, D.C. 82–3
  opening editorial 76–7
  rightward shift 93–4
public opinion 4–5, 11, 15–17, 20, 26–7, 40, 42–3, 55, 59, 62
public sphere 3–5, 11–12, 14–18, 20–22, 32, 40, 42, 48, 55, 83–4, 105, 149
public use of reason 16

Quarterly, The 1, 31, 33, 35, 38–41, 43, 47–52
  Tories 25, 35, 37, 39–40, 44, 48, 50

Ramparts 90, 109, 135
Re-view of war 55, 63, 69, 71, 73
  Iraq War 66, 72
  Vietnam War 61, 64–8, 70, 72, 109, 121, 135
  World War I 56–7, 59
review 1, 3, 9
  etymology 9
  institutionalization 21, 29, 31–7, 44–8
  review form 1, 7–10, 15, 29, 31, 40, 45, 47–9, 52, 156
Review of the State of the British Nation 11; *see also* Defoe, Daniel
Revue internationale 4

Salmagundi 138
Schmitt, Carl 89, 96, 99–101, 155
Seven Arts 55, 57, 59–61, 65–6, 137; *see also* Bourne, Randolph
Signs 112, 118
Silvers, Robert 64–5, 67
Social Text 53, 118, 128, 131, 136, 142, 145–8, 150
  Sokal hoax 128, 146–8
Spectator, The 11, 17–21, 24–8, 32–3, 36, 149
state, concept of the 1–2, 11–12
  stato 12
Steele, Richard 11, 13, 17, 19–20, 23–4, 28
  Censor of Great Britain 27
  Member of Parliament 13, 28

Tatler, The 11, 17–24, 26–8, 32, 34, 36, 56
Telos 2–3, 7, 53, 105, 112, 116–17, 134, 138, 140

anti-statism 2, 87, 95–103
artificial negativity 88–9, 96–8
"conservative turn" 89, 93, 101
criticism of emerging neoliberal
    policies 98, 103
federalism 89, 99–101
focus on Eastern Europe 96
founding 84–6
Habermaniacs 87
influential contributors 85
"linguistic turn" 88
Marxism 84–8, 96, 102–3
North American critical theory 7, 90
on-line presence 155
organic negativity 88, 97–8
populism 89, 99–101, 123
relationship to New Left 86–7
theory 72, 86, 94, 131–4, 136–7, 140, 142–3, 145–50
Thesis Eleven 97, 118, 131, 141–5

view and re-view 1–3
    authority of critic's view 11, 14–15, 17, 28, 33, 40, 43–5, 48, 111–12, 129
    critical re-view 3–6, 17, 55, 73, 112, 156
    state's view 1, 3, 5–6, 11, 16, 32, 43, 45
    surveillance 156
visible government 8

Westminster Review 1, 31, 33, 35, 37–53, 72, 102, 131
    "Men and Things in 1823," first essay 42–3
    philosophic Radicalism 40, 46–7
    review of reviews 49–52
    utilitarianism 35, 43–4, 46
Wilson, James Q. 78, 94, 135
Wolin, Sheldon 9, 121, 131, 133–9, 149–50; *see also democracy*
    criticism of overtheorization 149
    epic theory 134, 136, 138
    "Political Theory as a Vocation" 133